The School in the Community

Edited by
Rosemary C. Sarri
and Frank F. Maple

❖

National Association of Social Workers, Inc.
1425 H Street N.W.
Washington, D.C. 20005

ACKNOWLEDGMENTS

The production of this volume and the many workshops related to the NASW school social work project were the responsibility of many people, and any statement of appreciation will necessarily fall short. Yet certain individual contributions deserve special mention.

The one person most responsible for this undertaking was Sam Negrin, director of the project and a member of the NASW staff. Mr. Negrin wrote the initial project proposal, which resulted in a grant funded by the National Institute of Mental Health (grant MH 11795). It was because of his untiring efforts and dedication to the improved delivery of social work services in schools that the project was conceived and sustained. Mr. Negrin was supported in his efforts by Jerry Kelley, who along with the undersigned, was educational codirector of the project.

The planning committee, under the chairmanship of Horace Lundberg, included Mary Louise Dillon, Charlotte Hayman, Betty Lacy Jones, Edward King, Pat Mancini, John Morgan, Ruth Schwartz, and Richard Staples. Among those who contributed greatly to the regional institutes on school social work were Alex Mindes, David Blumenkrantz, Sue Wheat, Mary McAllister, and Virginia Upson. Special acknowledgment is made to Wallace Lornell for his continuing support and guidance.

The project editors received considerable assistance from the efficient services of the NASW Publications Department, directed by Beatrice Saunders. Special recognition is given to Patricia Ann Lynch, editorial adviser, and Wendy Almeleh, senior editor, for their help in preparing the manuscript for publication.

Special thanks are extended to Milton Wittman and Margaret Daniel of NIMH, without whose encouragement and support this project would never have been initiated.   —F.F.M.

◊

Contents

3

II   INNOVATIVE STRATEGIES AND PRACTICE APPLICATIONS

Foreword

The Kerner commission report placed on the doorsteps of the schools much of the responsibility for the race riots of the 1960s.[1] In reaction to that report, as well as being aware of the need to strengthen school social work's contribution to American education, the NASW Council on Social Work in Schools undertook a three-year project to expand the school/community linkage role of social workers in schools. Jointly funded by the National Institute of Mental Health and NASW, the project produced a national workshop and twelve regional institutes. This book was developed out of these activities.

In the early days of school social work, practice tended to focus on emotion, motivation, and personality. Traditional social casework skills were readily transferred to the school setting and contributed greatly toward maximizing the educational experience. School social workers, as vital members of the pupil personnel team, still carry responsibility for assuring the availability of high-quality casework services to children and their families who need mental health services. As these roles became familiar and acceptable to the education systems that employed social workers and pressures for individual services increased, more and more school social workers tended to avoid such tasks as influencing school policy or changing systems. This tendency was reenforced by the educational establishment's resistance to social workers' assumption of functions and the real threat of job loss when the system interpreted change efforts as criticism or attack.

What further exacerbated the problem was that the educational system, faced with increasing demands by various groups for decreasing

---

[1] *Report of the National Advisory Commission on Civil Disorders* (New York: Bantam Books, 1968).

[2] Ibid., p. 25.

5

funds, came to view pupil personnel services as the first to be cut from school budgets. Not surprisingly, few school social workers were prepared to assume a change-agent role when it meant fighting the very system that employed them. They were caught between the rigidity of the educational establishment and the rising voices of parents and community groups who were clamoring for change and rebelling against the school system's failure "to provide the educational experience which could overcome the effects of discrimination and deprivation." [2]

Against this background, the project undertook to promote a professional action role for social workers in the schools. In so doing, NASW recognized that many workers needed training in and knowledge of service delivery systems, institutional dynamics, and institutional change strategies necessary for assuming this role. Added to this was the lack of support from the school system and, to some extent, from the social work profession. Thus the project attempted to provide the information it thought school social workers needed and to help educate them so they might see not only the political problems facing education and the dynamics that perpetuate these problems, but also develop strategies for dealing with them.

High-quality education is the responsibility of all citizens. But it should be of special concern to social workers whose historic mission has been the improvement of the human condition. Thus social workers may join with others to press for new attitudes and methods that consider education as a right for all children—not a privilege—the right of all children to go as far as their innate abilities will carry them.

SAM NEGRIN
Project Director
NASW School Social Work Project

October 1972

Preface

"Social Change and School Social Work in the 1970s" was the theme of the National Workshop in School Social Work held at the University of Pennsylvania in June 1969. One important aim of this workshop, sponsored by the National Association of Social Workers and the National Institute of Mental Health, was to stimulate innovation and change in school social work throughout the United States. Another primary objective was to encourage school social workers to assume significant leadership roles in facilitating effective social change during a period of crisis and upheaval. To achieve these goals, the following four components were related to the objectives just stated:

1. A national planning committee was selected to represent different regions of the United States. This committee was responsible for planning national and regional events.

2. The National Workshop in School Social Work met for one week at the University of Pennsylvania and provided key leadership for developing regional and state activities. At this workshop there were school social workers who performed highly differentiated tasks: state directors and supervisors; city administrators; individual, group, and community practitioners; school principals; social work editors; psychologists; public school teachers; and students.

3. The third component involved a variety of state and regional conferences held over an eighteen-month period in nearly all regions of the country. These conferences provided an opportunity for further consideration of issues raised at the national workshop. They also led to the development of many innovative projects in school social work, some of which are reported in this book.

The fourth component was preparation of this book on school social work, which incorporates some of the major papers presented at the several conferences and also reports noteworthy innovations and demonstration-research projects developed in conjunction with the total project. Space limitations have prohibited inclusion of many excellent papers and reports. Those that have been included were selected by the editors and the national planning committee as having the greatest import for school social work throughout the United States.

Part I of this book includes a series of papers that present findings about and analyses of some of the major issues in education today. Special emphasis is placed throughout on the implications for school social work. This section is followed by Part II, which presents a series of papers on practice innovations. These reports are not meant to be inclusive of all types of innovations in school programs. Rather, they were chosen to emphasize approaches that represent different trends in practice.

Rosemary C. Sarri analyzes some major issues and problems confronting American elementary and secondary education. Goals and means are being challenged today by persons within and outside educational organizations. Problem-solving is hampered by the tremendous size of the educational enterprise and by unwieldy bureaucratization. This paper provides a context for considering subsequent proposals for new educational strategies and technologies.

Findings from an extensive national survey of the activities and roles of school social workers are discussed by Lela B. Costin. Costin reports that social workers define their activities in terms of individual remedial services and give little attention to modifying school conditions that contribute to the emergence or maintenance of problem behavior among students. She proposes several general strategies for augmenting system change and emphasizes the importance of recognizing that the school is primarily an educational institution, rather than a context for providing therapeutic services to selected children.

Change in the social institution called education is the focus of the paper by Alfred J. Kahn. Kahn points to the current dissatisfaction with the operation of many human service organizations, including the public school. He raises questions about how the school can develop structures and mechanisms to achieve greater effectiveness and more participation by both majority and minority groups. The changing social milieu of the school; the new roles and expectations of students, the problems in obtaining and allocating resources, and increased skepticism by the public are all factors that have important implications for the roles of school social workers.

The expectations of a state commissioner of education are succinctly presented by Carl Marburger. Marburger chastises school social workers for their inadequate assessment of problems within the school-community environment and emphasizes the need for integrated multilevel strategies if greater effectiveness is to be achieved.

A provocative presentation of several models of practice in school social work is offered by John J. Alderson. Alderson focuses his analysis on four service delivery models: traditional-clinical, school-change, community-school, and mediating-problem focused. These are discussed with reference to their respective goals, type of client system, perceptions of source of problem behavior, conceptual base, worker strategies and methods, and major worker roles.

Simon Wittes presents one strategy for resolving social conflict in educational organizations. His focus is on the positive use of conflict to effect system change. Findings are presented from a study of seven school systems in which serious problem behavior and conflict occurred. The change strategy involved the used of problem-solving mechanisms in which administrators, teachers, parents, and students worked together to change school conditions and practices. Emphasis was placed on the need to shift from the arbitrary use of power and authority to participatory decision-making.

Behavior modification techniques are used extensively in education today, and the paper by Richard B. Stuart is a cogent analysis of much of the research and literature on classroom management and social control. Stuart emphasizes that the classroom should be the content and format of instruction. Many instructional alternatives for classroom teachers are presented and analyzed. This paper has special relevance for social workers who work with teachers and for staff development and training of both teachers and social workers. Stuart also alerts practitioners to the potential unanticipated consequences of intervention systems that may accelerate the identification of secondary deviance, which may be negative for many students.

The last paper in Part I is a stimulating analysis of labeling theory as it applies to school social work. Edward J. Pawlak discusses several of the major theoretical perspectives on social deviance and labeling. His analysis highlights the utility of this approach for the practitioner in that it makes obvious alternative conceptualizations of the sources and manifestations of deviant behavior. Individual- and organizational-level variables are considered. The paper concludes with a presentation of new strategies for school social workers in the modification of information systems and in the role of an ombudsman-advocate.

Helen Nieberl opens Part II by emphasizing the need to change from delivering preset services (such as casework, group work, and community organization) to a problem-focused approach that starts with problem-identification. This approach is noteworthy in that pertinent data are gathered about the school and its community to determine the various factors that affect student learning. Service is designed to enhance learning outcomes and is directed toward the interpersonal, school-system, and community levels.

John J. Stretch and Phillip E. Crunk provide invaluable data on the consequences and use of indefinite suspension. They offer guidelines for modifying school systems that extensively utilize punitive measures for disciplinary purposes.

Linda P. Wassenich's paper on systems analysis may be effectively utilized in conjunction with the Nieberl and Stretch-Crunk papers. It proposes a means of using the systems approach to identify targets of change without depending on the written referral process, thus enhancing the potential for designing services to meet high-priority school needs.

Jerry W. Willis and Joan S. Willis identify specific strategies for changing school systems from within through generating administrative support. The key strategies include involvement of significant system members in the recognition of problems and generation of solutions. System reinforcements to maintain change efforts and modeling procedures to initiate change are additional strategies described.

The paper by Betty Deshler and John L. Erlich examines the development of the school-community agent program in a large urban setting. It updates the older approaches developed in the Detroit Public Schools and points to a new model for improving school-community relations through the full and significant involvement of grass-roots people in decision-making. The focus is on the local school—not the higher bureaucracy of the overall system.

A project to teach school social workers to engage in community organization activities is presented by Jeffrey Lickson. It complements the Deshler-Erlich article in its description of the training required to implement their model.

The role of the school social worker in the secondary school is described by Johanna M. Bielecki. Her approach emphasizes direct service to adolescents, including drug-users, through a walk-in, self-referral system in a suburban community. The concept thus enhances volunteerism on the part of clients, a vital aspect in advocating student objectives in school settings.

The last two articles in Part II describe the implementation of innovative approaches at the state level through statewide in-service workshops. First, Claire Gallant and Barbara MacDonald describe how they, as state consultants, set up, operated, and evaluated the workshops and their impact.

Second, the article by Frank Maple presents a learning package designed to give all the details involved in teaching the shared decision-making concept. This concept and its subparts are pictured in relation to two-person transactions. The rationale, teaching design, worksheets, and all materials utilized in the workshops are presented. These are intended to serve as models for others who wish to describe the step-by-step process involved in implementing one or more innovations.

ROSEMARY C. SARRI
FRANK F. MAPLE

October 1972

PART I

Current Patterns
and Framework
for Practice

Education in Transition

Rosemary C. Sarri

Public schools today are in a period of crisis. One need only pick up a newspaper to be made aware of the serious difficulties facing students, parents, boards of education, teachers, and others affiliated with education. Along with many other social institutions in the United States, education is experiencing a period of great soul-searching, turmoil, and conflict.

Among the contributing factors are race relations and racial conflict, problems of poverty, increased voter resistance to support for local education, and increasing alienation of the young as reflected in high dropout rates, drug abuse, crime, serious underachievement, and—last but not least—intergenerational conflict. The latter has already resulted in increased open rebellion in both junior and senior high schools in all types of communities, and all indications are that the future will bring even more disruption unless effective means for problem-solving are developed. School personnel and boards of education are expected to be able to respond in new and nontraditional ways to resolve these myriad problems, but it is unlikely that their responses will be sufficient, since these problems involve the political, economic, and cultural systems as well as education.

Few would disagree that the United States is presently threatened by increasing disintegration of its entire social, political, economic, and civic structure. The public school is one of the social institutions that is expected to play a significant role in resolving problems that are contributing to this disintegration. When state and national programs of urban renewal, income maintenance, pollution, housing, civil rights, and education depend, as they do, on the intelligent support of local communities, the failure of the present school system to produce enlightened leaders is frightening at the least. Any study of these problems from a long-term perspective would suggest, as Conant has said, that education is an essential prerequisite if satisfactory solutions are to be found.[1]

No part of the United States has escaped problems in education. These problems are manifested in a variety of forms, some of which will be examined here. Other articles in this volume will extend this analysis, and several tentative solutions to some of the problems will be proposed.

By definition education is a social institution committed to social change and innovation. Leonard says: "To learn is to change. Education is a process that changes the learner." [2] In the late fifties the educational system demonstrated an ability to adapt its curriculum, at least in selected areas, as a consequence of public concern. At the same time education is a conservative social institution concerned, as Parsons says, with "pattern maintenance" for society.[3] Schools have assumed major responsibility for the preparation of youths for adult social roles. In the United States this has led to great emphasis on technological training for an industrialized society.

The demands of today are shifting and will doubtless change even more in the future, but many schools still place primary emphasis on values that are no longer relevant. Furthermore, bureaucratization of the school system has aggravated this conservatism because of its resultant rigidity, inflexibility, and stultification of education. Most of the criticism being directed at the educational system today is aimed at its intransigence in the face of vastly different environmental conditions and altered expectations of parents and students alike. There is

---

[1] James B. Conant, *The American High School Today* (New York: McGraw-Hill Book Co., 1959); Conant, *Slums and Suburbs* (New York: McGraw-Hill Book Co., 1961).

[2] George B. Leonard, *Education and Ecstasy* (New York: Dell Publishing Co., 1968), p. 18.

[3] Talcott Parsons, *Social Structure and Personality* (New York: Free Press, 1964); and Parsons, "The School Class as a Social System," *Harvard Educational Review*, Vol. 20, No. 3 (August 1950), pp. 297–318.

16

thus a great need to stimulate those elements of the system that will foster innovation and change.

The Public School Mandate

The public school confronts a serious dilemma in the requirement that it educate all children without regard to ability, interest, or prior preparation and often with fewer resources than are believed essential for such an ambitious task. It is expected to accommodate a student population with a wide range of personal attributes and social backgrounds. It is apparent from any study of the present ferment about education that the school is expected to perform multiple roles in society, but insufficient attention has been given to consideration of the means to achieve these ends and their feasibility for all types of students in differing neighborhoods and communities.

It is generally accepted that the school's primary mandate is to prepare individuals to meet the requirements of adult occupational roles, but it is also expected to further students' character development and prepare them for responsible citizenship in a democratic society. The school is held responsible for enhancing the educational attainment of all while providing varied educational opportunities for those who wish to take advantage of them. It has been viewed as the link through which all youths, poor and rich, enter the mainstream of American society.

The importance of the educational system to society is highlighted by the 1968 Report of the National Advisory Commission on Civil Disorders:

> Education in a democratic society must equip the children of the nation to realize their potential and to participate fully in American life. For the community at large, the schools have discharged this responsibility well. But for many minorities, and particularly for the children of the racial ghetto, the schools have failed to provide the educational experience which could help overcome the effects of discrimination and deprivation.[4]

This report further elaborates the relationship between the malfunctioning of the educational system and the civil disorders that have taken place in many communities. The evidence of this and other research

---

[4] *Report of the National Advisory Commission on Civil Disorders* (New York: Bantam Books, 1968), pp. 424–425.

studies clearly indicates that many youths at the bottom or periphery of society are denied education that is appropriate to their needs. Problems result because education (at least completion of secondary school) has increasingly become a significant criterion for entry into the labor force. Educational failure for whatever reasons inhibits successful access to the occupational system and thereby induces frustration that makes people—young people especially—prone to violent types of problem-solving.

The status of education in a highly industrialized society affects its development as a social institution, for it is viewed as a major social investment requiring a great commitment of resources over a long period of time. It has become increasingly obvious in recent years that education is heavily involved in political processes at the state and federal levels. Clark asserts that education as a social institution mediates the supply and demand of workers and the assignment of social statuses.[5] It has a mandate from the larger society to select students for adult roles by differential evaluation of their ability and performance. In discussing this role he has noted:

> . . . in the complex society, with its elaborate division of labor, one's occupational future is more open and much more likely to be won by dint of individual achievement. The process of allocating young people too has become complicated and heavily intertwined with formal education and training.[6]

In another context he analyzes the relationships between education and the economy:

> Education's expanding role in occupational preparation, which thrusts it into the economic order, is the aspect of modern education that has greatest influence in changing its nature and altering its relations to society.[7]

Many research findings have documented the importance of education in employment, for today few persons enter professional or managerial careers without a college degree, and most clerical and sales workers have at least a high school diploma. Assuming that the cur-

---

[5] Burton R. Clark, "Sociology of Education," in Robert L. Faris, ed., *Handbook of Modern Sociology* (Chicago: Rand McNally, 1964), pp. 734–769. In this article Clark discusses the several functions of education today.

[6] Burton R. Clark, *Educating the Expert Society* (San Francisco: Chandler Publishing Co., 1962), p. 83.

[7] "Sociology of Education," p. 739.

rent situation is likely to prevail, it is important to understand the educational processes involved in career assignment and to determine if the school's mandate is being fulfilled as it was expected to be. For it is more than slightly possible that commitment to certain ends over a period of time will produce unanticipated and sometimes undesired consequences.

There is evidence that vocational education has a secondary status in the public school because the occupations for which persons in vocational curricula are being prepared have a relatively low status in the larger society. Vocational training programs receive fewer resources and have less-adequate teachers, even though it could be argued that the reverse is required. Some schools in the inner city have almost no vocational training programs, while schools in the suburbs have equipment that goes unused because their students are uninterested in such training.

In accord with its goal to prepare students for responsible citizenship in a democratic society, the so-called comprehensive school was developed in the United States.[8] However laudable this objective, experience has brought certain problems to the fore. Among the more serious of these are the negative consequences of the tracking system. The comprehensive school was developed so that students preparing for college could be educated together with those preparing for immediate entry into employment. This necessitated a plan for tracking students into differentiated curricula to meet variations in ability, interest, and future career expectations. Articulation with higher education was attempted and largely achieved, but—in particular for males—there was almost no articulation between the vocational track and the industrial structure. Vocational education has not kept pace with technological changes and it does not provide adequate preparation for participation in a rapidly changing labor force.

Another failing of this system has become apparent in the face of increasing evidence that children from working-class backgrounds are often locked from their earliest days in the elementary school into tracks that it is difficult to leave. There was an implicit assumption about flexibility in the tracking approach, but no provisions were made to obtain systematic and continuous findings about the actual operation of the system. As a result educators and laymen were unaware of its

[8] See Franklin J. Keller, *The Comprehensive High School* (New York: Harper & Brcs., 1955).

rigidity and biases vis-à-vis certain groups. Basically people believed in the Horatio Alger myth of an open society and an open educational system for all, but no one bothered to ascertain how the system was in fact operating.

Demise of the Community

The absence of a sense of community is recognized by many observers of American society. In the last century Toennies, the German sociologist, wrote of the attributes of a community in which persons learn to share common experiences and traditions, as contrasted to the community in mass society.[9] More recently Reich, Toffler, Goodman, Friedenberg, Leonard, and others have, in a variety of ways, expressed the need for a new type of vital community in which the enhancement of human potential and satisfaction are viewed as primary objectives for all.[10] Group membership is considered as an end in itself and members are encouraged to share common values and commitments.

The lack of community has affected education as a social institution, but in turn education has contributed to the demise of the community because of its overemphasis on specialization, fragmentation, and bureaucratic conformity. Newman and Oliver assert that the present situation can be attributed to the overemphasis placed on individual and societal needs as two polar extremes, with little or no attention given to the vitality of the groups that bridge the individual and society.[11] Quite obviously the alienation of the young today is at least partially attributable to the lack of institutional mechanisms for facilitating the participation of youths in significant societal decision-making.

American society has insisted on a protracted period of formal socialization for its young people, and the public school has been assigned key responsibility for this. "Adolescent moratorium" covers the ages between 15 and 20 or 25 and is accompanied by a lack of effective participation in all spheres of life. Recent legislation to increase the rights of 18-year-olds represents a new trend, but it is

---

[9] Ferdinand Toennies, *Community and Society,* Charles P. Loomis, trans. (East Lansing: Michigan State University Press, 1957), Book 1.

[10] Charles A. Reich, *The Greening of America* (New York: Random House, 1970); Alvin Toffler, *Future Shock* (New York: Random House, 1970); Edgar Friedenberg, *Coming of Age in America* (Boston: Beacon Press, 1965); Leonard, op. cit.; Paul Goodman, *Growing Up Absurd* (New York: Random House, 1960).

[11] Fred Newman and Donald Oliver, "Education and Community," *Harvard Educational Review,* Vol. 37, No. 1 (Winter 1967), pp. 61–106.

unlikely that the occupational sphere will change rapidly. There are several signs in the informal social structure that youths are seeking their own community—for example, in the development of a variety of forms of communal living and in the challenges to administration in education.

Other problems have arisen because of the concept of neighborhood school, which also had a laudable objective at one time but now results in total separation of the slum and suburban child from one another. The reliance on local financing through property taxes has aggravated this situation. Current plans for busing and decentralization of decision-making are only partial solutions. As Sexton has shown, schools in poor neighborhoods are disadvantaged in almost every way.[12] Some federal programs, such as Title I, were designed to alleviate this situation, but they lack the stability and resources needed if communities are to make long-term commitments.

Size and Bureaucratization

The sheer magnitude of the educational enterprise in the United States further aggravates the situation. It is estimated that there are more than 46 million children enrolled in public elementary and secondary schools today, and this number is expected to exceed 63 million by 1980.[13] There are single buildings that handle more than 4,000 students, and educational parks for 20,000 are envisaged. Size alone appears to be an inhibiting factor in effective education in many communities. The attempts at various patterns of decentralization are but one recognition of this problem. It can no longer be ignored.

An almost inevitable consequence of this problem has been an overemphasis on bureaucratization and control that negates the educational goals being sought. It is estimated that about 30 percent of the United States population is engaged in education in some capacity, making it one of the nation's largest institutions.[14] Public schools at present consume up to 40 percent of state and local tax expenditures, with per capita costs continuing to rise each year.[15] Still another problem is

---

[12] Patricia C. Sexton, *Education and Income* (New York: Viking Press, 1961).

[13] *Projections of Educational Statistics to 1979–80* (Washington, D.C.: U.S. Government Printing Office, 1971).

[14] Ibid.

[15] *Digest of Educational Statistics, 1970* (Washington, D.C.: U.S. Department of Health, Education & Welfare, Office of Education, 1970), p. 22.

the concentration in urban areas—21 percent of the public school population lives in cities of 50,000 or more.[16]

Opportunities for flexible planning in education are inevitably more constrained in large cities where competition for land and other resources is keen. Metropolitan school districts that are planned to cope with the consequences of racially segregated communities are especially questionable because of their size.

Despite its gigantic size the public elementary and secondary system is amazingly uniform. Initially this finding is somewhat surprising, because only broad limits are set by law as to what actions may and may not be taken by the school system. Considerable leeway is left to the local board of education and the individual system. However, because of standardization of curricula and certification of teachers at the state level, homogeneity rather than heterogeneity has been the formal outcome.

Student role behavior is also highly prescribed because all are expected to achieve above the minimal level academically and at the same time to conform to specified behavioral codes. These role prescriptions are reinforced through a variety of mechanisms such as standardized examinations and through elaborate behavioral control policies that are often linked to requirements for academic performance.

Given the situation of having to take all children irrespective of background, personality, or other attributes, the system has structured within it the potential for deviance. Not all students are adequately prepared, sufficiently motivated, or responsive to classroom behavioral standards; the school therefore engages in specialized efforts to implement educational goals for these students. Within limits it seeks to increase students' motivation to achieve academically, to ameliorate personal and social stresses that circumscribe learning, and to cope with behavior that jeopardizes classroom processes.

When the source of deviance may be actual inability to conform to the school's requirements, stemming from physical defect or inadequate intelligence, the system may assign the student to a special class or school. Goals for special education often represent marked departures from other goals of the school, and this in itself may complicate problems in establishing goals priorities. In addition some special education programs may unwittingly aggravate the problems they were intended

---

[16] *National Education Association Research Bulletin,* Vol. 45, No. 2 (May 1967).

to solve. Elder reported that the continuation schools in California became "dumping grounds" for students who were unable to function in regular classroom situations.[17] Greater concern is typically expressed about special programs for students who are unwilling or unmotivated to conform to the school's requirements.

The extent of the seriousness of the consequences of the school's failure to provide adequate education for substantial numbers of students is apparent in any examination of studies of elementary and secondary education and in the vividly written case reports of such people as Kozol and Silberman.[18] These failures cannot be attributed to a lack of innovative efforts, especially in large metropolitan communities where the problem is at least as serious as anywhere. Much money and time have gone into a wide variety of demonstration efforts, but frequently these have been discontinued prematurely or because expectations for outcome were plcaed inordinately high. Insufficient attention has been given to the problems of implementing innovative programs, in particular to the use of an organizational perspective in initiating and evaluating such special programs.

There is now considerable pessimism about the failures of elementary and secondary education, especially in the urban ghetto school. Despite the commitment of considerable resources, serious underachievement continues, misconduct interferes with learning, and the premature school dropout rate is reported to be increasing in many states. Students as well as parents are exerting pressure on the schools to improve educational opportunities and to do so by increasing their participation in decision-making about curricula, personnel, and policies. Demonstrations, boycotts, strikes, and the like are becoming increasingly prevalent

[17] Glen H. Elder, Jr., in "The Schooling of Outsiders," *Sociology of Education,* Vol. 39, No. 4 (Fall 1966), pp. 324–342, presents data from a study of continuation schools on the West Coast that deal with the public reputation of the school and its articulation with meaningful adult occupational roles. Similar problems have been observed in the 600 Schools in New York City—where students are sent when the local schools cannot cope with them—despite considerable effort to alleviate some of their negative consequences through special projects of such agencies as Mobilization For Youth.

[18] *See* James E. Coleman et al., *Equality of Educational Opportunity* (Washington, D.C.: U.S. Government Printing Office, 1966); U.S. Civil Rights Commission, *Racial Isolation in the Public Schools* (Washington, D.C.: U.S. Government Printing Office, 1967); Jonathan Kozol, *Death at an Early Age* (Boston: Houghton-Mifflin, 1967); Charles E. Silberman, *Crisis in the Classroom* (New York: Random House, 1970).

—sometimes initiated by teachers, other times by students, and sometimes by other community residents.

The School As a People-Changing Organization

As a human service organization the school is primarily concerned with changing people, but in a more general sense with processing people into new statuses and careers. Included in this general category of human service organizations are mental hospitals and clinics, general hospitals, juvenile courts, family and children's agencies, prisons, and agencies for the retarded and physically handicapped. All of these are variously mandated by society, some for the socialization of persons so that they will be prepared to fulfill social role requirements and others for the treatment and resocialization of those who are not meeting conventional social requirements. The school is classified primarily as a socialization agency, although it also fulfills the functions of a social control agency. It is assumed that the majority of students are developing along normal gradients and are able to learn to fulfill their socially prescribed roles. In contrast, in agencies in which resocialization is the primary mandate, it is assumed that clients have demonstrated an inability to fulfill normal role prescriptions for given statuses.

This distinction breaks down in the process of analysis because all organizations involve their members in socialization and resocialization. The bank, the factory, and the university all require changes in those who participate in these organizations. The changes in attitudes and loyalties required of a bank employee, however, are necessary but not sufficient for organizational goal attainment. The changes sought by the public school in its students are substantive goals of academic and social learning. Variations among schools are expected in the priorities assigned in these two areas, but most teachers, administrators, and students would agree that a student is not merely expected to acquire specific knowledge and skills; he is also expected to develop his capabilities in learning and in meeting behavioral requirements for the enhancement of cultural values.

The nature of change in primary group members is what differentiates people-changing organizations from other kinds of bureaucracies. These change goals are pervasive—that is, the range of activities in which the school seeks to influence students extends outside the organization. This influence is expected to be relatively permanent in the form of new and different modes of behavior, new identities, and new self-perceptions. The process of inducing change is also important because it has a moral and value-laden quality. For example, it is generally accepted that one may only use socially approved methods of inducing behavioral change. The process is further confounded because the student is a reactive organism capable of directly influencing the learning process at all points and in highly significant ways.

Reliance on professionals for significant decision-making has been a characteristic of public schools as it is of many human service organizations. Teachers, school administrators, social workers, counselors, and other special services personnel all have substantial authority in the public school. The statuses of students and parents differ in terms both of the quality and quantity of authority they possess relative to that of the staff. It has been suggested by Cuban, Clark, Janowitz, and others that professionalism has dramatically increased social distance among teachers, parents, and students.[19]

Until recently teachers and administrators have assumed that they had nearly absolute autonomy in all crucial decision-making about the operation of the schools. This authority is now openly challenged by minority groups as well as by affluent middle-class parents. Clark has proposed several alternative conceptions of public education, all of which involve shared participation in decision-making. He argues for a new definition of education as follows:

> Public education can be more broadly and pragmatically defined in terms of that form of organization and functioning of an education system which is in the public interest.[20]

In his analysis of the urban ghetto school Janowitz argues that professionalism has contributed to the development of a "specialization" model of education. This model, he asserts, is a failure in the effective education of children. He proposes a new model—aggregation—that is focused on and built around teacher-student interactions within the classroom and community. Development of these interpersonal relationships is viewed as essential to education. The teacher is responsible for creating the conditions that enhance learning.[21]

[19] *See* Larry Cuban, "Teacher and Community," *Harvard Educational Review,* Reprint Series No. 3, *Community and the Schools,* pp. 63–82; Kenneth Clark, "Alternative Public School Systems," *Harvard Educational Review,* Vol. 38, No. 1 (Winter 1968), pp. 100–113; Morris Janowitz, *Institution Building in Urban Education* (New York: Russell Sage Foundation, 1969).

[20] Op. cit., p. 111.

[21] Op. cit., pp. 35–60.

Malperformance

This discussion of education in the current scene would be incomplete, especially for a social work audience, if attention were not paid to student malperformance—to the individual and organizational factors producing or associated with deviant behavior, to the failures of many schools, and to organizational strategies for resolving the problems of student and school malfunctioning. These problems are of such a serious nature in many communities today that they threaten the survival of schools. In other communities police and public officials are required to be present continuously "to preserve law and order."

It is known that standards for academic achievement and for desirable conduct vary among schools and even within the same school. These variations mean that such types of malperformance as underachievement, poor classroom conduct, and failure to adjust are not identically defined. Because of variations among schools and, to some extent, among teachers in the same school in standards of judgment, the aspects of pupil personality, performance, or ability presumably at issue in one situation are therefore not the same as those relevant in another situation.

In addition there are many differences among schools in terms of their curricula, resources, competence of teachers, student population, and school organization. These variations produce wide differences in the learning environment, in opportunities for achievement or adjustment, and in conditions that shape the meaning of the school experience for students.

There are also significant differences among schools with respect to their procedures for identifying and coping with student malperformance. In one school students manifesting difficulty may become targets for the full complement of remedial services. In another school such students may encounter relative indifference; when attention is given, it may result in loss of status or privileges for these students, perhaps leading eventually to their exclusion from classes and even suspension from school.

The theoretical frameworks for study of deviant behavior developed by social scientists such as Cohen, Lemert, Friedson, and Erikson are especially useful for analyzing malperformance in the school.[22] Mal-

---

[22] See Albert Cohen, *Deviance and Control* (Englewood Cliffs, N.J.: Prentice-Hall, 1966); Edwin Lemert, *Human Deviance, Social Problems, and Social Control* (Englewood Cliffs, N.J.: Prentice-Hall, 1967), pp. 40–66; Kai Erikson,

performance is used to refer to behavior that violates valued norms in the school and/or community to the degree that, if it persists, it will lead to the assignment of a status that has negative consequences for the person whose behavior is so defined. These consequences may be both of a long- and short-term nature, as Erikson suggests:

> Deviance is not a property inherent in certain forms of behavior; it is a property conferred upon these forms by the audiences which directly witness them. The critical variable in the study of deviants, then, is a social audience rather than the individual actor, since it is the audience which eventually determines whether or not any episode is labeled deviant.[23]

Within this framework student malperformance may be viewed as social or interactional in that it is a resultant of adverse interactions between characteristics of the student and school conditions. Given conditions of the school interact with attributes of the student population to enhance or impede educational attainment.[24] Certain aspects of school organization and practice contribute, often inadvertently and unwittingly, to the very problems they are designed to alleviate. For example, special classrooms for malperforming students may have negative consequences in that they serve to stigmatize the student and may lead to consistent informal discrimination, or they may foster organized stereotypical behavior. Thus no type of malperformance must be considered either as a unitary phenomenon or as inhering primarily in the attributes of the students, but rather as a result of the interaction between school and student.

The school defines the conditions under which given behavior becomes deviant as well as defining deviance as such. These definitions vary widely, making it possible for a behavior that is formally proscribed in one situation to be ignored or even sanctioned in another.

Student difficulties are social in that they are manifested within the social context of the school through the interaction of other students, with teachers, and with academic tasks. These problems assume relevance as they are assessed in terms of the social objectives and

"Notes on a Sociology of Deviance," in Howard Becker, ed., *The Other Side* (New York: Free Press of Glencoe, 1964), pp. 9–21; Eliot Friedson, *Disability as Social Deviance,*" in Marvin B. Sussman, ed., *Sociology and Rehabilitation* (Washington, D.C.: American Sociological Association, 1965), pp. 71–99.

[23] Op. cit., p. 18.

[24] Benjamin Hodgkins and Robert Herriatt, "Age-Grade Structure, Goals, and Compliance in the School: An Organizational Analysis," *Sociology of Education,* Vol. 43, No. 1 (Winter 1970), pp. 90–105.

values of school personnel. Such behaviors have their own origin in and are currently shaped by social relations with other students, in experiences in the school, and elsewhere.

Once the student has been identified as a deviant, this may significantly affect his public identity, his self-image, and his motivation to achieve. Furthermore, such identification has important implications for how the student is subsequently dealt with by the school, for how his school career is shaped, and, ultimately, for his life chances.

Summary

The picture of contemporary American elementary and secondary education presented here is not an optimistic one. The system is characterized by overbureaucratization, fragmentation, inability to adapt to changing conditions, tremendous pressures of size, racism and ideological conflict, lack of adequate resources, and feelings of alienation, indifference, and powerlessness on the part of those who are most deeply affected by the system. It is apparent that society is confronted with major problems in the education of the young. It is also probable that any adequate solution to these problems will involve types of change that are not yet fully apparent in the proposals and demonstration projects that have been initiated in a number of communities. For example, a variety of efforts are directed toward resolving problems resulting from racism and segregation, but few of these have achieved the level of success necessary to generate widespread support, despite legal efforts to facilitate the process.

Despite this pessimistic view of the contemporary situation, there are signs that provide a basis for optimism about the future. There is acceptance by many of the extent of the problems and a willingness to begin to work toward their resolution. Obviously this recognition is an essential precondition for change. A new concept of community is emerging in many areas—sometimes associated with efforts toward decentralization and community control of schools and in other situations as attempts to experiment with new forms of social interaction or with alternative forms of education. Questions such as "Who owns the schools and for what purpose?" are being examined seriously.

The present design of American education tends to isolate persons according to age and formalization of instruction. Education cannot be equated with "schooling," which is defined as formal instruction in a unit that has only that purpose. Unfortunately, much of present

28

social policy suggests that education is for the young and should be provided in a "school." Increased leisure time and the need to retrain a given individual for new occupations several times during his life indicate that education must be conceived of as a pervasive and open social institution. There are suggestions that the population is being overeducated, but perhaps the opposite may be true in terms of future societal needs. Effects are now being made to involve older adults as well as parents and interested community residents in a broadened concept of education for community living. When coupled with a policy fostering community control of schools, this offers a potentially exciting solution to many of the most serious problems of today, especially in the urban community.

The recent reports of the Joint Commission on the Mental Health of Children and of the 1970 White House Conference on Youth contain detailed recommendations for increasing the effectiveness of education as a vital social institution.[25] Although both reports are focused on children and youths, both state explicitly that solutions are not to be found in the isolation of the young. They also emphasize the need for education as an open and permeable social institution.

Thus this analysis of education in transition suggests that there are formidable problems that obstruct and inhibit education as a vital social force. But it has also been suggested that tentative solutions are on the horizon if we will but try to see them.

---

[25] Joint Commission on Mental Health of Children, *Crisis in Mental Health: Challenge for the 1970's* (New York: Harper & Row, 1970); White House Conference on Youth, "Task Force Recommendation," presented to the Subcommittee on Children and Youth of the Committee on Labor and Public Welfare, U.S. Senate, August 2, 1971.

Social Work
Contribution to
Education in Transition

Lela B. Costin

Two generally well-known, urgent problems provided the stimulus for
a national study of school social workers that is the subject of this
paper: (1) unanswered questions pertaining to the recruitment and use
of social work personnel and (2) disturbing conditions in the public
school and in the community that influence the nature of school social
work.

The manpower shortage is an increasingly familiar problem in school
social work, as it has been in the field of social welfare as a whole.
For the past twenty years the number of social workers employed
in the public school setting has increased steadily. Even so, the total
number has remained far short of the growing demand—and projections of demands based on increases in the school population do
not take into consideration the extent of needed social services for new
school programs resulting from federal legislation such as the Economic
Opportunity Act and the Elementary and Secondary Education Act.
It is clear that new answers to staffing problems must be found.

The second problem providing impetus for the study is unsatisfactory school and community conditions, as reflected in the large numbers
of children who fail to learn, who drop out of school, or who graduate

from high school poorly prepared for an effective transition into either higher education or employment. These conditions and practices are well known and well documented. Here are but a few of them:

1. Inequality of educational opportunities stemming from continuing widespread racial and economic segregation.

2. Persistent stereotyped beliefs that low-income and nonwhite children have limited capabilities, resulting in lowered expectations of them.

3. Faulty school practices related to control of pupils' behavior.

4. Placement of value on conformity to the detriment of individuality.

5. Lack of communication between the school and the community it serves and between the school and the home.

6. Irrelevance of much of the educational process for different population groups, which intensifies children's feelings of alienation from their school and from the larger society.

7. Learning experiences that fail to offer children and young persons the opportunity to feel involved—experiences that instead are too often inflexible, repetitious, or unrelated to their present and future.[1]

We waste their fleeting youth. A warning issued in 1923 is still highly relevant. Hart, addressing the National Conference of Social Work, said, "The school occupies a strategic position for holding the mind of childhood to futilities" and for "being able to prevent the development of that freed social intelligence without which civilization has no future." He also speculated about needed qualities in school program and organization and what could be accomplished "if our social workers were willing to lose their jobs for the sake of such schools."[2]

The study that forms the basis for this paper focused on the tasks performed by school social workers. The intent was to develop a basis for assigning responsibilities to school social work staff with different levels of education and training.[3] A definition of school social work

[1] James S. Coleman et al., *Equality of Educational Opportunity* (Washington, D.C.: U.S. Government Printing Office, 1966); Walter E. Schafer and Kenneth Polk, "Delinquency and the Schools," *Task Force Report: Juvenile Delinquency and Youth Crime, Report on Juvenile Justice and Consultants' Papers* (Washington, D.C.: Task Force on Juvenile Delinquency, the President's Commission on Law Enforcement and Administration of Justice, 1967).

[2] Joseph K. Hart, "The Relations of the School to Social Work," *Proceedings of the National Conference of Social Work, 1923* (Chicago: University of Chicago Press, 1923), pp. 365–370.

[3] Lela B. Costin, "An Analysis of the Tasks in School Social Work as a Basis for Improved Use of Staff." Final Report to the U.S. Department of Health, Education, and Welfare, Office of Education, Bureau of Research, February 28, 1968.

was developed to include a description of the content of that field of practice. This description was based on a factor analysis of ratings by professional school social workers. These ratings expressed the workers' opinions as to the relative importance of a range of tasks for the attainment of social work goals within a public school setting. The study also measured these social workers' opinions as to the appropriateness of assigning the various tasks to nonprofessional staff.

The study sample was drawn from a roster of professional school social workers and represented all regions of the United States. More than 72 percent of the persons to whom questionnaires were sent returned them. These completed questionnaires provided the data for the analysis that follows.

School Social Work Content

The overall finding of the analysis of school social work tasks was as follows:

1. School social workers formulated a definition of their work that focused primarily on the individual child in relation to his emotional problems and his personal adjustment.

   a. Casework was seen as the primary method of giving service, although group work was acknowledged to be important. The principal technique was to interview the child to determine his feelings about his home, his school, and his problems.

   b. The goals in work with the individual child were centered on attempts to help him control or express his feelings appropriately, to help him understand his relationships to others, or to give him an insight into his emotional problems.

   c. The problems of the child in school were viewed as arising mostly from his personal characteristics or those of his parents and from their family functioning. In turn, little recognition was given to the impact of school conditions on a child or the total set of circumstances within the school that might be related to his poor adjustment.

   d. Emphasis was placed on helping the individual student accommodate himself to the existing school situation rather than on modifying patterns within a school's operations that might be generating difficulties for him and for other students as well.

e. Work with the child's parents was considered important mainly when this was necessary to clarify the child's problems or to obtain support for the social worker's activity with the child.

f. Consultation with the teacher was defined principally in relation to an individual child and the social worker's service. Omitted from consultation were areas of the teacher's work related to broader concerns in the school system and the community.

g. Activity with community agencies was defined in ways that supported the worker's efforts with an individual child—giving or obtaining information in order to facilitate referrals or supporting parents and encouraging them to use existing community services to which they had been referred.

2. In contrast with these highly rated tasks, school social workers rated as significantly less important work with children and their parents in relation to the child's educational goals, values, abilities, and interests and to the social and academic expectations and regulations of the school. Least important were tasks that focused on activities such as professional research, in-service training, publication of new findings and perspectives, recruitment of social work personnel, work with parents to help them understand and channel their concerns about problems of the school system, the improvement of working conditions in the school, consultation with administrators on the formulation of student welfare policies and work in the community to bring about new social welfare services or social change.

3. When opinions of school social workers in seven geographic regions of the United States were compared, they showed a pattern of consistent agreement on the definition of school social work just described. The agreement was almost as complete for social workers from school systems of varying sizes.

4. In spite of the acknowledged insufficient number of graduate social workers, professional social workers in the schools showed a reluctance to identify tasks that they were willing to assign to persons with less than their own level of education and training. They reserved for themselves responsibility for the core tasks—casework and group work services to the child and his family in relation to emotional problems and personal adjustment. They were willing "occasionally" to delegate some of the tasks involved in routine management of a work load or the provision of factual information or suggestions in educational counseling with the child and his parents.

This definition of school social work largely ignores the relationship of the school and its operations to other social institutions in the community. It commits its professional personnel to use their resources to provide a limited range of social work services without sufficient attention to the most pressing problems of schoolchildren and youths today, problems that would lend themselves to experimentation in the design of services and staffing patterns.

Correcting the Situation

The findings of this analysis make it hard to escape the conclusion that social work in the schools has arrived at a point in its history when the main body of its tasks and goals is not attuned to the urgent problems of the population being served. How can we begin to correct this situation?

SOCIAL WORK'S OBJECTIVES   Social work's objectives in relation to the school's purpose must be based on social work principles. Essentially the school's purpose is to provide a life setting for teaching and learning and the attainment of competence. Social work's obligation is to help make school a rich and stimulating environment for children and young people in which they can prepare themselves for the world in which they have to live. The school, then, must be related to the characteristics of its student body, the outside community, and the social conditions its pupils face, and it must carry out its teaching in ways that contribute to needed social improvements.

Some early social workers were keenly aware of the strategic position the school occupies among a community's institutions and were impressed by the opportunities presented to the school. Breckinridge, for example, in addressing the National Education Association in 1914, spoke of the magnitude of the school's task and the extent to which its importance had gripped the conscience of the community:

> To the social worker the school appears as an instrument of almost unlimited possibilities, not only for passing on to the next generation the culture and wisdom of the past, but for testing present social relationships and for securing improvements in social conditions.[4]

---

[4] Sophonisba P. Breckinridge, "Some Aspects of the Public School From a Social Worker's Point of View," *Journal of the Proceedings and Addresses of the National Education Association, July 4–11, 1914* (Ann Arbor, Mich.: National Education Association, 1914), p. 45.

Her plea was for a closer study of the school's failures and the consequent loss to the nation in social well-being. At about the same time as Breckinridge spoke, other social workers in settlement houses were recognizing the necessity for the school to relate itself closely to the present and future lives of its children. Wald wrote:

> Intelligent social workers seize opportunities for observation, and almost unconsciously develop methods to meet needs. They see conditions as they are, and become critical of systems as they act and react upon the child or fail to reach him at all.
> . . . Where the school fails, it appears to the social workers to do so because it makes education a thing apart—because it separates its work from all that makes up the child's life outside the classroom.[5]

For far too many children education has become a thing apart, separate from their vital concerns. The resulting pupil problems, as Vinter and Sarri have defined them, are a product of the interaction of pupil characteristics and school conditions.[6]

SOCIAL WORK RESPONSIBILITY If school social workers are to meet their professional obligations, they must move quickly to remedy the existing situation. One way is to assume more active responsibility for consultation with administrators and teachers in the formulation of school policy that directly affects the welfare of pupils. This means examining the symptoms and determining the causes of pupils' problems in the system, channeling knowledge about neighborhood and other cultural and community influences on pupils' lives, encouraging and aiding administrators in developing cooperative working relationships with community agencies.

A second area needing renewed attention by school social workers is liaison among home, school, and community. Many parents as well as children—in all socioeconomic groups—are alienated from the public school and feel that they have no effective way to channel their concerns to the appropriate school personnel or to affect the school's functioning. Increasing attention is being paid to the rights of parents in relation to the schools their children attend; to honor these rights implies more than simply giving attention to parents when

[5] Lillian D. Wald, *The House on Henry Street* (New York: Henry Holt & Co., 1915), p. 106.

[6] Robert D. Vinter and Rosemary C. Sarri, "Malperformance in the Public School: A Group Work Approach," *Social Work,* Vol. 10, No. 1 (January 1965), pp. 3–13.

school personnel want their cooperation in carrying out a school plan or procedure in relation to their children.

There is evidence that too often school social workers' relationships with community agencies are ineffective, to the detriment of troubled children. Anderson, in an investigation of the processes and problems in the referral of schoolchildren to mental health clinics throughout Illinois, found frequent impairment in the usefulness of school services and mental health clinics because of the inability of professionals in both schools and clinics to cooperate with each other. Such failure was reflected in petty jealousies and in lack of communication, coordination, and understanding.[7]

In addition to the need to develop more effective means of cooperation with existing community agencies, school social workers have the responsibility to give leadership in bringing about needed extra-school programs through work with other individuals and community groups and to interpret overall school needs and policies (not just those of social work service) to those persons in the community who are in a position to support and enhance the school's effectiveness.

The earliest function of school social workers was to serve as an authentic liaison among home, school, and community. They must again give considerable priority to this essential role. They must also continue to give direct service to students, singly and in groups. But toward what goals?

The definition of school social work presented earlier placed major emphasis on casework with the individual child in relation to his emotional problems, with goals centered on attempts to help him control or express his feelings appropriately, understand his relationships with others, and give him insight into his emotional problems. In today's world the focus of school social work must be shifted away from a major emphasis on emotion, motivation, and personality and toward such cognitive areas as learning, thinking, and problem-solving. Goals should center on helping students to acquire a sense of competence, a readiness for continued learning, and a capacity to adapt to change.

Several reasons support this shift in emphasis:

1. A greater proportion of young people must be prepared to suc-

---

[7] Richard John Anderson, "Procedures and Problems in Referring School Children to Mental Health Clinics." Unpublished doctoral dissertation, Illinois State University, 1968.

ceed in higher education if they are to acquire the knowledge and skills required for technological and professional occupations where manpower is badly needed and where they will be able to share in the responsibilities and rewards of full citizenship.

2. A capacity to adapt to change and to continue to learn is essential for the successful future of this country's youths. Regardless of what else may be predicted, it is certain that there will be change and stress in the world for a long time and that many of the solutions to life's problems will lie in learning and the capacities for problem-solving and decision-making.

3. Confidence that one can learn and succeed—a sense of competence acquired through learning—is an important contributor to individual mental health. Escalona stated it well when she said:

> One of the primary ego functions that sustain adaptation, and that provide means of coping with stress and of overcoming obstacles, is the capacity for formal structured learning. . . . The experience of learning, and the perception of the self as one who *can* learn, generates a sense of the self as an active being, and . . . as the carrier of power and competence. It also makes available a source of pleasure and of satisfaction that is not directly dependent upon the quality of interpersonal relationships. Last, not least, each instance of successful learning makes the world more intelligible.[8]

Target Groups

To what groups of children and young persons should school social workers direct major attention? The following three main groups should be given some priority.

PRESCHOOL CHILDREN The need for constructive programs for young children's daytime care and development is urgent. The ferment regarding day care and preschool education, reflected in attempts to reconceptualize daytime programs for preschoolers, is growing. In planning and administering such programs, the social work profession traditionally has stressed components of emotional care and protection and has termed its programs "day care service," implying that they are a form of supplemental family care. The education profession, on

---

[8] Sibylle K. Escalona, "Mental Health, the Educational Process, and the Schools," *American Journal of Orthopsychiatry,* Vol. 37, No. 1 (January 1967), p. 2.

the other hand, has given greater consideration to the child's social and intellectual development and has applied terms such as "nursery school education" and, more recently, "compensatory preschool education."

For many years both professions seemed content with this administrative distinction—care and protection through social work and social and intellectual development through education—and ignored the fact that these boundaries were artificial ones that contributed to insufficient and unsatisfactory programs on both sides. Hopefully, various developments are moving us toward a more generic definition of programs for the young child's daytime care and development outside his own home.

One such development is reflected in the findings of a study of child care and working mothers reported by Ruderman for the Child Welfare League of America.[9] In all seven geographic regions of her study, from 20 to 40 percent of mothers who had children under 12 years of age were employed—a sizable proportion—and this proportion is expected to increase. Ruderman's study confirms that working mothers reflect the community as a whole and come from all its subgroups. The great majority were middle-class whites with employed husbands and living in intact households. Under the umbrella of "working mother family" are a large number of both so-called normal and problem families, with children who have a wide range of individual characteristics.

What these young children often share are inadequate, makeshift, and unstimulating forms of care and education during their mothers' working hours. Only 3 percent of the child care arrangements of the working mothers in Ruderman's study were in formally organized day care or nursery school programs. With the nation's economy requiring and encouraging more mothers to work, how can we continue to ignore the necessity for attention to the development of these millions of young children who need an outside source of nurture, supportive emotional response, and a variety of stimulating experiences that will contribute to their cognitive and social development?

Another factor that is helping to move us toward broader attention to daytime programs for young children is concern about the learning

---

[9] Florence A. Ruderman, *Child Care and Working Mothers: A Study of Arrangements Made for Daytime Care of Children* (New York: Child Welfare League of America, 1968).

38

handicaps of culturally deprived children. Much of the impetus for attention to cultural deprivation grew out of social forces and changes in society, such as changes in the economic system, a greatly enlarged reliance on technology—bringing with it jobs that require proficiency in the use of language, mathematics, and problem-solving methods—and the civil rights movement. It was psychological theory and changes in the conception of man's nature and his development, however, that provided the basis for a reasonable expectation that preschool services could deal with cultural deprivation in a way that would increase substantially the average level of children's intellectual capacity. Certain changed beliefs based on psychological research showed the feasibility of manipulating the environment of children who were being reared in culturally deprived circumstances, not only through broad social change and welfare provisions, but through daytime programs that would utilize an understanding of the importance of a child's early sensory experiences—the extent to which he has a variety of things to see, hear, touch, and respond to with interest in the company of understanding and responsive adults.

This kind of knowledge about how a child's intelligence develops provided the scientific backdrop for the federal government's Project Head Start. This kind of assumption of responsibility at the federal level, together with the day care provisions in the 1960s under amendments to the Social Security Act, provide a more forthright assertion of public social policy in relation to programs for young children's daytime care and development than this country has ever had. It places an urgent obligation on education and social welfare to resolve the differences in their conceptions of day care and preschool education and to join forces to provide stimulating preschool programs available to all young children.

Why should school social workers become involved in this question when they already have so much to do? There are several reasons:

1. To ensure that when children enter school at age 6 the school's purpose will not be thwarted because of the inadequacies of these children's early experiences.

2. Because social work principles and methods have much to offer that is important in the conception and design of programs for children's daytime care and development.

3. Because school social workers occupy a pivotal position for leadership between the institutions of public education and public welfare.

In this matter we might say, as did Oppenheimer in 1924, that the school is "the strategic center of child welfare work." [10]

We might also take note of the fact that today an undesirable degree of "professional separatism" exists between the fields of child welfare and school social work.

NEGLECTED AND DEPRIVED CHILDREN A 'second target group for school social work attention is children between the ages of 6 and 12 who live in homes where they experience neglect by their parents and various other forms of extreme deprivation—economic, cultural, and social. These are among the nation's most vulnerable children. They live in disorder, reflected in their parents' failure to perform the essential tasks that help to hold a family together—tasks of money management, health care, food preparation, and housekeeping. In addition, the parents have pressing personal needs that take precedence over the needs of their children. Interpersonal relationships within the family are unstable; there may be constant dissension, absence of affection and trust, or extensive marital discord. Parents and children are isolated. Ostracism by the community and neighborhood is common— landlords, officials, and tradespeople tend to treat such families with disrespect.

These families have been labeled multiproblem families. Their children are children in trouble—seriously disadvantaged and in need of immediate help. These are children who have learned early the tragic truth that to the community—and usually to their parents—they are regarded as surplus. Their family, and others like theirs, has too many children; such families, the community says, have nothing to offer—society does not need them. They cannot escape the recognition that in the mainstream of society they are termed problems, with little chance for success.

It is true that many of these families receive considerable attention from child welfare workers and public assistance workers who carry a protective services caseload. But the traditional approach in protective services has been to focus on casework with the parents, whose demands and problems are so great that their children seldom receive direct attention from the worker. These children require and deserve

---

[10] Julius John Oppenheimer, *The Visiting Teacher Movement With Special Reference to Administrative Relationships* (New York: Public Education Association of the City of New York, 1924), p. 28.

help in their own right. School should be a place where they can receive constructive and caring attention in relationships in which they can be seen as individuals. School social workers must not assume that they need not give social work services to these children simply because their families are known to other community agencies.

THE DEPRIVED MIDDLE CLASS The last group of children is quite different from the neglected and disadvantaged children just discussed. These are middle-class children with affluent parents in the cultural mainstream of society. Sometimes their relative disadvantage is imposed from within their own homes, where they may be overprotected, neglected, ruled by rigid and dominating parents, or given no guidance at all. Their adult models may be shallow, unstimulating, insensitive, or dishonest. Here too one parent may be missing because of marital discord, separation, or divorce. Here too adequate parental attention may be lacking. The deficiencies in such homes are more easily concealed behind a façade of good neighborhoods, well-kept lawns, comfortable homes, polite speech, and other material disguises.

Because of their favored status and apparent success, we fail to recognize these children's handicaps and the school's effect on their development. Most of these children enter school with a capacity and readiness to succeed, often to find an outdated, mediocre educational system in which their talents are not cultivated. They too may be required to study what to them is irrelevant to their daily lives and their future. As they turn away, they are allowed to forgo true learning and to settle for doing their assigned homework, passing their courses, and accepting promotion through the system. They are kept in cultural ignorance of the world, its people, and its social institutions. And yet how these young people meet their future responsibilities as citizens is crucial to the survival of society.

Some authorities on education of the disadvantaged have included such middle-class youths in their definition of the educationally disadvantaged. An example of this kind of interest is as follows:

Having prepared him for college and employment, we have given little thought to how well he will perform as an adult, how much he will be responsible toward other human beings and cognizant that a concern for the welfare of others is ultimately a concern for one's own welfare. . . .
The very institutions we have established to perpetuate our Democratic society . . . will surely fall short of their purposes unless the people who

administer and operate them are themselves fully educated, thinking adults. . . .

We cannot expect such an approach as long as middle-class individuals —those who become our housing authority personnel, employers, realtors, social workers, and teachers—are themselves deprived of the full benefits of an educational process which prepare them for their personal and social roles.[11]

These three target groups of children and young persons are not the only ones who require new approaches. Among others who should be considered are, for example, predelinquent, aggressive youths between the ages of 14 and 16 who have hostile attitudes toward school and who get into trouble in school and in the streets—where they often spend much time because they have been suspended from school for their misbehavior.

Implications

Various important implications flow from this analysis of tasks in school social work. School social workers must revise extensively the static model of service into which their field of practice has drifted. To be effective, a new model must recognize the interdependent relationship of the schools to the community's other social institutions and functions, some of which also have serious problems—for example, the unstable family, the public assistance system, the juvenile court, and the labor market for low-income youths. Further, school social work service must be defined as a response to the most pressing problems of the school's pupils and to underlying conditions both within and outside the school system that impinge on large numbers of them. In redesigning social work service, the purpose of the school must be kept clearly in mind—that is, to serve, not as a therapeutic center, but as a life setting for children and young people in which learning is possible and competence can be acquired. Social workers in the schools must give up their traditional, almost exclusive, reliance on casework and use all the social work methods and alternative approaches within each of these methods.

Greater weight should be given to responsibility for consultation with administrators and teachers in the formulation of school policy that

---

[11] Mario D. Fantini and Gerald Weinstein, *The Disadvantaged: Challenge to Education* (New York: Harper & Row, 1968), pp. 38–39.

directly affects the welfare of children and young persons and their chances of succeeding in school. Equally important, the neglected role of liaison between home, school, and community must be revitalized. As school social workers begin to redefine their functions and interpret their revised goals, it should help to lessen some of the interdisciplinary confusion that exists among the various school specialists, especially psychologists, guidance counselors, and social workers.

Changes such as these will make it possible to experiment with new staffing patterns and to break away from outmoded patterns of work. Indeed, if the school social work role is derived from a definition of function that reflects such crucial conditions and problems within and outside the school system, then the appropriate social work role in the schools will not only *permit* but will also *require* differential use of social work personnel with various levels of education and training. Conversely, if the definition of school social work is kept narrow, primarily to reflect and meet the needs and abilities of the graduate social worker, it will be difficult to break through the problem of the growing demand for school social workers in the face of continued insufficient numbers of those with a graduate education.

A challenge issued by Addams in 1909 seems especially applicable to all who work in the schools today. In her book *The Spirit of Youth and the City Streets,* she wrote:

> We may either smother the divine fire of youth or we may feed it. We may either stand stupidly staring as it sinks into a murky fire of crime and flares into the intermittent blaze of folly or we may tend it into a lambent flame with power to make clean and bright our dingy city streets.[12]

---

[12] Jane Addams, *The Spirit of Youth and the City Streets* (New York: Macmillan Co., 1909), pp. 161–162.

The Schools: Social Change and Social Welfare

Alfred J. Kahn

Social work is a profession within the social welfare field. Social welfare, as an institution in American society, takes its cues from the social milieu. Therefore, to talk about new directions in school social work is to talk about society and social welfare, using the latter term in its broad sense.

Although the social milieu is the point of departure for any discussion of social welfare, it is hard to characterize the world in which we are living and to know what to make of the present social scene. For example, six or seven years ago the question of what automation was doing to American society was seen as important. Today hardly anyone talks about automation, although it may still be a major force.

At one time many people were certain that in a few years work would be redundant—that those who wanted to work would have to fight for the privilege of being in the labor force. All others would have a guaranteed means of support that would keep them out of the system and out of the way of those who really wanted to do the world's work. These were the projections of Utopians like Theobald, who took such projections quite seriously and presumably still does.[1]

---

[1] See, for example, Robert Theobald, *Free Men and Free Markets* (Garden City, N.Y.: Doubleday Anchor Books, 1965).

It may well be that these projections are reasonable for a period of twenty or thirty years from now, but it is certainly true that today society is working under the assumption that there is a lot of work to be done and that income should basically be related to participation in the labor force, except for persons in those categories to which we are willing to extend societal support. For example, we are willing to support students, we are willing to support old people under a variety of devices, and perhaps, if we are wise, we will do something for children as well.

Similarly, there was a great deal of talk about the impact of bureaucracy—of mammoth institutions—on our lives. A few years ago the intervention of bureaucracy between individuals and primary group experience was seen as a major social problem. Of course automation made the whole thing even worse.

Context for Decision-Making

These problems may all be important, but somehow they have become less salient for the moment than other problems we are now facing. The question to be asked now is: What is the essence of the social milieu that is going to shape present-day school social work? School social workers working with growing children, trying to set a framework for their growth and a context in which to help them develop their sense of community and of primary group experience, have to decide what the social situation is from which they operate.

SEPARATIST MOVEMENTS The situation we face today is something that we would not have expected six or seven years ago. There is a large militant and vocal separatist movement in the black community. There are the beginnings of a smaller, but sometimes equally vocal, separatist movement in Spanish-speaking communities. What context do these movements create for the children in these communities? Many social workers working in ghetto communities and urban school systems are dealing not with a small number of black or Spanish-speaking children, but with a population of minority group children who may comprise 50 percent or more of the school population.

In this context everyone—school social workers as well as children—is trying to develop some perspective on the separatist movement. What are its implications for services? What are its implications for the way these services are organized? How may the splits within minority communities over this issue be recognized and evaluated?

CRISIS OF LEGITIMACY There is one aspect of the immediate reality that directly affects social workers in the school system. The United States today is facing a major crisis—at both the local and national levels—of legitimacy and due process. That is, major questions have been raised that have challenged existing structures, value systems, and procedures—major questions about the validity of traditional ways of determining community policy, of implementing that policy, and of carrying through community programs. This crisis is a challenge to values, to traditional democratic due process, and to traditional political processes.

Some groups—perhaps out of guilt, fear, or the conviction that in order to right injustice one sometimes must do things in different ways, forgoing traditional processes—have accepted what is taking place. Others are not so accepting of challenges to tradition. Repressive steps have been taken. Decisions made under the pressures of protest groups are being revoked. Students have been imprisoned and procedures are being tightened in a variety of places. This does not affect only professional associations and universities; it is rapidly spreading to the high schools and junior high schools. What is the importance of it all?

When young people question the authority of teachers and parents, when they use tactics that meet none of the rules of due process or even of polite behavior, this represents a crisis in legitimacy. We must now decide whether we are dealing with a temporary aberration or a basic change in society. This has major implications for those who deal with young people and students. Is this a social revolution out of which will come new norms and new values? Or is this, rather, a temporary outbreak by a small minority who will soon be repressed? Either case could be argued. And there are intermediate positions. We are in a period of great conflict over the question of legitimacy and the use of repression. What will result is not certain, but the schools will be a major battleground. This means that the school social worker will have to question and define not only his relationship with a community that is in revolt against the traditional concept of a school system, but also his relationship with students who are in revolt against the traditional procedures within that system.

ANTIPOVERTY AND CIVIL RIGHTS MOVEMENTS The antipoverty and civil rights movements have been built on the social changes of the past decade. They grew out of both progress and great inequality. As benefits increase, the inadequacy of existing provisions is dramatized because people's expectations rise. It is not that people have less. Rather, they

46

have more—but their expectations are greater. They have learned that they can have even more, and that others do have more—more material resources, more human rights, more human dignity. As the threshold is raised, people's capacity to see beyond the horizon is raised.

Even larger numbers of American people have a vision of an industrial urban society that could be humanized, that could redistribute wealth as never before, that could guarantee a social minimum, that could implement values in ways that humanize the city. There is going to be a greater freedom from market forces and greater decision-making through political means on how to distribute the productivity of the country, which soon will reach a Gross National Product of $1 trillion. If we do nothing more than put a fair share of the increment of GNP into social welfare, we will have the kind of society that none of us dared dream about twenty years ago.

This is the context in which decisions must be made as to where the schools are going, where education is going, and where social work is going.

Problems of the Young

In the context just presented judgments will have to be made about youths, children, families, and educational institutions. Several problems of the young are striking.

ADOLESCENT ROLE IDENTITY One monumental problem society will face is that of adolescent role identity. As a result of the nation's standards of living, nutrition, and health, the age of puberty is constantly being lowered. It used to be said that the age of puberty drops three months in every decade. Even that no longer seems right. People are becoming sexually mature at a far earlier age than ever before.

Whereas in past societies sexual maturation occurred at about the time when adolescents were entering the labor market, this is not the case today. Our concerns for the education of the young join with the long period of training required to produce a productive and skilled worker to keep adolescents out of the labor market. Child labor and compulsory education laws were enacted to guarantee a minimal educational level for all. We want to maintain our children's dependency because we want them to stay in school. This is an important incongruity—socially defined dependency at a point of increasing physical maturity.

47

When are we going to face the fact that there are not just a couple of transitional years between childhood and adulthood, but rather a large piece of life? This transitional period is defined variously as from age 16 to 25, 18 to 25, perhaps 16 to 30. In this age group are people who lack a respected, economically viable life role. We either try to make them less mature than they are by denying them responsibility and rights or we impose burdens on them that the economy does not sustain. Young people are trying in new kinds of ways to create their own devices for coping with the problems they face. Much of what they do upsets the rest of the society.

The issues of identity and of the role of young people in today's society motivate a great deal of the behavior of young people today. The great altruism and self-dedication of the Peace Corps and Vista Volunteers give evidence of this, as does the escapist philosophy of the motorcycle clubs and societal dropouts. There is the altruism of the ghetto volunteers on the one hand, and delinquency and destructiveness on the other. There is the drug scene—and also the writing, music, and art. Yet these are all young people looking for a role in society.

Among other things, college and high school students are demanding a role in the running, not only of the institutions in which they are studying, but of the country as a whole. That their demands are justified is indicated by, among other gains made, the granting to 18-year-olds of the right to vote.

The evidence shows that these young people do have something to say and something to contribute. And what they are saying cannot be ignored.

Society is faced with several major questions here. Together with young people it needs to engage in social invention to solve the problem of increased maturity and enforced dependency. What can be done? Will young people be given stipends or salaries while they go to school— as is done in some countries—so they can have incomes they regard as their own? What kinds of socially responsible things can they do if they are not in the labor force?

SOCIAL VALUES Another kind of problem is involved in the cases of younger students in junior high and high school. These young people are asking such important questions as: What is of value? What is worthwhile? What is important? What is true?

They can see several different social patterns. In the ghettos they see upheaval, protest—a fight against injustice that takes the form of

48

undermining the legitimacy of social institutions, of saying that the establishment has cheated, enslaved, and fooled people. In the suburbs they see a world of affluence that is in many ways empty from the point of view of values. For many children childhood is defined as a time to study hard in order to get into a good college. The important question is how to get ahead.

Seeing all this, how can young people today believe and trust in themselves and others? Some young people join the value system of the rat race and become grade oriented. Others cannot quite make it in the rat race. They are not bright enough, do not have the familial supports, or are not rich enough. They become the hoods, the cop-outs, the drug-users, the runaways. Some youths become social delinquents, others become junior models of suburban America.

Contribution of the School

Can the school contribute anything to solving the problems of young people in American society? Does a part of the solution of the problem of identity—the search for responsible roles—lie with the school? There is another question beyond these: Does the school system have any role in the broader social service network? This writer feels that the answer is "yes." The premise is this: Apart from his service role, a social worker in any institution must help shape its forms and policies.

A SOURCE OF INFORMATION How does the individual learn about his rights and benefits in this society? How does he learn about social security, housing, retirement plans, and health services? The citizen needs sources of information. The schools have the opportunity to provide this necessary access to the system for all families with children. The school could become an access point within the social service network—a system of information, advice, referral, and advocacy that goes far beyond the problems of individual children.

One must, of course, ask whether this would be a good thing for the schools to do. What would it do to the role of the school in the community?

ASSISTANCE TO COMMUNITY GROUPS One of the specific problems today, perhaps the biggest problem, is the deprived minority group member in the urban setting. What can the schools do about the civil rights revolution? What can they do to accelerate in some way what society is trying to do to solve this problem?

49

There are a number of possibilities. Technical assistance to community groups is one. The school is a center of knowledge and competence. Schoolteachers and school resources may be the only place in many parts of the country to which local community people can turn when they are deprived. Schools could provide technical assistance to people who want to create Model Cities programs, an antipoverty program, or other strategies to cope with deprivation on an organized basis.

This does not mean going out and organizing, although that is a possible role, and certainly school social workers could provide community extension. They could provide training and information programs extending beyond literacy needs into the field of community services and social welfare.

COMMUNITY CONTROL This brings up a more difficult problem—that of the school as a battleground for community control. Deprived minority group members often feel that they can break out of their situation by gaining some control over school policies, just as suburban parents have in their school systems. The struggle will involve the problems of increased community control and protection of union rights, of community control and maintenance of professional standards. The same battle will emerge shortly in the public welfare and health fields as well.

Social workers in the schools have to think carefully about this question of community control. They will have to ask themselves such questions as these: How do I feel about community control? How can I cope with it? How can I help communities make decisions about it? Am I a community organizer? Am I neutral or not? On whose side am I? What role do I play? What skills and knowledge do I have? Ultimately school social workers will have to inject some sense and thought into the whole issue of centralization/decentralization that is dealt with today largely by rhetoric.

The truth is that no modern society can decentralize everything or allow complete community control in any area. The issue is rather what kinds of policies may be set at each level, so that participation, diversity, autonomy, self-expression, implementation of goals, identification with the system, and community competence may be maximized. Complete community control is totally unrealistic because funding, standards, and requirements come partly from outside. So is a totally central administration because schools need to individualize their constituencies. The question becomes: What pattern will now emerge? For school social workers there is an additional question: How do the more traditional issues, such as helping with deviance, breakdown, truancy, poor functioning, and poor learning, fit into the picture?

Task of the School Social Worker

The task of the school social worker could be defined as doing all those things within the school system that will help the child to function as a student. The school social worker must give the teacher, the child, and the family the support they need. At the same time these services ought not to be provided in such a way as to define the school as a treatment facility.

Not all communities have mental health clinics. School social work in the casework role goes far toward filling this gap: supporting the teacher with classroom adjustments, working with families, working with children on a short-term basis, coping with school emergencies, making referrals, integrating services. Some school social workers see this as their role. However, there are certain issues that should be discussed. On the one hand, the British Seebohm Committee has examined the whole pattern of social service and has made the case that the school social worker be based in a local general social service outlet. In this way he will be able to assume a full treatment role and there will be no question about his identification. School social services will be integrated with family services.[2] On the other hand, there are some advantages to the school social worker in being part of an educational institution to assure credibility and help shape school policies.

School social workers ought to explore the limits of the institution in terms of community organization, social action, or treatment and, while recognizing what they cannot do, should retain their identification with the school as an institution.

---

[2] *Report of the Committee on Local Authority and Allied Personal Social Services* (London, England: Her Majesty's Stationery Office. 1968). The operational pattern in London keeps social workers in the schools.

Social Work Contributions and Present Educational Needs

Carl Marburger

It is not an easy task to find new ways of coping with old and new problems in the schools. In these chaotic times, to refocus school social work services to meet high-priority needs and to develop new approaches to improving both instructional and maintenance systems are high-priority tasks not only for those in the social work profession, but for all school personnel. Hopefully the identification of major roadblocks in school social work services will have an effect on and applicability to other school services as well.

One of the prime strategies may be a refocusing of school social work services based on needs that are identified by persons other than social workers. Some pertinent findings from a study made in New Jersey in 1964 by the State Department of Education are instructive. School social workers and the administrators who employed them were asked to react to a list of sixty-one tasks. There was marked disagreement between the social workers and superintendents as to which of these functions the workers should perform. And, surprisingly, there was a noticeable disparity of thinking among the social workers themselves as to the importance of the various tasks.

52

Perhaps there may be less disagreement over functions now. Determination of this could be valuable. Even more valuable would be identification of the needs of the population being served. A long, hard look should be taken at their most pressing needs in an attempt to relate the social worker's role to them in an effective way. Perhaps school social workers have permitted their sights to become too narrow, focusing only on the superficial aspects of school problems. Perhaps too much attention has been given to the student and his home environment, without equal concern for the school environment. The social worker should be a bridge between the home and the school. Frequently—and especially in the urban situation—he is not; often he cannot relate to either environment. Most important, perhaps too much attention is being concentrated on the most easily identifiable target—the emotionally disturbed—without sufficient parallel strategies being developed to deal with the much larger and more explosive problem area of the environmentally disadvantaged.

The Beadleston Act

Take, for example, the Beadleston Act enacted in New Jersey in 1955. This act requires all school districts to provide special education services for the handicapped, with the state to pay 50 percent of the cost of such services. The act's definition of disability, however, is too narrow to encompass the core problem of urban schools. It does not provide special education services for children who suffer language disability resulting from a disadvantaged background.

In spite of this deficiency, the Beadleston legislation has had a real impact on the quality of educational services for the disabled. It has also had a significant effect on the role of the school social worker by more sharply defining that role. A number of controversial tasks that school social workers may originally have assumed simply because no one else performed them have been taken over by a new professional—the learning disability specialist.

Similarly, there has been better separation between the roles of the school psychologist and the school social worker. The psychologist has taken over those areas in which there had earlier been disagreement, such as interpreting mental retardation to parents in terms of academic achievement and interpreting the meaning of tests to parents. Such tasks logically are a function of the psychologist. Perhaps the greatest confusion still exists between the roles of the school social worker and the school nurse. Here role differentiation has emerged slowly—mostly through trial and error—and sometimes the resulting tensions have hampered overall team functioning.

The Beadleston legislation has had a profound impact on the expansion of school social work services in New Jersey schools. It immediately assigns school social workers and other members of the child study team to the area of special services. It mentions no less than thirteen specialists who are to participate as needed on a team basis in the identification and classification of handicapped children. The child study team members are assigned primary responsibility for the formulation of the educational prescription and its subsequent implementation.

The law states specifically that a social worker must participate in the identification, classification, and program planning for children whose difficulties are manifested by emotional disturbance. As a result the number of school social workers in New Jersey has increased at a steady pace. In 1958 there were 80 school social workers in the public schools; in 1968 there were 380. However, in spite of these gains there has been little change in the school social worker's view of his role and the relative importance of his various tasks.

Office of Education Study

In this regard a study of school social work tasks undertaken by the U.S. Office of Education's Bureau of Research is pertinent. In this study school social workers rated 107 representative tasks as to relative importance.[1] The findings and interpretations were distressing.

School social workers gave low priority to helping the child and his parents in relation to the child's educational problem. The importance of the learning situation was generally ignored; instead, social work goals were seen as focused primarily on work with the individual child in relation to his emotional problems or personal adjustment. Relations with community agencies were usually limited to information exchange or a source of referral for the family. There was a persistent tendency to support the status quo without attempting to effect change in conditions at the school, in the home, or in the neighborhood that could be contributing to the child's problems. The problem was almost always

---

[1] See Lela B. Costin, "An Analysis of the Tasks in School Social Work as a Basis for Improved Use of Staff." Final Report to the U.S. Department of Health, Education, and Welfare, Office of Education, Bureau of Research, February 28, 1968.

seen as arising from within the child or his family instead of from a possible interaction of the child and the school.

Another finding of great significance was that there was much reluctance to analyze social work tasks with the idea of defining differential levels of practice. Unless greater clarity is achieved in this area, the public schools will have little or no criteria with which to recruit or assign social workers with varying degrees of training.

Bringing Social Work Closer to Education

It is safe to assume that much of social work practice is being brought closer to the core problem of education by reason of required procedures such as those outlined in the Beadleston Act. This law gives orderly direction to the child study teams, spelling out the steps whereby appropriate facilities are to be sought if the local district is unable to provide for a child. Home instruction is the last option, after all other educational possibilities have been exhausted. Before this last step can be taken, however, placement in privately operated nonprofit schools must be considered. The educational program for each child is approved on an individual basis.

However, although many New Jersey children with special needs are having those needs met for the first time, the approval of large numbers of children for non-public school placement indicates that many school districts are seeking an easy way out of the problem rather than trying to solve it by making changes in the classroom or the educational system. Here, then, may be one of the greatest challenges school social workers will face.

It may be necessary to discard the medical model. Mental health concepts have been invaluable, especially in pointing out the importance of the child's self-image. However, by drawing on sociological concepts, the school social worker should begin to offer leadership in a new dimension. A new look at and concern for social factors related to and possibly responsible for drastic changes in the child's home-school situation could be added to the traditional concern about the removal of children from their homes, the related concern for the feelings of the family, and the interest in the child's adjustment at the residential center or day care facility.

The two categories of "social maladjustment" and "emotional disturbance" are responsible for most of the school referrals for placement. Not only the school social worker, but also the psychologist, the learning disability specialist, and the school administrator must be made aware of the debilitating effects of poverty and racism, rapid and devastating social changes, and the results of urban decay and their effects on children. School curricula and practices have not adjusted themselves to new community needs, principally because the needs have not been clearly identified. With increased numbers of children who do not learn or who act out their frustration in deviance of one kind or another, the school social worker has a commitment and a charge to seek out the causes, ask some hard questions, and learn how to bring about change—not only in the child and his parents, but in the staff and curriculum as well.

Those in state leadership positions have equal obligations and responsibilities. By paying greater attention to what kinds of candidates are admitted to the field, by being aware of the impact of legislation on the practice of professionals, by making more explicit the job performance expectations of other personnel groups on local, county, and state levels, and by facilitating workshops and group discussions of the factors in the social structure contributing to deviance or delinquency, administrators can spur professionals into relinquishing outmoded models and undertaking new approaches and strategies. Schools of social work and sociology, educational leaders, and state governments must combine their efforts to utilize the social worker as an agent of change.

The Enemy Is Us

Let us close with a bit of Pogo's philosophy: "We have met the enemy and he is us!" *Us* is the state departments that set unrealistic credential requirements. *Us* is professional groups whose primary concern is the protection of their territories. *Us* is teachers and administrators who do not know how to share decision-making. *Us* is *not* the children— who can learn if we will but help them and let them.

Models of School
Social Work Practice

John J. Alderson

Current practices in school social work are subject to heavy criticism. Some of this is clearly justified. It is the author's impression, however, that when this criticism denigrates the contributions that individual school social workers have made and are making, the criticism falls short of its purpose.

Without question shortcomings exist in current practices and efforts at service delivery in school social work. Kraft has asserted:

> It is not possible to cite a single innovation introduced by school social workers (since the origin of this specialty in 1906) which has modified the institutional practices of American education in any significant way. Similarly, far too few significant contributions are being made by social workers in the great debates on up-grading inner-city schools, combating the evils of racial and class isolation, etc. Nor is this to be expected, considering the way the role of the school social worker has evolved over the past five decades. On the other hand, some school social workers, operating as counselors and psychotherapists to individual children, have no doubt offered significant help to these children.
>
> . . . Despite the fact that "school social work" has been on the scene for more than 50 years, the overwhelming majority of schools in our day, including many of those with the highest educational standards,

do not now and never have employed the services of school social workers.[1]

This has the ring of harsh indictment. It is difficult to refute the factual picture on which Kraft bases his statements. It is evident that there is a tremendous unevenness in coverage on the national, state, and local levels. Using Florida as an example, fifteen of sixty-seven counties do not have school social work services. In counties with such services there are wide disparities in educational levels of personnel, ratio of services to population, and role definition of those performing these services.[2] There continue to be question and concern about the best appropriate mix of social work education and teacher training of the school social worker.

Another area of ongoing concern is the role of the school social worker. Is he primarily a highly skilled clinician within the school? Is he primarily an attendance counselor? Is his role to teach the education personnel mental health concepts and methods of working with students? Is he an institutional change agent? Should he have primarily a community organization focus? Is he an ombudsman?

The preceding was intended to demonstrate the difficulty of attempting to discuss systematically a concept of practice models. The current scene in school social work is such that the supporting foundations in both theory and practice are unsteady.

Nevertheless, examination of this aspect of school social work practice is necessary. The current restlessness and dissatisfaction of the profession, consumers, public schools, and educational training institutions require that an effort be made to bring together current thinking and practices, to chart emerging developments, and to begin to develop perspectives on the next steps in school social work.

Definition and Usefulness of a Model

Of what use is a theoretical model? It is important to deal with this question, since it is not uncommon to encounter among practitioners a certain apathy or antipathy toward theoretical models and a

[1] Ivor Kraft, "Towards a New Conception of Social Work in American Society," pp. 26–27. Unpublished paper, School of Applied Social Sciences, Case Western Reserve University, January 1968.

[2] Statement based on data supplied by Mrs. Annabel Brantley, consultant, School Social Work, State of Florida Department of Education, for school year 1970–71.

reluctance to change earlier theoretical formulations. A wise teacher of social work practice (Florence L. Poole, professor emeritus, Jane Addams Graduate School of Social Work) once emphasized that to learn to practice in social work one has to get theory into one's performance muscles. The task, as related to models and new theory in general, involves "stepping back"—at least for a time—from possibly routine and rather smooth performance operations, to view theory and sort out relevant aspects for service delivery.

Kogan has described a theoretical model as "a scheme or map for 'making sense' out of the portion of the real world which he is seeking to account for, explain, or practice." [3] Chin speaks of models as "mind holds" that are of practical significance to the practitioner in diagnosis and planful activity, adding that "nothing is so practical as a good theory." [4] Lathrope holds that practitioner models, which combine elements of prescriptive, expository, and research models, contain protocols of observation and action by which the practitioner governs his practice.[5]

A number of significant articles devoted to the subject of social work practice models have appeared. These have served to order and encompass the major currents, thoughts, and concepts that appear in the literature and in practice.[6]

Kelley identified several models of school social work practice: (1) generalist, (2) direct service, (3) team leader, (4) consultant, and (5) community organizer. In selecting a model for practice Kelley

[3] Leonard S. Kogan, "Principles of Measurement," in Norman A. Polansky, ed., *Social Work Research* (Chicago: University of Chicago Press, 1960), p. 90.

[4] Robert Chin, "The Utility of Systems Models and Developmental Models for Practitioners," Warren G. Bennis et al., eds., *The Planning of Change* (2d ed.; New York: Holt, Rinehart & Winston, 1969), p. 298.

[5] Donald Lathrope, "The General Systems Approach in Social Work Practice," in Gordon Hearn, ed., *The General Systems Approach: Contributions Toward an Holistic Conception of Social Work* (New York: Council on Social Work Education, 1969), p. 49.

[6] For recent examples *see* Jack Rothman, "Three Models of Community Organization Practice," *Social Work Practice, 1968* (New York: Columbia University Press, 1968); Catherine P. Papell and Beulah Rothman, "Social Group Work Models: Possession and Heritage," *Journal of Education for Social Work,* Vol. 2, No. 2 (Fall 1966), pp. 66–77; Werner A. Lutz, "Emerging Models of Social Casework Practice," p. 32, unpublished paper, University of Connecticut School of Social Work; Joan W. Stein, *The Family As a Unit of Study and Treatment* (Seattle: Regional Rehabilitative Institute, School of Social Work, University of Washington, 1969).

recommended that the worker meaningfully involve others in the school and community and then make "a professional estimate of what is around him and within him that will help determine how he should function." [7]

Several practice models for school social work will be identified and described in this paper. Although this is viewed only as a beginning, an effort will be made to be comprehensive. The data for this examination will be based largely on what has appeared in the literature. No effort will be made to develop a comprehensive overriding theoretical scheme, since this is clearly premature in a field in a state of flux in a rapidly changing society. The models represent an effort to bring together a view of the current practice scene in school social work.

A number of identifiable practice models appear to be emerging. Some of these approaches place emphasis on certain objectives, concepts, activities, tactics, or skills that have always been a part of the school social worker's role. However, the models draw these concepts and/or tactics together in an identifiable pattern to reach specific objectives.

For the purpose of this presentation, four models are identified: the (1) traditional-clinical, (2) school-change, (3) community school, and (4) social interaction models. An additional approach—indirect services—will be considered briefly. At this point it does not have the theoretical bases of the other models identified. It will, however, be described as an approach that may be used as part of any of the other models.

As is true of all theoretical models, no one model may actually apply in all respects in an actual practice situation. It seems possible that some features of all models could possibly be drawn on and combined in specific situations. The models are delineated and defined according to major theoretical conceptions that seem to identify the given model. It is the author's intent that one or more of the models or some of the central ideas will provide impetus for further discussion and formulation of school social work practice.

Two areas are arbitrarily excluded here—differential staffing and the team or interdisciplinary approach. This is not meant to minimize their importance. It is a basic premise that the models described contain relevant considerations for service delivery that are compatible

---

[7] Jerry L. Kelley, "Factors Which Affect a Model for School Social Work Practice," *The Supportive Role of School Social Work Services in Helping the Seriously Disturbed Child* (Des Moines: State of Iowa, 1967), p. 32.

with the differential staffing approaches and the interdisciplinary team concepts. One of these models or parts of two or more of them could be incorporated into service delivery packages using differential staffing or an interdisciplinary team approach.

Service Delivery Models

For each of the four models several dimensions will be developed for purposes of description and analysis:

1. *Focus*—where the intervention efforts are centered in relation to identified client needs and/or problems.

2. *Goals*—the aims of the service delivery model.

3. *Target systems*—"the person, family, group, organization, or the specific system—person or group—that is being helped." [8] In some instances this may be designated as the unit of attention or client system.

4. *View of sources of difficulty*—this relates to the conceptual base in that the perception of the sources of difficulty is related to the theoretical bases of the service delivery model.

5. *Worker tasks and activities*—the "various movements of the worker in any given client-worker system," with an emphasis on "categories of activity rather than on small discrete movements." [9]

6. *Major worker roles*—"a cluster of alternative activities that are performed toward a common objective." [10]

7. *Conceptual base*—the specific body of theoretical knowledge from which the model draws heavily in relation to its focus, goals, identification of client system, and view of sources of difficulty—a determinant of worker tasks and activities.

8. *Major theoreticians*—mainly social workers who have written and described certain features of the various models. Frequently these are workers who have drawn on a broad conceptual base, such as psychoanalytic theory or social science theory; generally, but not in every

[8] Allen Pincus and Anne Minahan, "Toward a Model of Teaching a Basic First Year Course in Methods of Social Work Practice," in *Innovations in Teaching Social Work Practice* (New York: Council on Social Work Education, 1970), p. 40.

[9] William Schwartz, "The Social Worker in the Group," *Social Welfare Forum, 1961* (New York: Columbia University Press, 1961), p. 157.

[10] Robert J. Teare and Harold L. McPheeters, *Manpower Utilization in Social Welfare* (Atlanta, Ga.: Social Welfare Manpower Project, Southern Regional Education Board, 1970), p. 34.

case, they have applied these conceptualizations to the school setting. In other instances the individuals have contributed to the development of theory and method in school social work practice and in an original sense to the practice of social work in the school.

TRADITIONAL-CLINICAL MODEL The traditional-clinical model is in all likelihood the best known and most widely applied model of school social work practice, as reflected in the literature.[11] This model is closely related to Lutz's description of the clinical-normative model, is the most highly developed, and is reinforced through a foundation in the literature.[12]

The focus of the traditional-clinical model is largely on individual students identified as having social and emotional difficulties that block attainment of their potential in school. A definition associated with this model is as follows:

> School social work, better known as visiting teacher work, is a specialized form of social casework. It is identified with and is a part of the program of the public school. It is a method of helping individual children use what the school offers them.[13]

The goals of this model are largely those of enabling the identified students to function more effectively within the school framework and make optimum use of their school experience. The target system or unit of attention is primarily the students and their parents.

The perception of the major sources of difficulty is largely derived from psychoanalytic theory, ego psychology, and casework theory and methodology. This view posits an emotional or psychic difficulty within the child that stems primarily from difficulties in parent-child and familial relationships. The school is largely viewed as benign and not dysfunctional in relation to the child's difficulty.

---

11 *See,* for example, Grace Lee, ed., *Helping the Troubled School Child: Selected Readings in School Social Work* (New York: National Association of Social Workers, 1959); *Social Work in Schools* (New York: National Association of Social Workers, 1960); John C. Nebo, ed., *Administration of School Social Work* (New York: National Association of Social Workers, 1960). For a discussion of the literature of the forties and fifties, *see* Lela B. Costin, "A Historical Review of School Social Work," *Social Casework,* Vol. 50, No. 8 (October 1969), pp. 446–449.

12 Werner A. Lutz, op. cit., p. 32.

13 Ruth E. Smalley, "School Social Work as a Part of the School Program," *Bulletin of the National Association of School Social Workers,* Vol. 22, No. 3 (March 1947), pp. 51–52.

Worker strategies, tactics, and techniques for this model primarily revolve around the casework method. The activities of the worker, in the traditional sense, may be summarized as follows:

1. Casework services to the child having difficulty in school.
2. Interprofessional relationships with teachers and other school personnel.
3. Casework services to parents.
4. Work with community social agencies.
5. Interpretation of the program to the community.[14]

The major worker roles are those associated with social casework—primarily enabling and supportive activities with the student and his parents and collaborative and consultative activities within the school directed toward assisting the individual child. Some of the early writings foreshadowed the more recent conceptualizations. For example, note was made of the unique character of individual schools, which, although not couched in system terminology, is similar to the view of the school as a social system that is a major component of the school-change model.[15]

Despite the barrage of criticism directed toward it, the traditional-clinical model has had surprising durability. In all likelihood this model remains the predominant mode of school social work practice in the United States today. This is due to several factors. The benign view of the school is quite acceptable to school personnel. Generally this model as traditionally practiced holds school conditions as given; the individual students need to adapt and adjust to the normative conditions within the school. The model has been utilized to a large extent in relation to attendance functions of the school social worker. In many states these functions continue to be a large component of the job of the school social worker, and much of the activity related to attendance still involves home visits and interviews with students and their parents. Additionally, this model has proved durable in schools located in middle-class neighborhoods, especially when there is a lack of profound community disruption and change. In these areas many of the parents are geared to the office interview, and goals and objectives for their children, as related to the school, are largely compatible with those of the school itself. Thus the school, community,

[14] John J. Alderson, "The Specific Content of School Social Work," in Lee, ed., op. cit., p. 40.
[15] Ibid., p. 39.

parents, and students are largely geared to accept the normative conditions associated with this model.

Recently expansions of the clinical-normative model have appeared, and there is growing emphasis on direct services to individuals, families, and groups. In addition there is greater emphasis on consultation. An expanded worker role can make this model more viable with respect to current conditions. In a pupil personnel demonstration project (which included such innovative practices as a strong advocacy role for disadvantaged families), an integral part of the role of the school social worker was psychosocial evaluation.[16]

The traditional-clinical model is besieged and struggling, but it is far from ready to be counted out of the current scene. The model now has few defenders. It has many who are willing to attack it as an outmoded model for the practice demands of the 1970s.[17]

SCHOOL-CHANGE MODEL The school-change model could also be termed an institutional change model. The major focus of this model is dysfunctional conditions of the school, especially as related to school norms and conditions. Its goals are to alter dysfunctional school norms and conditions—that is, those conditions that seem to pose barriers to enhancing the social and educational functioning of students and that actually serve to exacerbate or even create the students' difficulties.

The client system in this model is thus viewed as the school in its entirety. All persons within the school—students, teachers, administrative personnel, custodians, and so on—are potential targets for intervention.

The sociological concept of deviance plays a part in the development of the model. Students identified as deviant may become imprisoned in their roles and have difficulty in moving toward more productive role functioning within the school. Shafer has noted that a child's school career may be ruined by conversations in the teacher's lounge that

---

[16] "Center's Social Worker Uses Psychosocial Evaluation as Communication Instrument," in *Pupil Personnel Services Demonstration Center*, Conyers, Georgia, Rockdale County Public Schools, No. 10 (February 1969), p. 3.

[17] *See*, for example, Lela B. Costin, "What Directions for School Social Work," in John J. Alderson, ed., *Social Work in Schools: Patterns and Perspectives* (Northbrook, Ill.: Whitehall, 1969), pp. 149–150; Warner Bloomberg, Jr., "The Missing Dimensions of the School Social Worker's Role: Advocate and Reformer," in *Patterns for Innovative Practice: Proceedings of the School Social Work Conference, 1967* (Springfield, Ill.: Office of the Superintendent of Public Instruction, 1968), pp. 69–85. Conference sponsored by the Illinois School Social Workers in cooperation with the Office of the Superintendent of Public Instruction.

label him as a troublemaker—a label that may follow him throughout his school career.[18]

Another important conceptionalization is that developed by Bower, who speaks of institutional goals becoming displaced. Running through this model is the suspicion—and supporting evidence is available—that certain school norms or institutional policies get in the way of students' accomplishments and optimal functioning. Bower maintains that all too frequently management of the behavior of students—not education—becomes the primary goal of the school.[19]

Vinter and Sarri stated a basic premise of this model when they proposed that patterns of student malperformance be viewed as "resultants of the interactions of both pupil characteristics and school conditions."[20] Based on this conceptualization school social workers are called on to do the following:

1. Address themselves more fully to the conditions of the school and not limit their efforts to contacts with students.

2. Assist teachers and administrators in identifying those school practices and arrangements that inadvertently curtail learning and adjustment.

3. Find ways to serve specific individuals while simultaneously dealing with the sources of student difficulties within the school.[21]

Direct work with students—especially group work—has been associated with this approach along with advocacy, consultation, mediation, and negotiation with teachers, administrators, families, and agencies.

Wittes viewed the major task of school social workers as changing an often unyielding educational system. He indicated the following activities as legitimate:

1. Helping students to articulate and diagnose the problem they see as crucial and critical in their school.

2. Serving as ombudsmen, either in an individual capacity or through a trouble-shooting group. Students could utilize this mechanism for grievance procedures.

---

[18] Walter E. Shafer, "Deviance in Public School: An Interactional View," in Edwin J. Thomas, ed., *Behavioral Science for Social Workers* (New York: Free Press, 1967), pp. 51–59.

[19] Eli M. Bower, "Building Bridges Over the River Kwai: Goal Displacement and Constriction in Human Institutions," *Psychology in Schools*, Vol. 5, No. 4 (October 1968), pp. 310–316.

[20] Robert Vinter and Rosemary C. Sarri, "Malperformance in Public School: A Group Work Approach," *Social Work*, Vol. 10, No. 4 (January 1965), p. 4.

[21] Ibid., pp. 12–13.

3. Setting up informal groups of teachers, students, and administrators to enable each to voice concerns and settle conflicts.

4. Forming change-agent and/or problem-solving teams made up of students, teachers, and administrators who would look at the school as a system, assess its difficulties, and engage in change activity.[22]

A premise of Wittes's formulation is that the social worker is a change agent in relation to the school itself, uses himself directly as an agent of change, and serves as a catalyst for developing mechanisms for change.

The model has rendered a genuine service in focusing on conditions of the school that may be dysfunctional and lifting the sights of school social workers from a psychopathological view. Through bringing social science concepts to bear, a different mode of intervention activities is called for, as contrasted with the traditional-clinical model.

The school-change model, which carries with it a strong component of advocacy coupled with a stance that views the school itself as the target system, imposes a greater burden of risk-taking on the worker. Concomitantly it necessitates greater skills in working with the power structure within the school in such a way that the worker himself is not blocked, made ineffectual, or removed from the scene as a result of his activities. Knowledge of organizational behavior and skills in effective negotiation are essential to effective practice within this model.

A deficiency of the model as depicted in the literature is that it seems to focus almost exclusively on the school itself as the major factor in producing difficulties within the student. In this sense it appears to draw a boundary line around the school and ignore other major systems impinging on the child, especially community and familial factors.

COMMUNITY SCHOOL MODEL   The community school model holds great promise. The increasing interest in this approach appears to be related to increased disturbances in school-community relations, fuller recognition and attention to the problems of inner-city schools, and the ongoing concern about juvenile delinquency, dropouts, unemployed youths, and disadvantaged groups. Reflective of this fact is that more school systems are adopting a community school concept.[23]

Developments in this model are in some ways analogous to the early

---

22 Simon Wittes, "Conflict Resolution in Secondary Schools," this volume.

23 Kelley pointed this out (op. cit., p. 31) in noting that on August 27, 1962, the New Haven, Conn., public schools had adopted a community school policy in which the school was defined as an educational center for both children and adults, a neighborhood community center for citizens of all ages, a com-

roots of school social work practice in which community concerns about children moved social work into the schools. The community school model is emerging with a fuller scope than the concepts of work with the community that formed a part of the traditional-clinical model. Earlier conceptualizations were largely oriented toward providing liaison services in relation to individual students.

Few articles have appeared that are specifically related to community aspects in the role of the school social worker. Nebo urged that school social workers become involved in community organization, stating that social workers have been guilty of "talking among themselves." He added: "No school social worker can function successfully without using the method of community organization." [24]

The community school model is largely focused on deprived or disadvantaged communities, which generally have been out of step with the goals and norms of the school, have less understanding of the school, and are more mistrustful of it. Although Hourihan maintained that the community approach was relevant to all schools and communities and predicted that increasing numbers of school social workers will abandon traditional approaches and adopt more creative modes of operating—including a community-oriented approach—the major description of these activities has been related to inner-city schools and schools with a predominantly disadvantaged population.[25] There is, however, another aspect that appears to be growing. This relates to the intervention of the school social worker when communities and schools are undergoing drastic changes, such as integration.

The major goals of the community school model are to develop community understanding and support of the school, to develop school programs to assist disadvantaged students, and to alleviate conditions of deprivation that affect the child's learning and social functioning capacities within the school. Deshler has stated:

The major premise in which the role is based is the principle of educating the "whole" child. If we are to educate the whole child, we must be

munity services center, and a center for neighborhood or commmunity life in which the school assists citizens in the study and solution of significant neighborhood problems.

[24] John C. Nebo, "The School Social Worker As Community Organizer," *Social Work,* Vol. 8, No. 1 (January 1963), p. 105.

[25] Joseph P. Hourihan, "The Expanded Role of the School Social Worker," in Alderson, ed., op. cit., p. 134.

aware of all forces that play on the child, all the hours of the day; not just when he is with us in school.[26]

Merl, in depicting the need for greater community involvement, stated that the social worker in the school "needs to go where the problems, needs, people and possible solutions are or might be found." He added that the worker must "reach out—and not wait to be sought out."[27] It is also evident that federal legislation related to poverty, civil rights, and other areas was a factor in moving social work more strongly toward a community orientation. Programs such as Project Head Start were influential in the development of greater outreach services to families and communities by school social workers.[28]

The target system within this model is that of the community area surrounding the school, interacting with the school, sending students to the school. Within this model the community has at least an equal primacy with the school itself as a target for intervention.

Sources of difficulty include poverty, disadvantage, deprivation, and other social conditions that have an impact on students and school personnel. School personnel may lack full understanding of cultural differences and the effects of poverty and may need particularized knowledge and skills in order to work more effectively.

Hourihan described the following range of tasks and activities of the community social worker:

1. To gain a knowledge of the children and their parents, the kinds of problems the children face at home, what their parents' problems are, what the community problems are with which the children and their parents have to deal, and the depth of these problems.

2. To report and interpret to members of the school staff the dynamics of the community and the operant societal factors.

3. To involve himself in community activities.

4. To enable community members to ask questions, raise issues, and restructure those elements of the community that fail to meet the needs of its children and youths.

---

[26] Betty Deshler, "The School-Community Agent in the Detroit Public Schools." Unpublished paper, February 1965.

[27] Lawrence Merl, "The Social Worker as a Link Between School, Home, and Community," in *The Supportive Role of School Social Work Services in Helping the Seriously Disturbed Child* (Des Moines: State of Iowa, 1967), p. 39.

[28] Robert B. Rowan, "The Impact of Federal Legislation on School Social Work," *Social Work*, Vol. 12, No. 2 (April 1957), p. 115.

5. To educate the community with respect to programs provided by and in the school, assist it to participate in these programs, and help it to understand the school's educational program.[29]

Recent articles place emphasis on the school social worker's role in intervening in conditions of school-community unrest. Walton, Reaves, and Shannon describe a crisis team approach to school and community conflict. They state that "the crisis team was not restricted in its movement within the school or community," and add that "at various times the crisis team played the roles of mediator, enabler, advocate, organizer, and developer on behalf of the pupils, teachers and school administrators."[30] In this approach the social worker serves as part of an interdisciplinary crisis team that was dispatched when a breakdown in school-community relationships occurred. Newton stresses the educational role of the social worker in assisting members of various races and cultural backgrounds to achieve a fuller understanding of one another.[31]

A critical analysis of this model would focus on several points. One point is the readiness of school social workers to function along the lines of orientation called for in the model. This relates both to the requisite skills and the attitudinal set of workers. It is evident that many of those currently practicing in the schools need additional training and skills to carry out these activities. Indications are that some schools may not be ready for the social worker to work so fully in relationship to the community. Street, in speaking of the problems of inner-city schools, noted that educators have a "special defensiveness and attention to keeping the boundaries of the school system impermeable."[32] Additionally, when the activities of the worker are focused on the community, school personnel may have difficulty in recognizing the benefits to students that accrue on a more indirect basis.

Questions about the identification and loyalties of the worker may arise. In this respect it should be noted that active advocacy in relation

---

[29] Op. cit., p. 133.

[30] Maxine Walton, Gloria D. Reaves, and Robert F. Shannon, "Crisis Team Intervention in School Community Unrest," *Social Casework*, Vol. 52, No. 1 (January 1971), p. 12.

[31] Josephine K. Newton, "The Pupil Personnel Worker in Racial Conflict," *Florida Pupil Personnel Quarterly*, Vol. 3, No. 3 (Spring 1971), pp. 4–5.

[32] David Street, "Educators and Social Workers: Sibling Rivalry in the Inner City," *Social Service Review*, Vol. 41, No. 2 (June 1967), p. 158.

to the community and the notion of assisting the community to raise questions about the school may place the worker in a difficult change agent position with respect to his employing agency. This brings up the question of effectiveness. Many workers are aware of situations in which social workers functioning as advocates of community groups have jeopardized their positions because of the employing agency's concern that the worker has aligned himself against it.

Street cites risks involved in pressuring educators to the point at which collaboration becomes impossible. He called on community organizers to develop "expertise in guiding a local group to make a useful criticism of the school, not a diffuse and wholly self-initiated one." [33]

It is the author's contention that for full effectiveness in this role the worker must maintain a dual identification with the community and the school and become highly skilled in mediation and advocacy. Schools of social work are now educating their graduates to work more fully with the community. Ongoing staff development is important to enable existing school social work personnel to develop the knowledge and skills requisite to the community school model.

SOCIAL INTERACTION MODEL   Social interaction "denotes reciprocal influencing of the acts of persons and groups, usually mediated through a communication. This definition includes the interaction of a person with himself." [34]   The model is deliberately set in this broad framework owing to key features of the approach, including (1) attention to the interactional field, (2) a deemphasis on specific methodology, and (3) emphasis on tasks in social interaction that emphasizes a social problem and on behaviors and actions of all participants in a social process.

This practice model is derived in large part from the work of Schwartz. His model for social work practice, which he termed the mediating model, emphasized the relationship between the individual and his nurturing groups. Schwartz used the term symbiotic to describe this relationship, positing that each needed the other for growth. [35]

---

[33] Ibid., p. 163.

[34] Julius Gould and William L. Kolb, eds., *A Dictionary of the Social Sciences* (New York: Free Press, 1964), p. 657.

[35] William Schwartz, "The Social Worker in the Group," *Social Welfare Forum, 1961* (New York: Columbia University Press, 1961).

Although Schwartz originally developed his model in relation to work with groups, the generic nature and applicability of the model for all social work practice are evident.

The major task of the worker is "to mediate the process through which the individual and his society reach out for each other through a mutual need for self-fulfillment." [36] To extend this view to the school setting, the worker views the student as a part of school, family, and community systems, all of which interact with and need one another. In this approach the worker's awareness of the forces impinging on the child help the worker to direct his attention toward the relationship and toward forces affecting the various systems as they interact.

Schwartz raises the following questions:

Who is my client? Whom do I represent? To whom do I belong? Is it the system, in this case the school, or is it the client, in this case, the child and the family? Is it the system that hires me (and aids me by the way), or the member who is having trouble? [37]

Schwartz goes on to indicate the difficulties that occur when the social worker fixes his sights either too strongly on the student, thus attempting to manipulate the system to meet the child's needs, or too strongly on the system, without sufficient regard for the individual functioning within the system. He answers this dilemma by stating:

The social worker has responsibility for both the individual and the social; for both the child and the school. It then becomes unnecessary, in fact, dysfunctional, for him to try and make choices and declare allegiances for one or the other. His job, as I said, is not to range himself one against the other, but to help them recognize their common ground and work it out together. [38]

Schwartz identifies five major tasks of the worker in the mediating model:

1. Searching out the common ground.
2. Detecting and challenging obstacles.
3. Contributing data not available to the client.

---

[36] Ibid., p. 154.

[37] William Schwartz, "The Use of Groups and School Social Work Function," p. 2. Unpublished paper presented at the Fourth Annual Conference of the New York State School Social Workers Association, Saratoga Springs, N.Y., May 10, 1969.

[38] Ibid., pp. 4–5.

4. Lending a vision. In this activity the worker shows himself to be invested in people and their interactions with other important societal systems and institutions.

5. Finding the requirements and limits of the situation. The walls and boundaries establish the context for a working contract.[39]

Gitterman has applied the model in practice with groups in the school setting, specifically illustrating the value of this approach in work with disadvantaged and/or alienated students.[40] Shulman has pointed up the need for further elaboration of the model to provide functional guidelines when working with the community or the individual and has developed some preliminary thinking in these directions.[41]

Bertrand, although not writing specifically about the school setting, has described a problem-centered approach to practice that is "characterized by comprehensive, open-ended thinking around any single presenting problem and action-oriented practice based on the assessment of needs of client or client groups in their situations." [42] A problem-focused practice model has been depicted by Spitzer and Welsh, who have demonstrated an application of the approach in the school setting. The approach delineates a five-step process that ranges from defining the problem through intervention and evaluation of results. The problem-focused stance

> requires of the social worker the ability to be creative, innovative, purposeful, and fully identified with the basic value system of the social work profession and its emphasis on the inherent worth of every individual. The worker has to have knowledge of the various client systems with which he will be interacting. He needs the skills that will allow him to become effectively involved in relationships with individual persons and families, with small groups and neighborhood groups, and within large and small systems and institutions.[43]

The relationship of these approaches to the social interaction model

---

[39] "The Social Worker in the Group," p. 157.

[40] Alex Gitterman, "Group Work in Public Schools," in William Schwartz and Serapio R. Zalba, eds., *The Practice of Group Work* (New York: Columbia University Press, 1971), pp. 45–71.

[41] Lawrence Shulman, *A Casebook of Social Work With Groups: The Mediating Model* (New York: Council on Social Work Education, 1968), pp. 68–71.

[42] Patricia Bertrand, "Teaching Multi-Methods as an Integral Part of Problem-Centered Social Work Practice," Occasional Paper No. 7 (Madison, Wis.: University of Wisconsin School of Social Work, 1968), p. 8.

[43] Kurt Spitzer and Betty Welsh, "The Problem Focused Model of Practice," *Social Casework*, Vol. 50, No. 6 (June 1969), pp. 324–325.

is related to their generic nature, the deemphasis on a specific method, and the mandate for worker involvement and intervention with systems interacting with the target system.

There are a number of strengths in this model as applied to the school setting. The model is broadly enough focused for the worker to engage himself fully with major systems interacting with the target system. In some ways this model appears to be an elaboration of the earlier discussions of the importance of the school social worker's serving as a link among school, family, community, teacher, and child. This concept, placed in the context of the mediating model, defines the worker's role as that of linking or mediating among these various systems.

The social interaction model places less emphasis on advocacy than do some of the other models. The worker, in viewing various systems as clients, makes strong efforts to enhance the functioning of these systems, searches out commonalities, assists in removing obstacles, and opens up and facilitates communication and transactions.

The emphasis on mediation is generally viewed as a strength. Operationally it could become a weaknness in that the worker may be prone to mediate too much and may be reluctant to take advocacy measures when power structures are resistant to change in relation to those who are powerless. While recognizing this possible deficiency, the model appears to have great potential strength and to avoid some of the pitfalls of the other models. With its broad stance it would appear to lend itself to differential staffing, since staff at various levels could function in a number of ways, using various methods in combination in working with interacting systems.

INDIRECT SERVICES   An indirect services approach is being used more frequently by school social workers. Typically indirect services are defined as consultation, supervision, and administration. Kelley described a consultation model of school social work practice, noting that it considerably increased the school social worker's sphere of influence.[44] It is additionally evident that some school social workers spend a large proportion of their time working in one or all of these three methods. A number of recent articles call for expanded use of consultation in social work practice as a means of delivering service more adequately.[45] Berlin declared that the traditional role of

---

[44] Op. cit., p. 20.

[45] See, for example, Costin, op. cit., pp. 159–160; Hourihan, op. cit., p. 140.

the school social worker is doomed by sociocultural pressures. He urged extensive use of consultation to achieve a greater impact on the needs of students.[46]

The author is reluctant to term the indirect services approach a model, since it appears to be a set of methods that could be used in any of the four models described. The goals, purpose, and guiding conceptualizations for the use of indirect services would enable it to be a significant aspect of any of the models described.

Conclusion

School social work—as is true of the entire social work profession—is searching. The search is for "newer modes of analysis, a new synthesis, and new concepts" to guide practitioners in delivery of significant helping services to clients.[47] A unified practice model remains illusory at this time.

Each of the models described has both strengths and limitations, some of which were noted in a brief critique of each. The social interaction model has great potential. It can be applied effectively by an individual practitioner in one or several schools or may be used as a basis for services provided by a large staff comprising different levels of personnel. It has sufficient scope in its guiding conceptualizations to provide a means of linking or orchestrating the various competences, levels, and specialized functioning of social work staff.

Ultimately, of course, school social workers must sort through and assess the utility of the available knowledge, assess their own and their school's and community's specific resources and problems, and choose, in concert with others, to assist clients toward enhanced social functioning.

---

[46] Irving N. Berlin, "The School Social Worker as Mental Health Consultant." Paper presented at the 1966 Pacific Northwest Regional Institute, National Association of Social Workers, Seattle, Wash.

[47] Donald Lathrope, "The General Systems Approach in Social Work Practice," in Gordon Hearn, ed., *The General Systems Approach: Contributions Toward an Holistic Conception of Social Work* (New York: Council on Social Work Education, 1969), p. 61.

Conflict Resolution in the Secondary School

Simon Wittes

The development of creative means of intervention and of change strategies in school systems are currently being defined as important parts of the social worker's role in the schools. In this attempt some of the conclusions and results of various projects conducted by CRUSK are relevant and may shed some light on the issues school social workers are examining.[1] The kinds of projects, the issues and problems that have been uncovered, and the strategies that have evolved all have meaning for the school social worker.

Specifically the question of conflict resolution in schools will be examined in the light of a project that was designed to intervene in high schools undergoing serious disruption and conflict. The goals of the project were twofold: (1) to attempt to understand the nature of the disruption and its underlying causes and (2) to help develop change strategies to deal with the crisis in ways that were educationally relevant and productive.

Seven schools were chosen for the study based on a number of criteria. The basic criterion was the extent to which disruption had taken place or the extent to which the administration feared that dis-

---

[1] CRUSK stands for the Center for Research on the Utilization of Scientific Knowledge, Institute of Social Research, University of Michigan, Ann Arbor, Michigan.

ruption would occur. Other criteria included organizational patterns, school size, racial mix, number of students, and so on.

The locations of the schools ranged from California to New Jersey. Suburban, urban, and small-city schools were included. The racial composition ranged from 95 percent black to 100 percent white. A consultant located in each of the schools was to serve as an on-site worker in that specific system. Part of his task would be to design a change strategy using the conflict that had occurred in the school.

This paper will discuss first some of the issues that were common to the various schools, the types of disruptions that occurred, and the types of administrative response. Also to be examined will be some of the models of intervention used and the results of these interventions. Finally, implications of these change strategies for the role of the social worker in the schools will be considered.

Portrait of a School in Crisis

As has been stated, one of the criteria for selection was the existence in the school of a history of disruption or strong potential for disruption. By disruption is meant increasing rates of vandalism, property damage, wastebasket fires, false fire alarms, fights between individual students, fights between groups of black and white students, protest demonstrations, walkouts, stabbings, and shootings.

Why do these disruptions occur? How does a school respond to these disruptions? To answer these questions, let us look at one of the schools in the project, a school that typifies not only the causes and issues underlying the disruptions, but also the reaction of the administration.

The high school in question was located in a community of about 30,000 people, approximately 70 percent white and 30 percent black, and had approximately 3,400 students. Within the first week following the opening of school in September 1967, the local youth council of the National Association for the Advancement of Colored People, as a result of much dissatisfaction and unrest owing to the fact that the community did not have a swimming pool available for use by black people, made a number of demands on the high school administration. They requested a hearing on these demands. Following this there was a protest by some black students regarding the procedure for selecting a homecoming queen in the school. This was followed by a dis-

76

turbance in the cafeteria during which chairs were overturned, plates were thrown, and students were pushed around.

The administration responded by suspending students. Protests followed the suspensions, and the administration stepped up its level of response by calling in the county police. To maintain law and order sixteen policemen were placed outside the school and four policemen were stationed inside.

The situation quieted down and remained quiet for about three weeks. Then there was a series of mass disturbances and demonstrations and the expulsion rate went up again. The administration reacted by increasing the number of policemen. As a result, eventually forty armed policemen were patrolling the school. It cost the Board of Education about $100,000 to maintain this police protection.

In spite of this, a group of two hundred students collected in the hallway one day. The police moved in on the students, but the students were not ready to disperse. The policemen responded by spraying them with mace. There was a tremendous increase in tension, and the administration closed the school.

By this time the administration thought the students had learned a lesson. They reduced the number of policemen in the school from forty to ten. But they also installed closed circuit television cameras in the school's hallways, with a monitoring setup in the principal's office that permitted him to view every hallway.

About this time CRUSK entered the system in response to a call for help from the superintendent of schools. The image that confronted the project members was one of barricaded doors, uniformed policemen, and monitoring TV cameras. Is this what we want our high schools to look like in the future? What can be done other than this to maintain some sense of safety for faculty and students? What kinds of responses can be made other than repressive measures, which are unproductive and costly? These are the questions CRUSK sought to answer.

UNDERLYING ISSUES As a way of illustrating some of the issues underlying the disruptions that occurred, let us examine more closely a confrontation between a number of students and the superintendent of schools. The study group called together about a hundred of the students who had been involved in the disruption. Meeting first in small groups, the participants attempted to define the issues the students saw as important. In the afternoon representatives of the student groups met with the superintendent and his staff.

Lack of administrative foresight. The following is an excerpt from the tape recording of that confrontation in which one student talked about the lack of planning on the part of the administration:

> . . . when they had riots in Watts and Chicago this previous summer, before we started school in September, you knew that we were an integrated school . . . ; you also knew that we would probably feel the way those teen-agers felt then. Or you should have known. I felt that you should take each school in your district . . . and analyze the problems that would probably arise in September. If you had analyzed the problems and looked at those riots and saw the causes, then maybe in September you would have been better adjusted and it wouldn't have took you by surprise, and you would have been able to handle the situation better . . . .

Discrimination by teachers. Students also expressed concern over discrimination on the part of teachers:

> Now, a Negro will come into class, and he comes late, he gets an after-school appointment, which is right because he has no business coming late. And when the white boy comes into class and don't get one, then that's not right. . . .

The students felt that the teachers did not respect them as human beings and individuals, although the teachers wanted this type of respect from the students.

Injustice. Students' comments also reflect some of their feelings about violations of basic principles of justice and fair play:

> . . . when the kids went in [the auditorium] to talk, . . . they were in there to help solve the problem. And first Doc says to take your ID card and we'll excuse you from class by the name on the ID card. So everybody gave their ID cards. . . . Now they're sending a letter to our parents. And your parents have to come back and . . . sign a paper.
>
> . . . . .
>
> We're in this school to learn. And my mother said . . . when you go up there . . . and you say I promise not to do this, or you bring your parent in, or write a note, that you're admitting to something you've never done. I was in there because I was concerned. I'm not involved in it. . . . And I don't feel that it's right for me to bring my parents up there.

References were made by students to the procedure requiring students who engaged in disruptions and who were suspended to pledge their good behavior as a condition for reenrollment. Moreover, partially as a result of a bomb scare, teachers inspected students' lockers for explosives and weapons. Students, administrators, and teachers were caught in an intolerable situation in which mutually conflicting interests and responsibilities were at stake. The human waste and tragedy is not only that they were caught in that bind; the greater tragedy is that their history together had so divided them that they could no longer rationally explain and adjust their positions to one another.

THE ADMINISTRATION'S VIEW   These, then, are some of the issues that were uncovered in this school. Let us now look at the attitudes and actions of the administration, using the same high school project as the basis of inquiry. The administrators, principals, and superintendents of the system were asked to get together and talk about the disruption in the high schools and to explore what they saw as the underlying reasons for that disruption.

Outside intervention. What emerged from these discussions was that the administrators seemed to have a clear grasp of some of the basic causes and dynamics of disruption, but at the same time they tended to interpret what was going on in such a way as to limit or deny their responsibility for acting. For example, they saw the trouble as resulting from outside intervention—by the local chapters of the Congress of Racial Equality and the NAACP and the local militant group. These groups, in the view of the administrators, were using the schools as part of some larger plan of attack. Yet, in a seeming contradiction they recognized that the students, as members of the community, were themselves using the community to further their demands.

It was found that both views were true—that there was a high degree of interdependence between the students in the school and the various community groups. Community groups had taught the students how to build a power base in order to bring about change, and the students had raised various issues in the schools that allowed these groups to come into the school. Significantly, part of this interaction was in response to the fact that the administration considered the demands that had been made by students as childish and illegitimate until such time as sufficient power was brought to bear. Then all of a sudden the demands became legitimated. The administration did not deal with the issues, either in terms of their educational value or their relevance to the students, but rather with the strength of the power base behind the issues. They did not move until sufficient pressure was brought to bear on them.

Another example of this problem of perception was raised in the conspiracy issue. Many of the administrators said that if one looked at the similarity of issues and demands that were being presented in various high schools throughout the nation, and if one also looked at the similarity of the strategies being used, it would become obvious that a definite conspiracy existed. When this issue was probed further, it became evident that to some extent the administrators were using the idea of a conspiracy as a reason for not looking at their own system or the relevant issues.

Alienation of students. The administrators suggested that many students felt alienated from the schools. They knew that in many cases the curriculum was not relevant to the students; for example, vocational training was nonexistent. They also felt that the students perceived that as individuals they were not important, that nobody—teachers or administrators—cared about them. Some mentioned that it was often impossible for a teacher to demonstrate a sense of caring for a student out of fear of recrimination and rejection by other faculty members. This feeling of alienation was found to be one of the great disruptive forces.

Interracial conflict. Another problem was the administration's conception of the relations among students. In many cases what began as not necessarily an interracial conflict among students came to be so defined by the administration. This apparently resulted from the school personnel's view of themselves as experts in teaching and handling students. Disruption in the school is a reflection on the staff's abilities. However, if the cause of the disruption was interracial conflict, the teachers could then excuse themselves by saying that no one can really deal with interracial tensions. This perception interestingly enough contradicts the interpretation the students placed on that violence.

> The problem of this school is the colored kids were all up in rebellion against the administration, and the white kids were all up in rebellion against the administration. And they wanted to talk and they wanted some action. . . . But they never got a thing; . . . nothing was ever done. And so it just started up again. And I guess now that after they had a little trouble, . . . somebody's listening to us.

· · · · ·

. . . all the fighting wasn't because of any prejudice against each group. It was just because it was the only means we could take toward being able to talk to the administration.

. . . . .

Like if I went to fighting . . . as a means to accomplishing something, it wouldn't be because of prejudice. . . . But it's just that I can't go directly to Mr. ———. If I went to speak to him, why, I'd be turned around before I even got to his office. And the same . . . with white boys. So my only means is to cause trouble. And I can only do that by fighting, and then I can get to talk to him.

. . . . .

We had a problem that confronted everybody in our group. We sat down and we talked and we decided that the problem was that the students had no way of communicating with the administration on a level that they would be heard and really listened to. So they did the only thing they knew how to do to get attention: This was to riot, or *revolt* is a better word. . . . They revolted so that the administration would pay some attention to them. . . . The only time you listen to us is when we riot. So what *other* method do you want us to use?

This is an important point. The students were saying that there was no issue of racial antagonism between groups. Rather, they saw the administration as the common target of their concern and their activity. As students (both black and white) began to realize that their target was the administration, the tension that existed among them diminished and their combined efforts focused on the administration. This is not to say that there was no racial tension. There was. The critical point is that once the students began to see common problems in relation to the administration, interracial collaboration became possible.

Nature of students' concerns. One of the most important questions raised in the school was the nature of the students' strategy and concern. Did the students or teachers know why the school had been disrupted? Was such disruption deliberate or spontaneous? Did the students want to take over, to be heard, or what?

Once again there was a fundamental difference in perception. The teachers either thought the students did not know what they wanted or that they wanted to "run things." The students said that what they wanted was "a little bit of voice in what goes on around here." In many conflict situations students are asking for more influence or power in setting policy and making decisions that affect their academic and personal lives. By and large these requests have not met with a sympathetic or positive response from teachers and administrators.

Administrators, who are used to wielding power without much political accountability to students, have responded in three general ways:

1. To deny that there are problems, to gloss over possible issues, and as far as possible to ignore the evidence of discontent and rebellion.

2. To distort, consciously or unconsciously, the position and grievances of students. The students' rhetoric, laced with the language of control and vengeance, often lends itself to such a distorted escalation of fear and anarchy.

3. To use repressive force. Repression may take many forms in schools, among them suspension, expulsion, or introduction of the police.

Patterns of Response

These responses raise many questions. Sometimes students' requests are quite legitimate and should be considered carefully and openly. The responses made by administrators and teachers—especially denial or repression—usually tend to confirm many students' preconceptions of the school and society as closed and inaccessible. Strongly repressive tactics may indicate to students that the school has decided to escalate the level of conflict. There are several serious problems that arise from this response.

1. Students may feel compelled to adopt more disruptive tactics in order to achieve a dialogue. Another imminent danger of this level of response is that for many trivial offenses teachers pull students out of the classroom and send them to the office. Once such administrative programs were available, some teachers no longer tried to exercise local control over the classroom and ended up by losing all control.

2. It must be remembered that students are always learning from the behavior of their teachers and principals; frightened or extreme responses do not teach students enlightened ways of responding to conflict, controversy, and dissent in their own lives.

3. Further, concrete political realities sometimes make these postures problematic because school administrators may not be able to get away with them; they may not work. Students now may have a kind of ultimate power in the school because they can close the schools down almost any time they organize to do so.

School administrators must begin to recognize the fact that they do not have unilateral and arbitrary power as they once had. The legal and objective facts of school life may not have changed, but the articulation of a group consciousness and thus a base of power among students has begun to emerge. In many schools large numbers of students feel that if they organize they have enough power to be able to disrupt the ongoing activities of the school to such an extent that they can bring the school to a grinding halt. Administrators can no longer run right over students. They must sit down with them and engage in some kind of negotiation or bargaining. At this point everybody confronts a dilemma that needs professional resolution, because few people know how to negotiate or bargain.

It is clear that students do not know how to bargain. They are just learning to recognize the issues and to create and escalate the conflicts that may get issues to the bargaining table. Once in such a situation students often maintain discussion at such a level of rhetoric that it is impossible to bargain, or they are so glad to talk that they are easily co-opted with some minimal form of tokenism.

Adults are not any more skillful, certainly not when pushed from behind by community and professional groups that are opposed to "permissiveness" and "anarchy." Bargaining is sometimes seen by adults as a way to cool off tensions and avoid resolving issues; the pitfall here is that as soon as this sort of bargaining is over, conflict and protest will break out even more vigorously. Many efforts at bargaining fail simply because of the participants' lack of values, skills, or ability to perform in such settings. These, then, are some of the more important issues provoking disruption in the high schools and some of the more salient patterns of response.

A Review of Causes

Let us first briefly review the causes of school disruption, because they are a basis for thinking about new role definitions for school social workers. These are as follows:

1. The high school curriculum and the effect to which it is relevant to the lives of the school's students.

2. The nature of classroom instruction. Students do not want to become passive recipients of what someone else thinks is critical information. They want a relaxed classroom atmosphere, individualized instruction, independent thinking, and stimulating discussion.

3. The extent of teacher and administrative control over students.

This review is by no means exhaustive; it is, rather, only illustrative. There are other issues, to be sure, that did not exist in the high school that has been examined here in depth. For example, in many schools students still have to raise their hands for permission to go to the bathroom. Girls still have to bring notes to be excused from physical education because of their menstrual periods. Students are still being punished physically. All of these add up to a dehumanizing atmosphere in which the student has little say and even less control.

Implications for the Social Worker's Role

What are the implications for the role of the school social worker? In what ways can the worker intervene in disruptive or potentially disruptive situations to bring about resolutions that humanize the school system and make it more responsive? There are various possibilities.

OMBUDSMANSHIP The CRUSK studies showed that many disruptions broke out in reaction to long-ignored and/or suppressed grievances. Often students themselves had difficulty articulating these grievances; as a result neither they nor the administration could deal with the problems. School social workers could perform a valuable task in meeting with groups of students and helping them to diagnose and articulate the problems they see as crucial and critical in their school. Once students begin to look at the issues and articulate them, school social workers can play an important role in helping them to devise and implement change strategies.

Social workers need to study their potential role as ombudsmen: trouble-shooters within the school whose task it will be to inquire into and probe the misuse of and disrespect for human resources. The parallel here is to teachers' unions with their grievance procedures. Why should students not have their grievance procedures as well?

UNDERSTANDING CHANGE FORCES School social workers could also help students to understand their community, to go out into the community and seek the forces for change within it. For example, in the high school under study it was the students who involved the NAACP in order to bring pressure to bear. What better way is there for students to learn about the community and political processes than by such involvement?

REDUCING ALIENATION A third possibility is to deal with the problem of personal alienation. There is a lack of human contact between students and teachers, between teachers and administrators, between

84

students and administrators. School social workers could set up informal meetings of students, teachers, and administrators to help them get to know each other as people and to voice the concerns each has. What may begin to emerge from such meetings are the common concerns that all people in the system have and the degree to which they are locked into their given roles because of external pressures. This interchange and interaction might be a starting point for whatever change efforts school social workers want to engage in.

A similar effort would be to bring students together in informal discussion groups. There is probably as little communication among black, Spanish-speaking, and white students as there is between students and teachers or administrators. The formation of small groups with skilled workers helping people talk to each other can be a valuable contribution to the high schools.

LESSENING INTERGROUP TENSION Social workers could also design activities in the schools that will allow for the understanding of intergroup tensions. They could work toward the implementation of a course on intergroup relations using the school as a laboratory for research into the question of how groups relate to each other. Activities could be designed to help students from different groups to understand each other's cultures.

INFORMATION-PROCESSING Another role could grow out of the kind of information that school social workers get from students. Students know what is happening, and school social workers know—or should know—all kinds of students. From these students they acquire a variety of information on what is happening in the school. What do school social workers do with that information? It is not suggested that they violate confidentiality. It is suggested that this is important information, information that has to be put back into the system in a manner that allows for reevaluation, reassessment, and the choosing of new directions. School social workers could play an important part in the formation of structures that could use this information in meaningful ways. What is suggested is the formation of what might be called a change agent or problem-solving team, a team comprised of students, teachers, and administrators who would be assigned the task of looking at the school as a whole system, assessing its difficulties on the basis of actual data, and engaging in change activity.

Another aspect of the school social worker's role that has been suggested by CRUSK's research is the role the worker can play vis-à-vis the system. Is he an advocate or the traditional facilitator and mediator? On whose side is he? What are his skills? Where are his commitments?

Models of Intervention

CRUSK is now working on a project involving three high schools and one elementary school. Change agent teams composed of students, teachers, and principals have been set up. The development of these teams over the first six weeks was fascinating. They began by taking as change goals limited tasks, such as the elimination of study hall. Slowly they gained cohesiveness and a sense of their own strength, and they began to develop strategies that were more far reaching. This development of course began to cause problems. For example, in one high school, as the team gained strength the principal, as part of the change agent team, came to feel threatened by his seeming loss of authority. He tried to reassert his authority by making such demands as that he have sole power to call meetings. This tactic failed and the principal began to complain to the superintendent of schools. In spite of the principal, this team has brought about a great number of innovations, such as reading laboratories, the post of vice-principal for innovation, and industrial placement of students.

Different models of intervention have been tried in various schools in order to assess their effectiveness. In some models the consultants work only with students. In others they work with all involved parties: the community, the school board, the administration, students, and faculty. In still others they work with the administration alone.

In one model of intervention an attempt is being made to develop an internal change agent team with an outside consultant. The purpose is to discover to what extent the outside consultant can withdraw and let the team take over. Hopefully teams such as this one will work with other schools in their system and, again hopefully, the role of the outside consultant may be lessened.

There are many aspects of the system as a whole with which the school social worker can deal. Many workers find students the most exciting group with which to work. Others may find it easier to work with principals. Some can operate as teams relating to different parts of the system. Others can relate to school boards or to the community.

There is enough evidence to indicate that school systems are not going to change until pressure of some sort is brought to bear. Student-generated or community-initiated pressure brings about substantial movement for change. CRUSK's analysis suggests that this kind of confrontation will increase. At the same time it has also been found that this kind of confrontation leads to repression or chaos because the managers of educational institutions have not learned creative and effective ways of responding.

No confrontation or response will be educationally significant or relevant until such time as the changes that have been discussed here become institutionalized and new organizational forms and processes are developed in the schools. What is crucial to this development are new patterns of management, new curricula, new instructional designs, and new professional role systems. In this task school social workers will be as much a part and have as much to offer as any other group.

A multipronged approach to school system change is suggested that includes the development and institution of new organizational forms and processes. This approach holds the greatest promise for meaningful resolution of the crises and disasters that presently plague those caught up in the educational system. The alternative to a creative new approach is clear. The choice is ours.

Behavior Modification Techniques for the Education Technologist

Richard B. Stuart

As evidenced by the rising rates of school dropout and student rebellion, parent protest and legal challenge, American education must be said to be in a state of crisis. Compounding the problem, teachers, psychologists, school social workers, and school administrators appear to be suffering from a technological lag, making efforts to apply the (at best) partially successful solutions of the 1940s and '50s to current problems. It is only when professionals in the education field and its ancillary services include present-day advances in their practice that even a partial solution to the current crisis may be expected.

This paper is addressed primarily to school social workers. Following a brief review of selected aspects of the history and current status of school social work, a detailed account will be presented of the application of behavior modification to school social work practice. It will be suggested that the traditional model of the social worker as offering individual counseling to troubled youngsters is archaic and must be replaced by the model of an "education technologist"—with the teacher as the primary client. While the application of behavior modification to the school setting is an evolving technology, many aspects of the approach have already been validated and extensive reference will be made to supportive research.

School Social Work in Perspective

During the early part of the twentieth century when school social work was just beginning to gain professional acceptance, social workers were in the forefront of social reform.[1] The change targets of these early social workers were the living conditions endured by schoolchildren and their families and educational practices.[2] The chief technique used was the facilitation of information exchange between parents and schools, focused on the needs of children in general and geared to promote system change.

With the rise of the mental hygiene movement in the United States during the first quarter of this century, the target of school social workers became amelioration of the psychosocial stress reactions of individual children, and the chief means of intervention became some variant of relationship therapy.[3] As the target and technique changed, so too did the nature of the presenting problems seen by school social workers. Referrals during the first quarter of the century focused on problems related to academic performance, gradually shifting later to an emphasis on behavioral and personality problems.[4] As Costin succinctly concludes:

If the literature of the period correctly reflects its practice, then a transition was fully completed from the earlier focus on school and neighborhood conditions and social change to a clinical orientation in relation to the personality needs of the individual school child.[5]

---

[1] Lela B. Costin, "A Historical Review of School Social Work," *Social Casework*, Vol. 50, No. 8 (October 1969), pp. 439–453.

[2] *See* Edith Abbott and Sophonisba P. Breckinridge, *Truancy and Nonattendance in the Chicago Schools: A Study of the Social Aspects of the Compulsory Education and Child Labor Legislation of Illinois* (Chicago: University of Chicago Press, 1917).

[3] *See* E. M. Everett, "The Importance of Social Work in a School Program," *The Family*, Vol. 19 (March 1938), pp. 3–8; Grace Lee, ed., *Helping the Troubled School Child* (New York: National Association of Social Workers, 1959); H. E. Weston, "School Social Work 1953," *Bulletin of the National Association of Social Workers*, Vol. 30, No. 2 (December 1954), pp. 20–30.

[4] *See* Jane F. Culbert, *The Visiting Teacher in the United States* (New York: Public Education Association of the City of New York, 1923); Mildred Sikkema, *Report of a Study of School Social Work Practice in Twelve Communities* (New York: American Association of Social Workers, 1953).

Table 1

Approximate Proportion of Children with School Difficulties (Academic and/or Behavioral) Related to Given Factors, as Reported by School Social Workers

Related Factors	Number of Responses [a]	Proportion of Children (percentage of responses)				
		0	20	40	60	80
Genetic and health factors	320	5	62	17	16	—
Family experiences	344	—	8	11	71	10
Peer experiences	331	9	83	8	—	—
Experiences in school	347	—	67	13	4	16

[a] Unequal numbers are probably attributable to the vagueness of the question.

While other areas of social work practice have begun to focus attention on broader social issues, school social work appears to have remained in the grip of a mental hygiene orientation. Costin conducted a careful investigation of the self-descriptions of activities pursued by a national sample of school social workers, concluding as follows:

The description of school social work revealed by this study appears to reflect the school social work literature of the 1940's and 1950's, and shows little or no general response to the concerns expressed in both education and social work literature of the 1960's.[6]

Costin's results ere echoed in an informal investigation by the present writer. A total of 347 school social workers in the Midwest were asked to respond to questions about the judgments and values underlying their conceptions of school social work practice. The results have clearly indicated that an overwhelming proportion of school social workers believe that family experiences predominate over school experiences in accounting for the difficulties that students encounter in school (see Table 1). Consistent with this, when asked to choose one group as an exclusive target for intervention, 66 percent indicated a preference for working with parents, 6 percent for working with students' peers, and 38 percent for working with teachers. Finally, when asked

---

[5] Op. cit., p. 446.

[6] Lela B. Costin, *An Analysis of the Tasks in School Social Work as a Basis for Improved Use of Staff* (Washington, D.C.: U.S. Department of Health, Education & Welfare, 1968), p. 266.

Table 2

School Social Workers' Ranking of the Reasons for School Success [a]

Reason for School Success	Number of Responses [b]	Ranking (percentage of responses)				
		1	2	3	4	5
Learning is intrinsically rewarding	311	22	23	22	14	19
Parents create a positive attitude toward school	346	2	25	4	26	43
Peers have a positive attitude toward school	290	26	21	17	16	20
Teachers are skillful in classroom social behavioral management	347	20	26	12	27	15
Teachers are skilled in presenting materials	344	11	19	36	17	17

[a] The categories are in ascending order of success from 1 to 5.
[b] Unequal numbers are probably attributable to the vagueness of the question.

to explain school success, a strong plurality gave prime weight to "learning as an intrinsic reward" and to parents' positive influence; comparably less weight was given to the skill of the teacher in classroom management or the presentation of educational matter (see Table 2).

Taken together, the data generated by Costin and the writer suggest that many school social workers may be following procedures that are not well adapted to the crisis conditions met in contemporary education. Drawing on four types of evidence, data can be adduced in support of this notion.

First, it can be shown that whereas teachers view behavioral problems in educational terms, mental health professionals—including school social workers—continue to draw often unrestrained inferences from these problems to their presumed underlying causes.[7] The effect of this difference in approach is an almost hopeless disjuncture between

[7] See Allan Goldfarb, "Teachers' Ratings in Psychiatric Case Findings," *American Journal of Public Health*, Vol. 53, No. 12 (December 1963), pp. 1919–1927; J. F. Walsh and J. D. O'Connor, "When Are Children Disturbed?" *Elementary School Journal*, Vol. 68, No. 7 (April 1968), pp. 353–356.

educational and mental health professionals, with teachers tending to refer fewer children and mental health workers spending inordinate amounts of time in case-finding activities.

Second, it can be shown that, despite this search for cases, other professional groups in the community (for example, the police) are more effective in the detection of children with severe behavioral or personality problems than are workers within the schools, as measured by referrals to outside treatment agencies.[8]

Third, it can be shown that present service conceptions have led school social workers into sharp conflict in jurisdictional or territorial disputes with other professional groups within the schools (for example, school psychologists, guidance counselors, and crisis and helping teachers) and in outside social agencies (such as child guidance clinics), with an inevitable decremental effect on service.[9]

The final argument against the present conception of school social work practice as individually oriented treatment is suggested by simple arithmetic. A one-to-one service model cannot possibly meet the present demand for service, even granting the questionable assumption that its techniques are the best available.[10] For example, in 1967 the state of Michigan recorded 2,042,000 public school admissions and 82,200 public school teachers, a pupil-teacher ratio of 24.8 to 1. Approximately 500 professional school social workers were employed in Michigan in 1967. If these were to be evenly distributed with respect to the state's schoolchildren, each worker would have responsibility for 4,084 children.

Several studies completed in the past have shown that from 2 to 3 percent of school-age children are faced with such severe emotional and/or behavioral problems as to be incapacitated for school. Rogers suggested that approximately 12 percent of all elementary school chil-

---

8 Shirley Jenkins and Mignon Şauber, *Paths to Child Placement: Family Situation Prior to Foster Care* (New York: Community Council of Greater New York, 1966).

9 *See* J. K. Fisher, "Role Perceptions and Characteristics of Attendance Coordinators, Psychologists, and Social Workers," *Journal of the International Association of Pupil Personnel Workers*, Vol. 10, No. 1 (January 1966), pp. 1–8; R. O. Rowen, "The Function of the Visiting Teacher in the School," *Journal of the International Association of Pupil Personnel Workers*, Vol. 9 (December 1965), pp. 3–9; M. C. Shaw, "Role Delineation Among the Guidance Professions," *Psychology in the Schools*, Vol. 4, No. 1 (January 1967), pp. 3–14.

10 Richard B. Stuart, *Trick or Treatment: How and When Psychotherapy Fails* (Champaign, Ill.: Research Press, 1970).

dren present serious problems, and Ullmann showed that 8 percent of high school students evinced such problems.[11] Accepting 10 percent as a probable proportion of individuals requiring service, this would equal an overall caseload of 408.4 children and families per worker per year, a number vastly outstripping the realistic capacity of individual practitioners using even the most parsimonious treatment strategies currently available. For example, adopting the eight-sesion limit strongly suggested by Reid and Shyne for cases involving parent-child or marital difficulties, caseworkers wishing to serve all of their potential clients would be required to hold 4,867 interviews per year, or 135 interviews per week over a thirty-six-week school year—exclusive of conferences with teachers, counselors, school administrators, consultants, and social work staff.[12]

In summary it can be said that school social work is currently facing a technological crisis. With needs fast outstripping resources, both quantitatively and qualitatively, there is a clear and present demand for innovative service patterns. Vinter and Sarri have suggested three areas for such change.[13]

First, social workers must try to influence organizational/administrative patterns within schools to overcome schoolwide and often system-wide patterns of negative sanctioning, negative record-keeping, and negative expectations with respect to individual malperforming students.[14] In addition it can be argued that school social workers must also seek to influence organizations within and outside the schools in an effort to develop institutional support for new teaching environments, materials, and strategies that will increase the attractiveness and produc-

---

[11] See E. H. Martens, *Needs of Exceptional Children* (Washington, D.C.: U.S. Office of Education, 1944); C. R. Rogers, "Mental Health Problems in Three Elementary Schools," *Educational Research Bulletin,* Vol. 21, No. 3 (March 18, 1942), pp. 67–79; C. A. Ullmann, *Identification of Maladjusted School Children* (Washington, D.C.: U.S. Public Health Service, 1952).

[12] William J. Reid and Anne W. Shyne, *Brief and Extended Casework* (New York: Columbia University Press, 1969).

[13] Robert D. Vinter and Rosemary C. Sarri, "Malperformance in the Public Schools: A Group Work Approach," *Social Work,* Vol. 10, No. 1 (January 1965), pp. 3–13.

[14] Rosenthal and Jacobson have demonstrated that students expected by teachers to be "academic bloomers" will significantly outperform those for whom teachers hold neutral expectations. This finding is especially compelling because the teachers were given information about the students on a purely random basis. Robert Rosenthal and Lenore Jacobson, "Teachers' Expectancies: De-

tivity of schools for groups who are not motivated by current educational programs.[15]

The second and third recommendations call for the development of group intervention strategies that would permit refinement of effective intervention techniques and broadening of the scope of service, as well as the development of consultative skills in teachers that would equip them to control the social and task-relevant responses of all the school's children. Either of these approaches would greatly increase both the efficiency and efficacy of school social work service.

While no single technique can be expected to serve all needs, the final alternative would seem to have special merit. It can function both secondarily to prevent the continued deterioration of individual children's school performance and primarily to prevent school-related problems from developing in many other children.[16] It is toward the social worker in this latter role—that of consultant to teachers or "education technologist"—that the remainder of this paper will be directed.

Two Views of Student Problems

Acceptance of the role of education technologist will depend in part on the way students' problems are understood, since there is an interaction between the way in which problems are conceptualized by clinicians and the type of treatment strategy they use. During the reform era of social work, clients' problems were viewed as a logical outgrowth of the social contexts in which the behavior took place. The behavior

terminants of Pupils' IQ Gains," *Psychological Reports*, Vol. 19, No. 1 (January 1966), pp. 115–118. In addition, the work of Schafer and Polk on the effects of "secondary deviance" determination in public schools should be consulted. By this process students who are once labeled may be chronically doomed to negative expectations by teaching personnel, materially affecting their school performance. W. E. Schafer and Kenneth Polk, "Delinquency and the Schools," in Task Force on Juvenile Delinquency, the President's Commission on Law Enforcement and Administration of Justice, *Task Force Report: Juvenile Delinquency and Youth Crime* (Washington, D.C.: U.S. Government Printing Office, 1967), pp. 222–277.

15 *See* David Street, "Education and Social Workers: Sibling Rivalry in the Inner City," *Social Service Review*, Vol. 41, No. 1 (January 1967), pp. 152–165.

16 Emory L. Cowen and Melvin Zax, "The Mental Health Fields Today: Issues and Problems," in Emory L. Cowen, E. A. Gardner, and Melvin Zax, eds., *Emergent Approaches to Mental Health Problems* (New York: Appleton-Century-Crofts, 1967), p. 18.

was viewed as an adaptive response to unfavorable circumstances. Baer has termed this an "instrumental" property of behavior, implying that the behavior would be different if the environment in which it occurred were different.[17] The therapeutic strategy that emerges from this approach is an effort to ameliorate the situational factors associated with problem behavior and to lengthen the factors associated with more desirable behavior.

Following the advent of the mental hygiene approach, problems have been understood to be a consequence of intrinsic personality defects within the client. While these defects are in some instances attributed to a complex set of genetic, biological, and social forces, the essential therapeutic task has been seen as the modification of problem behavior leading to the reassertion of situational controls. Illustrated by both psychodynamic theories and even the newer cognitively oriented approaches, the implications of this approach are that defects in the person must be corrected, rather than focusing on change in the situations associated with these defects.[18] For example, someone chronically in debt would be termed a spendthrift despite the fact that the wages he earns are substandard.

When this conception of individual, as opposed to situational, responsibility is carried into the school, the child is held accountable for any deficit in his functioning while the school is credited with success in producing whatever positive changes are observed. In fact, however, the school carries the burden of responsibility for the success or failure of the child with respect to both academic and social performance. The teacher is assumed to have acquired the skills necessary to "teach" his students to make new responses in the presence of increasingly complex stimuli. The teacher is also assumed to have acquired the skills necessary to create an environment suitable to the acquisition of new skills by students. And yet Patterson, Shaw, and Ebner have observed:

[17] D. M. Baer, "Effect of Withdrawal of Positive Reinforcement on an Extinguishing Response in a Young Child," *Child Development,* Vol. 32 (1961), pp. 64–74.

[18] For a discussion of psychodynamic theories, *see* G. H. Pearson, "The Psychoanalytic Contributions to the Theory and Practice of Education," in Morton Levitt, ed., *Readings in Psychoanalytic Psychology* (New York: Appleton-Century-Crofts, 1959), pp. 338–354. For an example of a cognitively oriented approach, *see* William Glasser, *Reality Therapy? A New Approach to Psychiatry* (New York: Harper & Row, 1965).

In many respects the classroom is a barren wasteland when one compares it to other, normally reinforcing interactions. Most of the reinforcers in the system are highly formalized, such as grades and test scores. The control of social behavior is achieved more as a function of threatened or applied aversive consequences than by positive social reinforcers.[19]

In such an environment it is no wonder that children develop learning deficits and become socially disruptive. It may be that this is the behavior that is most rewarded!

In view of the defects observed within the schools, it is strongly suggested that the professional (whether teacher, psychologist, or school social worker) view the presenting problems of students as reasonable reactions to deficient environments. Granted, the social worker who makes this assumption runs the risk that he might be ignoring a pressing problem of some other etiology. If this is the case, however, the early, measurable failure of his efforts will alert him to this possibility.

On the other hand, the worker who seeks to change the individual rather than the classroom runs the following risks: (1) iatrogenic illness (that is, illness caused by the treatment) may well result from his efforts,[20] (2) if effective, there is a distinct probability that his efforts will not generalize into the classroom and the behavioral problems may quickly recur, and (3) defects in the educational system will be permitted to persist without change. Unlike the possible negative consequences of shorter term behaviorally oriented treatment, the ill effects of individually oriented treatment are slower to appear and—what is more often the case—do not permit remediation.

Studies of Student Behavior

Most requests by teachers for outside help center on behavioral rather than presumed dynamic problems. Repeated studies both in Europe and America have shown that teachers generally refer students for help

[19] G. R. Patterson, D. A. Shaw, and M. J. Ebner, "Teachers, Peers and Parents as Agents of Change in the Classroom," in Arthur M. Benson, ed., *Modifying Deviant Social Behaviors in Various Classroom Settings,* Monograph No. 1 (Eugene: Department of Special Education, University of Oregon, 1969), p. 15.

[20] Richard B. Stuart, "Assessment and Change of the Communicational Patterns of Juvenile Delinquents and Their Parents," in Richard D. Rubin, ed., *Advances in Behavior Therapy: 1969* (New York: Academic Press, 1970), pp. 221–230.

with problems related to poor study habits or poor social relationships.[21] While cultural differences (including differences in professional cultures) are naturally reflected in these referrals, teachers' requests for help apparently stress concerns with objectifiable target behaviors within the classroom.

Teachers also request aid in handling responses that occur with greater intensity or frequency in problem children but that occur in nonproblem children as well. For example, one series of studies has shown that hyperactivity—high rates of inattention, moving about the room, talking out of turn, or wriggling in one's seat—is manifested by "normal" students about once per minute and by "problem" students about five times per minute.[22] Thus the subjects of the teacher's concern are typically quantitative rather than qualitative in nature. Other studies have shown that the rate of task-oriented behavior—for example, visual focusing, reading, writing, and other responses previously determined as necessary prerequisites for task completion—varies from 20 to 80 percent of class time, but non-task-oriented behavior typically does *not* disrupt the attention patterns of neighboring students.[23]

In addition to stressing the actual response of the student, another approach to the selection of a target behavior includes the teacher's evaluation of the behavior. For example, one such approach uses the following three categories:

Appropriate behavior—any behavior which is proper and acceptable given the situation.
Inappropriate behavior—any behavior which is not proper or appropriate, given the situation, but can be ignored. Examples include: removing one's shoes and walking in stocking feet; tapping lightly on

[21] European studies include those of J. D. Cummings, "The Incidence of Emotional Problems in School Children," *British Journal of Educational Psychology,* Vol. 14 (Winter 1944), pp. 151–161; and W. D. Wall, *Education and Mental Health* (Paris, France: UNESCO, 1955). American studies include those of Rogers, op. cit.; Walsh and O'Connor, op. cit.; and R. H. Woody, "The Use of Electro-encephalography and Mental Abilities Tests in the Diagnosis of Behavioral Problem Males," unpublished Ph.D. dissertation, Michigan State University, 1964.

[22] Patterson, Shaw, and Ebner, op. cit.

[23] *See* L. A. Hammerlynck, J. W. Martin, and J. C. Rolland, "Systematic Observation of Behavior: A Primary Teacher Skill," in L. A. Hammerlynck and J. W. Martin, eds., *Education and Training of the Mentally Retarded* (Calgary, Alberta, Can.: University of Calgary, in press); Hammerlynck, "Direct Observation of Student Behavior to Validate Teacher Reports," paper presented at the Canadian Psychological Association meeting, Calgary, Alta., June 1968.

the table during a language or reading activity; leaving the table quietly during a table activity; or whispering to one's neighbor during an activity or when students are expected to remain silent and pay attention to the teacher.

Unacceptable behavior—any behavior which is harmful to the child or others around him, any behavior which . . . disrupts the class or a proportion of other students, and any behavior which involves breaking a rule the consequences of which have been clearly stated by the teachers. Examples include: eating paint or other toxic art material; leaving the table during a table activity and running around the room disturbing the other children; . . . .[24]

The advantages of this approach, which was used also by Wasik, Senn, Welch, and Cooper, are its ability to reflect differing social demands and its immediate cueing of the teacher as to his appropriate response.[25] It should be pointed out, however, that this system makes reference to social behavior; specification of academic or task behavior would require greater precision.

Finally, it should be indicated that in addition to individual students, entire classes might be the subject of observation and assessment. A wide range of observational systems is possible, depending on the values and intentions of the observer.[26] For example, investigators might be interested in fine-category observation of a single child and his teacher on a time-sampling basis or coarse-category observation of the rule-testing and enforcing behavior of an entire class and its teacher.[27]

---

[24] Martha Abbott, Katherine Howard, and Tim Walter, "Sullivan School Project: Final Report," p. 4. Unpublished paper, University of Michigan, 1969.

[25] B. H. Wasik, Kathryn Senn, R. H. Welch, and B. A. Cooper, "Behavior Modification with Culturally Deprived School Children: Two Case Studies," *Journal of Applied Behavior Analysis*, Vol. 2 (Fall 1969), pp. 181–194.

[26] *See,* for example, E. J. Amidon and J. B. Hough, *Interaction Analysis: Theory, Research and Application* (Reading, Mass.: Addison-Wesley Publishing Co., 1967); D. M. Medley and H. E. Mitzel, "Measuring Classroom Behavior by Systematic Observation," in N. L. Gage, ed., *Handbook of Research and Teaching* (Chicago: Rand McNally, 1963), pp. 247–328; J. S. Werry and H. C. Quay, "Observing the Classroom Behavior of Elementary School Children," paper presented at the conference of the Council on Exceptional Children, New York, April 1968.

[27] For the former *see* R. S. Ray, D. A. Shaw, and G. R. Patterson, *Observation in the School: Description of a Coding Form* (Eugene: Oregon Research Institute, 1968). For the latter *see* the minutes of a staff meeting of the Research and Development Center, University School, University of Michigan, undated (mimeographed).

One criterion for a useful system is its specification of student and teacher behavior. In addition Patterson and Harris have suggested that the system should permit observer reliability and generalization of observational data, be relatively free from observer bias, permit reliable sampling of behavior, and control for the effect of the observer on the data.[28] Both Patterson and Harris and Surratt and his associates have shown that the mere presence of an observer materially affects the nature of the data presented for observation.[29]

RESPONSE SPECIFICATION Hyperactivity and non-task-oriented behavior are relatively imprecise terms because children could engage in any of an enormous array of responses compatible with either behavior. It is therefore necessary to identify precisely the target of behavioral change in a process termed "response specification."

Reflexive behaviors that are under autonomic control are termed respondents. Operant responses are classes of behavior that produce some change in the environment.[30] For example, a child might raise his hand (response) and the teacher might grant permission for him to speak (a change in the environment). Most teachers are primarily concerned with operant responses. This paper will deal with their specification and control.

The second requirement of response specification is the selection of responses that occur in excess of once every ten to fifteen minutes.[31] This is necessary because effective behavior modification is often expedited by the chance to provide repeated learning opportunities. When target behaviors occur at intervals of several weeks or even several hours, it is often necessary to wait for a long time before sufficient experience has been accumulated to facilitate new learning, and ex-

---

[28] G. R. Patterson and A. W. Harris, "Methodological Problems in Observation Procedure." Paper presented at the American Psychological Association meeting, San Francisco, September 1968.

[29] P. R. Surratt, R. E. Ulrich, and R. P. Hawkins, "An Elementary Student as a Behavioral Engineer," *Journal of Applied Behavior Analysis,* Vol. 2, No. 2 (Summer 1969), pp. 85–92.

[30] J. R. Millenson, *Principles of Behavioral Analysis* (New York: Macmillan Co., 1967), pp. 159–163.

[31] *See* J. M. Ackerman, *Operant Conditioning Techniques for the Classroom Teacher* (6th ed.; Albany, Ore.: Linn County Mental Health Clinic, 1969). A simple method for calculating rates has been the use of a "nomogram." *See* R. C. Branch and S. I. Sulzbacher, "Rapid Computation of Rates with a Simple Nomogram," *Journal of Applied Behavior Analysis,* Vol. 1, No. 3 (Fall 1968), pp. 251–252.

periences intervening between training periods may mitigate the cumulative effect of this training.

Moreover, Patterson has suggested that behaviors occur in predictable chains with the more serious behavior taking place after a series of less disturbing premonitory responses.[32] Unpublished data by Stuart, for example, has shown that shouting by a 6-year-old brain-damaged child occurred at the rate of one episode per ninety minutes, but that he stamped his feet once in fifty-five minutes, said "no" in a loud voice once in seven minutes, and shook his head vigorously from side to side once in seventy-five seconds. Identification of this behavioral chain permitted early intervention in the behavioral cycle with two distinct advantages: repetition of control efforts permitted radical behavioral change without removing the child from the classroom and the amount of disruption of the class diminished as his outbursts decreased.

The third requirement of response specification is that it be a definite behavioral action rather than a nonaction. Lindsley has termed this the "dead man test," implying that dead students are best at "not talking out in class," while their live counterparts excel at "talking only when recognized" or "talking without recognition." [33] This requirement is essential because the nonoccurrence of an event cannot be counted.

The final requirement of response specification is the selection of a positive action to count in association with any negative action. There are two main reasons for this. First, teachers and others tend to concentrate spontaneously on the problem behavior of children identified as deviants. The clinician should avoid reinforcing this negative tracking. Second, as will be shown shortly, the technology for accelerating behavior is more powerful, as a general rule, than that available for deceleration. It is therefore essential to select as a behavioral target those responses amenable to acceleration.

It is desirable to establish a target rate at which the response is expected to occur when intervention is terminated. This decision is

---

[32] G. R. Patterson, "A Community Mental Health Program for Children," in L. A. Hammerlynck, P. O. Davidson, and L. E. Acker, eds., *Behavior Modification and Ideal Mental Health Services* (Calgary, Canada: University of Calgary, 1969), pp. 130–179.

[33] Ogden R. Lindsley, "Procedures in Common Described by a Common Language." Paper presented at the University of Kansas Ninth Annual Institute for Research in Clinical Psychology, July 1968. *See also* Ackerman, op. cit.

always "political" in the sense that it involves some compromise between the behavioral patterns emitted by the individual and the expectations of those judging his behavior—parents, teachers, and administrators, among others. If the rate is at the criterion level, no further action is needed. If the rate is below the criterion level, this rate constitutes a baseline and the evaluation of behavior must continue.

In evaluating the need for treatment based on rate data, as well as evaluating the changes mediated by treatment, Patterson, Shaw, and Ebner have developed an ingenious technique.[34] They measure the behavior of a so-called problem child, but at the same time measure the behavior of one other randomly selected child in the class. This gives a general measure of the behavioral climate of the class, facilitating interpretation of the observed rates by supplying a context for their evaluation.

ANTECEDENT CONDITIONS   If a response is an action that produces changes in the environment, then antecedents set the occasion for the response to occur. Management of antecedents is the province of behavioral engineers, architects, and professionals with a wide range of concerns. Some antecedents are favorable to the occurrence of a desired response; these are designated A+. Others, designated A—, are either unfavorable to the occurrence of the desired response or conducive to the occurrence of problem responses in the same situation. It is obvious, for example, that a well-constructed school (A+) will be more likely to be associated with good student performance than a dimly lit, cold, and poorly ventilated building (A—). In the same vein it is clear that loud music or noise in the halls is likely to interfere with effective study responses (hence A—).

There are four classes of antecedents. The first class is *instructional stimuli*—verbal or symbolic stimuli, such as rules or facial expressions, that serve to cue a response. If it is true that a well-managed class is (1) "a predictable one" [35] and (2) one in which the teacher controls more of the consequences than students,[36] then the teacher must

---

[34] Op. cit.

[35] D. E. P. Smith and J. M. Smith, *Teacher's Manual for the Michigan Language Program* (Ann Arbor, Mich.: Ann Arbor Publishers, 1968), p. 4.

[36] Carl Semmelroth, "How to Tell a Well-Managed Classroom When You See One." Paper presented at the Council for Exceptional Children, Denver, April 1969.

have a stable rule system composed of contingent rather than absolute rules. Contingent rules stress acceleration of positive responses and specify that if a desired response is emitted, a prescribed consequence will follow. Nonoccurrence of the desired response leads to absence of the consequence. In contrast, absolute rules stress deceleration of negative responses and specify that if negative behavior occurs, then a negative consequence will follow. Contingent rules lodge the responsibility for producing positive consequences with the student; absolute rules lodge responsibility with the teacher. Contingent rules are a more effective means of controlling behavior.

Smith has observed that rules must be enforced on at least 80 percent of the relevant occasions if they are to be at all effective.[37] In addition Madsen and his associates have shown that mere mention of rules is less effective than rule enforcement backed by positive attention to appropriate behavior.[38] Therefore it is clear that rules should be kept small enough in number and should be simple enough to permit teachers to use enforcement procedures readily. In addition rule systems should be free of contradictions and should provide an effective means by which both student and teacher may determine when desirable behavior has occurred.

Anyone who would generate a rule system must be aware that rule-testing is an inevitable consequence of rule-making. Smith and Smith have shown that rules will be tested at least twice in an effort to establish a basis for reasonable predictions of the consequences.[39] This means that teachers and others must be prepared to make appropriate responses in the face of possible apparent failure of rule systems, knowing that once the consequences of rule-testing are established, the rate of compliance with rules will increase.

A second class of antecedent conditions is *facilitating stimuli*—the essentials necessary if the response is to occur. For example, facilitating stimuli for the solution of algebraic problems are the tools for studying (such as a table, good light, and a quiet room), study materials, and the prerequisite skills (that is, arithmetic skills).

---

[37] *See* the minutes of a staff meeting of the Research and Development Center.

[38] C. H. Madsen, Jr., W. C. Becker, and D. R. Thomas, "Rules, Praise, and Ignoring: Elements of Elementary Classroom Control," *Journal of Applied Behavior Analysis*, Vol. 1, No. 2 (Summer 1968), pp. 139–150.

[39] Op. cit.

A great deal has been written about the effects of environment on learning and the design of effective learning environments.[40]   Similarly a great deal has been written about the value of such instructional aids as computers, teaching machines, and programmed instruction for selective use with students at all levels of education.[41]   The advantages of these approaches are that they permit individualized instruction and provide immediate feedback about the accuracy of responses so that all members of a large class can work simultaneously on different materials at different levels, while avoiding the practice of errors.

The third class of antecedent stimuli is *potentiating stimuli*—events manipulated by the behavior modifier in an effort to maximize the value of the consequences that will follow a response.[42]   For example, a teacher might schedule a game period for midafternoon when students are most likely to want a break, or he might read the first chapter of an adventure story (termed "reinforcer sampling" by Ayllon and Azrin[43]) that he plans to use as a reward for the completion of task behavior throughout the day.   In either case the likelihood that the student will work to attain the reinforcer is increased.

The fourth class of antecedents includes *discriminative stimuli,* which are indications that a positive consequence will follow a response, and *stimulus deltas,* which indicate that responses are unlikely to be followed by a positive consequence.   For example, a student might know that asking his regular teacher for permission to leave school early will be refused while such requests are likely to be granted by substitutes; the regular teacher is a stimulus delta for making such requests, the substitute teacher, a discriminative stimulus.

---

[40] *See,* for example, M. J. Ebner, "An Investigation of the Role of the Social Environment in the Generalization and Persistence of the Effect of a Behavior Modification Program," unpublished doctoral dissertation, University of Oregon, 1967; H. L. Cohen, Israel Goldiamond, James Filipczak, and Richard Pooley, "Training Professionals in Procedures for the Establishment of Educational Environments: A Report on the CASE Training Institute (CTI)" (Silver Spring, Md.: Institute for Behavioral Research, 1968).

[41] *See,* respectively, R. C. Atkinson, "The Computer Is a Tutor," *Psychology Today,* Vol. 1, No. 8 (January 1968), pp. 57–59; Alan Cleary and Derek Packham, "A Touch-Detecting Teaching Machine with Auditory Reinforcement," *Journal of Applied Behavior Analysis,* Vol. 1, No. 4 (Winter 1968), pp. 341–345; J. S. Birnbauer, S. W. Bijou, M. M. Wolf, and J. D. Kidder, "Programmed Instruction in the Classroom," in Leonard P. Ullmann and Leonard Krasner, eds., *Case Studies in Behavior Modification* (New York: Holt, Rinehart & Winston, 1965), pp. 358–364; C. H. Hendershot, "Programmed Learning: A Bibliography of Programs and Presentation Devices" (Bay City, Mich.: Hendershot

For some children good grades may be an indication of pleasant things to come. Superior papers might be posted on the bulletin board or read to the class or school staff; other students might expect to be granted money or extra privileges at home. Grades thus serve as a discriminative stimulus for approaching certain potentially reinforcing persons or situations. Will all children work to achieve good grades? Only those who have in the past enjoyed positive consequences associated with grades. Thus a discriminative stimulus or stimulus delta controls a response that has been learned through past experience. If a given child has not had experiences that add meaning to these events, he will not work to produce them.

CONSEQUENT CONDITIONS Antecedent conditions set the occasion for responses, increasing the likelihood that they will occur initially. If they are to recur, however, they must produce favorable consequences. If an operant response is a response that produces some change in the environment, then the changes or consequences produced by a given response must be regarded as the conditions exercising primary control over it.[44] Some consequences accelerate the likelihood that the rate of a response will increase: expressions of encouragement, payment for work completed, or an end to nagging. Other consequences decelerate the probability that a given response will be emitted: criticism, being ignored, punishment, loss of something of value, or being temporarily enjoined from engaging in a positive activity. In order for these consequences to exercise their control, however, they must occur; behavior is controlled by realities, not by expectations. For example, a child will work to achieve good grades if he receives some

Associates, 1967); F. S. Keller, "Good-bye Teacher," *Journal of Applied Behavior Analysis*, Vol. 1, No. 1 (Spring 1968), pp. 79–89; Keller, "A Programmed System of Instruction," *Educational Technology Monographs*, No. 2 (1969), pp. 1–26; K. E. Lloyd and N. J. Knutzen, "A Self-paced Programmed Undergraduate Course in the Experimental Analysis of Behavior," *Journal of Applied Behavior Analysis*, Vol. 2, No. 2 (Summer 1969), pp. 125–133; D. M. Eldred and G. W. Brooks, "Use of Programmed Instruction with Disturbed Children" (Waterbury, Vt.: Vermont State Hospital, 1966) (mimeographed).

[42] Israel Goldiamond, "Programs, Paradigms, and Procedures," in Cohen, Goldiamond, Filipczak, and Pooley, op. cit., pp. 27–28.

[43] Teodoro Ayllon and Nathan H. Azrin, *The Token Economy: A Motivational System for Therapy and Rehabilitation* (New York: Appleton-Century-Crofts, 1968).

[44] *See* B. F. Skinner, *Science and Human Behavior* (New York: Free Press, 1953).

recognition for his efforts. If he has merely been promised this recognition without ever having received it, his behavior is unlikely to be controlled by it.

The manipulation of consequences is a powerful means of behavioral control. When consequences follow solely on the occurrence of a given response, they are termed contingencies and their manipulation is termed contingency management.[45] A teacher may use recess as a contingency if recess is restricted to those who put away their materials properly or perform whatever the desired behavior is. Conversely, he may use recess noncontingently if he allows every child to go to recess regardless of whether he has put away his materials.

Two studies have evaluated the effect of contingent as opposed to noncontingent consequences in classroom settings.[46] Each of these studies has followed a six-step procedure common to current research in operant behavior:

1. A given response is specified, in the present instances, study behavior and cooperative play.

2. A base-line measurement is taken, reflecting the rate at which these responses occur in the environment prior to any manipulation.

3. The first experimental condition is instituted—noncontingent use of tokens in the first study and teacher attention in the second study, with measurement of the dependent variables (study and cooperative play) being continued.

4. The first experimental condition is terminated and the second condition—contingent use of tokens and teacher attention—is instituted, with continued measurement of the dependent variable.

5. The second condition is terminated and is replaced by a return to the first condition (a reversal that might equally have been a return to the original base-line condition), with measurement of the dependent variable continuing.

6. Finally, the second experimental condition is reinstituted, associated with a final measurement of response rates.

---

[45] Lloyd Homme et al., *How to Use Contingency Contracting in the Classroom* (Champaign, Ill.: Research Press, 1969).

[46] Don Bushell, Jr., P. A. Wrober, and M. L. Michaelis, "Applying 'Group' Contingencies to the Classroom Study Behavior of Preschool Children," *Journal of Applied Behavior Analysis*, Vol. 1, No. 1 (Spring 1968); pp. 55–61; B. M. Hart, N. J. Reynolds, D. M. Baer, E. R. Brawley, and F. R. Harris, "Effect of Contingent and Noncontingent Social Reinforcement on the Cooperative Play of a Preschool Child," *Journal of Applied Behavior Analysis*, Vol. 1, No. 1 (Spring 1968), pp. 73–76.

Both of these studies have shown that the rates of both study and cooperative play increase when consequences are applied contingently and actually *decrease* when consequences are applied noncontingently. These studies strongly support the suggestion that the many accelerative consequences available in normal classrooms—for example, attention, preferred seating locations, privileges such as use of special materials or participation in trips and games, among many others—should be made available on a purely contingent basis in order to maintain or augment the teacher's positive control of the class.

Consequences may have either of two characteristic forms: they may be informational or material. Information is anything that "removes or reduces uncertainty." [47] Feedback—"information about the effects of one's own behavior"—has great value.[48] Its function is to facilitate the planful control of the individual's behavior by "feeding back" to him the results of his own behavior.[49] In a real sense every operant consequence evokes behavior-regulating feedback in the sense that when a child learns that he may go to recess regardless of whether he has completed his work, this information will be useful to him in planning his next efforts.[50] However, some consequences are informational secondary to their material characteristics—as when we know that our work is appreciated when we receive an unexpected bonus check. Although it is recognized that there is a distinct overlap between informational and material consequences, they will nevertheless be discussed separately in the interest of clarity.

Informational Consequences Social reactions are a prime source of feedback because of their evaluative component and because they are often associated with eventual access to material reinforcers.[51] This is another way of saying that they have acquired or secondary value by virtue of having been associated with valued material consequences. For example, when a teacher tells a child that he may sit anywhere in

47 Fred Attneave, *Applications of Information Theory to Psychology* (New York: Henry Holt & Co., 1959), p. 1.

48 Stuart, "Assessment and Change of the Communicational Patterns of Juvenile Delinquents and Their Parents," p. 191.

49 Norbert Wiener, *The Human Use of Human Beings* (Garden City, N.Y.: Anchor Books, Doubleday & Co., 1956).

50 Skinner, op. cit., p. 59.

51 W. F. Hill, "Sources of Evaluative Reinforcement," *Psychological Bulletin*, Vol. 69, No. 2 (February 1968), pp. 132–146.

the room he chooses (privilege, a material consequence as used here), this permission is typically associated with smiles, attention, and positive words. The teacher's gestures and words in the future are likely to be accelerative consequences for the child.

Feedback may be used either to accelerate or decelerate responses. Implicitly, whenever one aspect of a response is praised, other aspects are neglected. It is to be expected that the praised aspect will be strengthened while the neglected, ignored, or extinguished aspects will be weakened. Beyond this, however, behavior modifiers may choose deliberately to remove positive feedback following certain responses, such as a sixth-grade child's solutions to fifth-grade problems, in an effort to motivate the child to undertake more complex sixth-grade problems. While decisive research on the subject cannot be cited, it is believed wise to avoid the use of simple extinction procedures because, as will be shown later, the control exercised by the behavior modifier may be weakened if such an approach is relied on. Instead it seems invariably wise to begin with the acceleration of a desired response, preferably one that is incompatible with the problem response, and only later resort to decelerative techniques to do away with any problem behavior that persists.

The use of positive attention has controlled a variety of behaviors in schoolchildren. Among preschool children, positive teacher attention has been shown to increase climbing, cooperation, crawling, and speech.[52] In one study a 5-year-old kindergartner who had not spoken

[52] See, respectively, J. S. Buel, Patricia Stoddard, F. R. Harris, and D. M. Baer, "Collateral Social Development Accompanying Reinforcement of Outdoor Play in a Preschool Child," Journal of Applied Behavior Analysis, Vol. 1, No. 2 (Summer 1968), pp. 167–173; Hart, Reynolds, Baer, Brawley, and Harris, op. cit.; F. R. Harris, M. K. Johnston, C. Susan Kelley, and M. M. Wolf, "Effects of Positive Social Reinforcement on Regressed Crawling of a Nursery School Child," Journal of Educational Psychology, Vol. 55, No. 1 (February 1964), pp. 35–41; D. W. Brison, "A Non-Talking Child in Kindergarten: An Application of Behavior Therapy," Journal of School Psychology, Vol. 4, No. 1 (Fall 1966), pp. 65–69.

[53] See R. V. Hall, Diane Lund, and Delores Jackson, "Effects of Teacher Attention on Study Behavior," Journal of Applied Behavior Analysis, Vol. 1, No. 1 (Spring 1968), pp. 1–12; R. V. Hall, Marion Panyan, Delores Rabon, and Marcia Broden, "Instructing Beginning Teachers in Reinforcement Procedures which Improve Classroom Control," Journal of Applied Behavior Analysis, Vol. 1, No. 4 (Winter 1968), pp. 315–322; C. H. Madsen, Jr., W. C. Becker, D. R. Thomas, L. Kosar, and E. Plager, "An Analysis of the Reinforcing Function of 'Sit Down' Commands," in R. K. Parker, ed., Readings in Educational Psychology (Boston: Allyn & Bacon, 1968).

in over a year spoke within four weeks when the teacher was attentive to him following each successive step toward effective speech (termed shaping or reinforcement of successive approximations). Among older schoolchildren teacher attentiveness has been used to increase rates of study and acceptable social responses.[53]

Unfortunately, both teachers and peer groups may serve to maintain problem behavior as well as desirable behavior.[54] For this to be true, the amount of attention offered to the child for negative behavior must almost equal or exceed the attention paid to positive behavior; Charlesworth and Hartup have shown that even nursery school children may exert a similar negative influence.[55] Much of this strengthening of problem responses is undoubtedly unintentional. For example, it has been shown that reliance on simple commands such as "Sit down!" may actually accelerate the rate of out-of-seat behavior and attention to crying may accelerate the rate of crying.[56] Faced with a class of perhaps twenty-five students and constrained by reliance on absolute rule systems, teachers may find it difficult to do other than pay attention to negatives; the need to reverse this tendency is clear.

The use of positive attention to increase the rate of a behavior incompatible with a problem response in order to extinguish that response has been convincingly demonstrated in several studies. In one, a child whose temper tantrums continued when she was held on the teacher's or principal's lap was brought under positive control within four weeks by reinforcement of appropriate social behavior and ignoring of inappropriate behavior.[57] In another demonstration a socially iso-

[54] *See* D. M. Baer and M. M. Wolf, "The Reinforcement Contingency in Preschool and Remedial Education," in R. D. Hall and D. M. Baer, eds., *Early Education: Current Theory, Research, and Practice* (Chicago: Aldine Publishing Co., 1968); F. R. Harris, M. M. Wolf, and D. M. Baer, "Effects of Adult Social Reinforcement on Child Behavior," *Young Children*, Vol. 20, No. 1 (October 1964), pp. 8–17; R. G. Wahler, "Child-Child Interactions in Free Field Settings: Some Experimental Analysis," *Journal of Experimental Child Psychology*, Vol. 5, No. 2 (June 1967), pp. 278–293.

[55] W. R. Charlesworth and W. W. Hartup, "An Observational Study of Positive Social Reinforcement in the Nursery School Peer Group," *Research Bulletin*, Vol. 108, No. 4 (1966).

[56] Madsen, Becker, Thomas, Kosar, and Plager, op. cit.; B. M. Hart, K. E. Allen, J. S. Buell, F. R. Harris, and M. M. Wolf, "Effects of Social Reinforcement on Operant Crying," *Journal of Experimental Child Psychology*, Vol. 1, No. 1 (February 1964), pp. 145–153.

[57] C. S. Carlsen, C. R. Arnold, W. C. Becker, and C. H. Madsen, "The Elimination of Tantrum Behavior of a Child in an Elementary Classroom," *Behavior Research and Therapy*, Vol. 6, No. 1 (February 1968), pp. 117–119.

lated child was brought to a pattern of social approach behavior by withdrawing effort to encourage him to join groups (which rewarded his isolation) and paying attention only to social approach responses.[58] This procedure has been used to accelerate the rate of task-oriented behavior while decreasing hyperactivity, aggression, and other socially disruptive responses of normal students as well as a variety of behaviors of brain-injured children.[59]

It is important to note that these changes have been achieved in work with individual children alone or in class, as well as with groups of children and entire classes. It is important to note that while some of these dramatic effects have been achieved with no increase in the overall amount of teacher attentiveness, it is clear that the teacher's attention must be radically redirected from negative to positive behavior.[60] Hall, Panyan, Rabon, and Broden have shown that in a class in which students studied 43 percent of the available time and teachers used positive feedback 1.4 times per session, the rate of studying increased to 77 percent of the available time following an increase to 17 teacher comments per session.[61] The total professional cost of this change was minimal, having been held to fifteen to thirty minutes with each teacher to introduce the procedure and several minutes with each on a weekly basis to review the results.

When efforts are made to use attention to accelerate a behavior incompatible with problem responses, Ackerman suggests as a general

[58] K. E. Allen, B. M. Hart, J. S. Buell, F. R. Harris, and M. M. Wolf, "Effects of Social Reinforcement on Isolate Behavior of a Nursery School Child," *Child Development*, Vol. 35, No. 2 (June 1964), pp. 511–518.

[59] *See*, respectively, K. E. Allen, L. B. Henke, F. R. Harris, D. M. Baer, and N. J. Reynolds, "Control of Hyperactivity by Social Reinforcement of Attending Behavior," *Journal of Educational Psychology*, Vol. 58, No. 4 (August 1967), pp. 231–237; Paul Brown and Rogers Elliott, "Control of Aggression in a Nursery School Class," *Journal of Experimental Child Psychology*, Vol. 2, No. 2 (June 1965), pp. 103–107; W. C. Becker, C. H. Madsen, Jr., C. R. Arnold, and D. R. Thomas, "The Contingent Use of Teacher Attention and Praise in Reducing Classroom Behavior Problems," *Journal of Special Education*, Vol. 1, No. 3 (Spring 1967), pp. 287–307; Hall, Lund, and Jackson, op. cit.; Hall, Panyan, Rabon, and Broden, op. cit.; R. V. Hall and Marcia Broden, "Behavior Changes in Brain-Injured Children Through Social Reinforcement," *Journal of Experimental Child Psychology*, Vol. 5, No. 4 (December 1967), pp. 463–479.

[60] M. H. Ward and B. L. Baker, "Reinforcement Therapy in the Classroom," *Journal of Applied Behavior Analysis*, Vol. 1, No. 4 (Winter 1968), pp. 323–328.

[61] R. V. Hall, Marion Panyan, Delores Rabon, and Marcia Broden, "Teacher Applied Contingencies and Appropriate Classroom Behavior." Paper presented at a meeting of the American Psychological Association, San Francisco, September 1968.

rule that the rate of attention for desirable behavior should equal 110 percent of the attention previously given for both positive and negative behaviors.[62] For example, if a child received two teacher comments per day for positive behavior and eight positive comments per day for negative behavior, the accelerated positive behavior should occur at the rate of eleven comments per day ($1.1 \times 2 + 8$). While data in support of this rule have not yet been published, it would appear at this time to be a reasonable guide.

Other than providing social feedback to children—a process that may make troublesome demands on the teacher—several investigators have used a variety of simple devices to transmit this information. Working with a physically handicapped 11-year-old boy, McKerracher used a light to indicate positive behavior and a buzzer to signify negative behavior; Quay and his associates used lights to signal positive behavior with normal elementary school children.[63] Several other investigators also used visual and auditory signals with normal and brain-damaged children, backing up the signals for positive behavior with reinforcements such as candy.[64] In addition Patterson has developed a "workbox" that contains a counter that can be reset and a light activated by a pushbutton controlled at some distance by a teacher.[65] The workbox has been used successfully to modify the behavior of a number of children. Even more complex light signal systems have been used to modify the behavior of groups of students or even entire classes.[66] In each of these instances lights have signaled

[62] Op. cit.

[63] D. W. McKerracher, "Alleviation of Reading Difficulties by a Simple Operant Conditioning Technique," *Journal of Child Psychology and Psychiatry,* Vol. 8, No. 1 (January 1967), pp. 51–56; H. C. Quay, J. S. Werry, Marjorie McQueen, and R. L. Sprague, "Remediation of the Control Problem Child in the Special Class Setting," *Exceptional Children,* Vol. 32, No. 8 (April 1966), pp. 509–515.

[64] See R. M. Addison and Lloyd E. Homme, "The Reinforcing Event (RE) Menu," *NSPI Journal,* Vol. 4, No. 2 (1966), unpaged; G. R. Patterson, Reginald Jones, J. Whittier, and M. A. Wright, "A Behavioral Modification Technique for the Hyperactive Child," *Behavior Research and Therapy,* Vol. 2, No. 3 (January 1965), pp. 217–266.

[65] G. R. Patterson, "Parents as Behavior Modifiers in the Classroom," in J. D. Krumboltz and C. E. Thoresen, eds., *Behavioral Counseling: Cases and Techniques* (New York: Holt, Rinehart & Winston, 1969), pp. 155–161.

[66] Surratt, Ulrich, and Hawkins, op. cit.; H. M. Walker, R. H. Mattson, and N. K. Buckley, "Special Class Placement as a Treatment Alternative for Deviant Behavior in Children," in A. Benson, ed., *Behavior Modification in the Schools* (Eugene: University of Oregon Press, 1969), pp. 49–80.

the eventual provision of a variety of material reinforcers. The dual advantages of this approach are that (1) the teacher is able to give increased amounts of feedback to students without disrupting his normal teaching routines and (2) feedback can be provided immediately following a desired response. Thus there is no danger of a teacher's forgetting to respond positively and there is no delay in the student's receipt of information necessary for his continued performance.

Another means of transmitting feedback from teachers to students is through the use of traditional grading procedures. In theory grades represent a reflection of the value of student output and should be associated with positive consequences in proportion to the value of the work done. In practice, however, there are five limitations to the value of grades.

1. Smith and Smith contend that grades can only be useful if they are positive. They state:

> Information feedback serves to increase motivation and stimulate change if the information is positive. But if it is negative, it can discourage both learner and teacher. In fact, evidence of failure is so punishing that people have built up effective techniques for ignoring information that might be negative.[67]

The techniques to which the authors refer include attacking the adequacy or relevance of the information, ignoring the information, or claiming that the essential aspects of performance have not been measured. In a partial test of this view, this author offered positive examination grades to one-half of a large graduate social work class; the other half of the class received negative grades. Seven days later he asked the class to identify their scores on the examination. Controlling for the level of grades, students who received positive information were significantly more accurate in their recall than were students who received negative information. Despite general knowledge of this tendency, positive grades are given infrequently.

2. A second limitation of grades is that grades should be secondary reinforcers because of their association with positive consequences. In point of fact, grades are typically used as a means of avoiding negatives rather than as a means of achieving positives. Skinner has observed, for example:

> The commonest practice in high school as well as college is still "assign and test." We tell the student what he is to learn and hold him responsi-

---

[67] Op. cit., p. 52.

111

THE SCHOOL IN THE COMMUNITY

ble for learning it by making a variety of unhappy consequences contingent upon his failure. In doing so we may give him some reason to learn but we do not teach.[68]

Unless positive incentives are associated with grades, grades will not acquire the property of secondary reinforcement. Some parents attach desirable consequences—such as money and extra free time—to good grades, but schools should not depend on parents to supply reinforcement for school-related behavior. Instead, schools should provide positive consequences such as the privilege of taking elective classes or coming to school at a later hour.

3. A third limitation is that grades typically are offered too late for either the student or teacher to make use of their information value. When tests come at the end of a unit of work, little can be done to overcome the deficits they reflect. If instead grades were offered at many intervals during a study activity, they could serve a regulatory function in the teaching process.

4. One explanation for the perpetuation of terminal grading is the assumption that grades are a reflection of student performance. This is the fourth limitation of grading procedures. In point of fact, the student's "learning" is a dependent variable that varies as a function of the teacher's skill in the management of the teaching situation. Traditionally students may fail, but teachers always pass.

> The existing practice of grading students assumes at bottom that the student is responsible for his learning and that his failure or success is a tribute to or a consequence of factors intrinsic to him. This idea of grading a school on the basis of its outputs assumes that all students can learn that the responsibility of the schools is to make that happen. . . . [69]

At the present time the person who occupies the relatively weaker position in an educational setting—the student—receives feedback. If the tradition were reversed—if teachers' reinforcement were made contingent on the grades earned by students—then teachers could use their relative position of strength to modify instructional conditions and thereby improve student performance.

5. Another limitation of grading procedures is the use of absolute rather than achievement ratings. Absolute ratings are measurements of student performance in comparison either to an arbitrarily determined

---

[68] B. F. Skinner, "Teaching Science in High School—What Is Wrong?" *Science,* Vol. 159 (February 16, 1968), p. 707.

[69] H. D. Gideonse, "Research Development and the Improvement of Education," *Science,* Vol. 162 (November 1, 1968), p. 544.

READERS PLEASE NOTE

Add to the Table of Contents:

Betty Deschler, MSW, Consultant, Mental Retardation Program,
Family and Children's Aid,
Jackson, Michigan
John L. Erlich, MS, Research Associate, School of Social Work,
University of Michigan, Ann Arbor, Michigan

ratio scale (grades are commonly assigned on the basis of the proportion of correct answers, the total number of questions being arbitrarily determined by teachers) or to the performance of other students. This curve grading introduces a double artifact: not only is the ratio scale arbitrarily determined, but students are denied exact information about the expected criteria for their performance prior to an examination, as a means of protecting the teacher from setting objective standards for measurement of his own performance as a teacher. In contrast to this approach, achievement ratings would compensate students according to the extent to which their performance improves from one test period to the next. The danger in a system that uses the student as a standard for his own evaluation is that students might unintentionally perform poorly at the outset. But if this approach were combined with traditional procedures, implying that students could receive certain privileges (for example, exemption from attendance at a given class or from homework assignments), this obstacle could be overcome.

If grades are (1) offered positively, (2) associated with accelerative consequences, (3) offered promptly, (4) understood to be indications of teacher achievement first and student performance second, and (5) offered as consequences for absolute and relative changes, then they can serve a useful function as a medium of feedback. If these criteria are not met, then it is doubtful that grades can be useful.

A final form of feedback in school settings is information about teacher functioning. Beyond grades, teachers may benefit greatly from information about their management of classes. Flanders has noted:

> As a group, teachers are isolated from systematic information about their own behavior. However, research indicates that teaching performance depends upon the range of behavior a teacher can produce, the self-control required to provide particular patterns of influence, a teacher's sensitivity in diagnosing the requirements of the moment, and his ability to predict the consequences of alternative actions. . . . Considerable improvement probably can be brought about by any program that provides reasonably intelligent teachers of average emotional adjustment with systematic information about their classroom behavior.[70]

To the extent that specific nuances of teacher behavior are associated with the differential performance of students, it would seem as though information about teacher behavior would be vitally essential to effective classroom behavior.

Several studies have contributed information about the criteria that

---

[70] N. A. Flanders, "Some Relationships Among Teacher Influence, Pupil Attitudes and Achievement," in Amidon and Hough, eds., op. cit., p. 24.

differentiate highly effective from less effective secondary school teachers. (It is probable that quite different patterns are associated with primary- and college-level teaching.) For example, Flanders has shown that two-thirds of classroom time is occupied with talk and two-thirds of this time is typically occupied with talk on the part of the teacher.[71] But Amidon and Giammatteo contrasted 33 teachers rated as superior with 120 not so rated by noting that superior teachers spoke 40 percent of the time in comparison to normative teachers who spoke 52 percent of the time.[72] Qualitative differences between the two groups showed that superior teachers used greater amounts of contingent praise and offered half as much direction and criticism. It has also been shown that student teachers talk more than experienced teachers and that effective teachers are more consistent in rule enforcement than ineffective teachers.[73] Thus the three principal factors that have been identified are the overall rates of verbal behavior by teachers versus that of students, positive versus negative comments, and rule enforcement versus rule neglect.

Three approaches have been used in efforts to bring teacher behavior into closer approximations to these objectives. First, teachers have been offered guidance outside the classroom as a means of improving student performance. This approach was illustrated by the work of Hall, Panyan, Rabon, and Broden.[74]

Second, teachers have been provided with feedback and their behavior has even been cued during class sessions. Assuming that verbal behavior of teachers and students is a valid index of other teacher actions, Amidon and Flanders have developed a system of classifying teacher behavior, including such indirect categories as acceptance of feeling or giving praise or encouragement and such direct categories as lecturing and giving directions.[75] When base lines have been established

[71] N. A. Flanders, *Teacher Influence: Pupil Attitudes and Achievement* (Minneapolis: University of Minnesota Press, 1960); Flanders, "Intent, Action and Feedback: A Preparation for Teaching," *Journal of Teacher Education,* Vol. 14, No. 3 (September 1963), pp. 251–260.

[72] Edmund J. Amidon and Michael Giammatteo, "The Verbal Behavior of Superior Elementary Teachers," in Amidon and Hough, eds., op. cit., pp. 186–188.

[73] Jeffrey Kirk, "Elementary School Student Teachers and Interaction Analysis," in Amidon and Hough, eds., op. cit., pp. 299–305; minutes of a staff meeting of the Research and Development Center.

[74] "Instructing Beginning Teachers in Reinforcement Procedures Which Improve Classroom Control."

[75] E. J. Amidon and Ned A. Flanders, *The Role of the Teacher in the Classroom* (Minneapolis: Paul S. Amidon and Associates, 1963).

for teacher behavior, this information is fed back to the teacher, who seeks to modify his performance to coincide with criterion levels of performance. While the criterion levels are not fully documented, the success of such an approach utilizing feedback mediated by others is being demonstrated.[76]

A third approach to the use of feedback to modify the teacher's behavior in class, developed by Smith and his associates, relies on self-shaping.[77] Teachers are asked to identify appropriate, inappropriate, and unacceptable classes of student behavior as well as the response they feel they should make to these behaviors. They are then merely asked to count the rate at which these behaviors occur. Smith has shown that the rule-enforcement responses of teachers can be accelerated from 50 to 80 percent of the relevant occasions by this method, with corresponding decreases of rule tests from a level of forty to fifty per quarter hour to a level of ten to twenty per quarter hour.

Similar changes have been observed elsewhere in a study demonstrating that teachers using self-shaping could radically modify the behavior of brain-injured kindergarten children.[78] Self-shaping is perhaps the least costly procedure and may well be the most generally useful because the teacher can resort to self-shaping whenever he believes it might be helpful. The tools of self-shaping are as simple as a chalk mark on the blackboard or a hash mark on an index card taped to a desk. More elaborate procedures might call for utilization of a counter.

Many of the foregoing approaches have depended on the provision of positive feedback to accelerate responses incompatible with poor performance, with a consequent withdrawal of attention from negative responses. In some instances this feedback has been self-produced, as in the self-shaping systems, while in the socially produced feedback conditions, normal social relationships, behavioral observers, signal systems, or grades have been the medium of feedback.

In essence these approaches have rested heavily on the manipulation of positive feedback. Negative feedback, while of questionable value, may be used in two additional procedures. First, negative feedback may be provided until desirable behavior occurs, at which time it is terminated. This is well represented by the teacher who stands in front of a class censoriously berating students until they come to order. The

---

[76] Kirk, op. cit.

[77] *See* the minutes of a staff meeting of the Research and Development Center.

[78] Abbott, Howard, and Walter, op. cit.

weaknesses in this approach are obviously that the teacher may become so aversive that he loses his influence or the students may be wise enough not to accelerate the teacher's negative behavior by compliance.[79] By the same token the primary use of negative feedback is subject to the danger that the person attempting to modify behavior might suffer a loss of influence and in addition run the risk of failing to provide necessary behavioral prescriptions for desirable responses. More will be said about the limitations of these procedures in the following section, in which material decelerative techniques will be discussed.

Positive reinforcement. Material consequences may be either concrete—such as candy, money, or an affectionate pat on the back—or privileges. Another term for accelerative consequences is positive reinforcement, which implies that when an event is followed or reinforced by a given consequence, its rate will be affected positively. This is a purely functional definition and suggests that events are positive when they work, not merely when the behavior modifier expects them to work. For example, candy offered contingently on the emission of correct reading responses by a young child might accelerate the rate of such responses, but it might also interfere with reading if the child interrupts his reading to eat his reinforcers. The determination of which consequences are accelerative is therefore an empirical matter.

There is strong suggestion that informational consequences may not be sufficient to compensate children for positive behavior. Millenson suggests that whereas teachers might be adequately reinforced by changes in their students' behavior (a fact that should be withheld from the attention of school administrators at bargaining sessions), students may need more tangible and immediate reinforcement.[80] Using the research methodology described, Reynolds and Risley demonstrated that the verbal behavior of a preschool child could not be accelerated through the mediation of social reinforcement alone, but that marked changes did occur when social and material reinforcers were used in combination.[81] Similar observations have been repeated elsewhere with preschool, elementary, and high school students.[82] Other than the

---

[79] Richard B. Stuart, "A Guide to Behavior Modification" (Ann Arbor: University of Michigan, 1969). (Mimeographed.)

[80] Millenson, op. cit., pp. 251–254.

[81] N. J. Reynolds and T. R. Risley, "The Role of Social and Material Reinforcers in Increasing Talking of a Disadvantaged Preschool Child," *Journal of Applied Behavior Analysis,* Vol. 1, No. 3 (Fall 1968), pp. 253–262.

obvious money and candy, a wide range of reinforcers is available in the classroom. Recess has been used most effectively, as have classroom games.[83] Other reinforcers include being permitted to give recitations in class, work with higher level academic materials, tutor slower learning or younger students, listen to records, attend special events, and participate in an endless series of other privileges common to virtually all classrooms.

Two difficulties encountered in the use of material consequences are the facts that (1) all children are not reinforced by the same things at the same time and (2) it is often not possible to deliver large reinforcements after small responses. To overcome these problems, Ayllon and Azrin have developed a token system of reinforcement.[84] This approach requires (1) specification of desirable behaviors, (2) development of a range of reinforcers formulated into a "reinforcement menu," [85] (3) assignment of values to the reinforcers in terms of the responses required to earn them, (4) development of a token or point medium to be given to the student following completion of the required tasks and to be exchanged by the teacher when the student chooses his reinforcer, and (5) rules for how and when reinforcing events may be used. Sherman and Baer have pointed out that the effective use of token systems depends both on training the recipient to value the tokens and the value he places on the selection of reinforcers ultimately provided.[86] They further note that the long-term effectiveness of token-aided behavioral change programs depends on the assumption by other agents in the environment (e.g., parents) of responsibility for reinforcing the behavior. They conclude, however, that on balance

[82] T. R. Risley, "Learning and Lollipops," *Psychology Today,* Vol. 1, No. 8 (January 1968), pp. 28–31, 62–65; Patterson, Jones, Whittier, and Wright, op. cit.; L. R. Miller, "A Note on the Control of Study Behavior," *Journal of Experimental Child Psychology,* Vol. 1, No. 2 (July 1964), pp. 108–110.

[83] J. G. Osborne, "Free-Time as a Reinforcer in the Management of Classroom Behavior," *Journal of Applied Behavior Analysis,* Vol. 2, No. 2 (Summer 1969), pp. 113–118; H. H. Barrish, Muriel Saunders, and M. M. Wolf, "Good Behavior Game: Effects of Individual Contingencies for Group Consequences on Disruptive Behavior in a Classroom," *Journal of Applied Behavior Analysis,* Vol. 2, No. 2 (Summer 1969), pp. 119–124; Hall, Panyan, Rabon, and Broden, "Teacher Applied Contingencies and Appropriate Classroom Behavior."

[84] Op. cit.

[85] Addison and Homme, op. cit.

[86] J. A. Sherman and D. M. Baer, "Appraisal of Operant Therapy Techniques with Children and Adults," in C. M. Franks, ed., *Behavior Therapy: Appraisal and Status* (New York: McGraw-Hill Book Co., 1969), pp. 192–219.

the advantages of token systems increasingly seem to outweigh their disadvantages and are steadily increasing in application.[87]

Indeed, the range of successful demonstrations of token systems with normal children in nursery school, elementary school, and junior high school settings has been impressive.[88] In addition, success has been met in applying token systems to the problems of disturbed children in special settings and with retardates in special settings.[89] What is especially impressive about these token systems is that they may be effectively administered by nonprofessionals, parents, and peers, and their cost relative to more elaborate systems (which, incidentally, have a lower probability of success) is quite low.[90] For example, Wolf,

---

[87] Ibid., p. 199.

[88] See, respectively, Bushell, Wrober, and Michaelis, op. cit.; Quay, Werry, McQueen, and Sprague, op. cit.; W. S. Wood, "The Lincoln Elementary School Projects: Some Results of an In-Service Training Course in Behavioral Psychology," Educational Technology Monographs, No. 1 (1968), pp. 3–26; David Giles, "Progress Report: East Side Youth Project" (Detroit: Neighborhood Service Organization, December 1969) (mimeographed).

[89] For programs with disturbed children, see H. S. McKensie, M. Clark, M. M. Wolf, Richard Kothera, and Cedric Benson, "Behavior Modification of Children with Learning Disabilities Using Grades as Tokens and Allowances as Back-up Reinforcers," Exceptional Children, Vol. 34, No. 10 (June 1968), pp. 745–753; K. D. O'Leary and W. C. Becker, "Behavior Modification of an Adjustment Class: A Token Reinforcement Program," Exceptional Children, Vol. 33, No. 9 (May 1967), pp. 637–642; Ethel Rabb and F. M. Hewett, "Developing Appropriate Classroom Behaviors in a Severely Disturbed Group of Institutionalized Kindergarten-Primary Children Utilizing a Behavior Modification Model," American Journal of Orthopsychiatry, Vol. 37, No. 2 (March 1967), pp. 313–314; M. M. Wolf, D. K. Giles, and R. V. Hall, "Experiments with Token Reinforcement in a Remedial Classroom," Behavior Research and Therapy, Vol. 6, No. 1 (February 1968), pp. 51–64. For work with retardates, see J. S. Birnbauer and J. Lawler, "Token Reinforcement for Learning," Mental Retardation, Vol. 2, No. 5 (October 1964), pp. 275–279; J. S. Birnbauer, M. M. Wolf, J. D. Kidder, and C. E. Tague, "Classroom Behavior of Retarded Pupils with Token Reinforcement," Journal of Experimental Child Psychology, Vol. 2, No. 2 (June 1965), pp. 219–235; P. A. Nolen, H. P. Knuzelman, and N. G. Haring, "Behavior Modification in a Junior High Learning Disabilities Classroom," Exceptional Children, Vol. 34, No. 3 (November 1967), pp. 163–168; I. H. Perline and David Levensky, "Controlling Maladaptive Classroom Behavior of the Severely Retarded," American Journal of Mental Deficiency, Vol. 73, No. 1 (July 1968), pp. 74–78; E. H. Zimmerman, J. Zimmerman, and C. D. Russell, "Differential Effects of Token Reinforcement on Instruction-Following Behavior in Retarded Students Instructed as a Group," Journal of Applied Behavior Analysis, Vol. 2, No. 2 (Summer 1969), pp. 101–112.

[90] See, respectively, A. W. Staats, K. A. Minker, William Goodwin, and Julie Landeed, "Cognitive Behavior Modification: Motivated Learning and Reading Treatment with Subprofessional Therapy Technicians," Behavior Research and

Giles, and Hall report a total average cost of $225 per child per year in contrast to a possible institutional cost approaching $100 per diem.[91]

Teachers, parents, and others who use token reinforcement can gain precise control over the behaviors with which they are concerned. They can immediately provide amounts of reinforcement directly proportional to the emitted responses. Three additional procedures have been used to further augment the potency of the system. First, "fines" have been levied against tokens earned as a way of decelerating undesirable behaviors. Following Wiener's demonstration of this response cost technique, Giles has demonstrated that it may not be useful with all persons, and Hall and his associates demonstrated that the proportion of task-oriented responses escalated from 47 percent to 65 percent when tokens redeemable for recess time were introduced, but the rate again spurted to 81 percent when students suffered fines for intervals of non-task-oriented behavior.[92]

A second technique that may be used is the mobilization of group support for the teacher's goals by giving tokens to the group for the positive behavior of one person, a few individuals, or the entire group. Lindsley originally described four formats for reinforcement: (1) individual reinforcement, (2) mutual reinforcement, in which all individuals in a group receive the same reinforcement at the same time, (3) joint reinforcement, in which each individual receives one portion of a reinforcement that must be pooled with others in order to realize a complete reinforcer for the group, and (4) communal reinforcement, in which one group reinforcement is given, requiring individuals to compete for its complete control or agree to subdivide or share it.[93] Drawing on Lindsley's alternatives, it is possible to give an individual points that are redeemable as reinforcements for the entire group.

Patterson, Shaw, and Ebner have effectively demonstrated that the behavior of several hyperactive children was well controlled by allow-

Therapy, Vol. 5, No. 4 (November 1967), pp. 283–300; Patterson, Shaw, and Ebner, op. cit.; Stuart, *Trick or Treatment: How and When Psychotherapy Fails.*

[91] Op. cit. *See also* Stuart, "Assessment and Change of the Communicational Patterns of Juvenile Delinquents and Their Parents."

[92] Wiener, op. cit.; Giles, op. cit.; Hall, Panyan, Rabon, and Broden, "Instructing Beginning Teachers in Reinforcement Procedures Which Improve Classroom Control."

[93] O. R. Lindsley, "Experimental Analysis of Social Reinforcement: Terms and Methods," *American Journal of Orthosychiatry,* Vol. 33, No. 4 (July 1963), pp. 624–633.

ing them to earn the privilege of distributing to the class candy or ice cream donated by their parents.[94]   In a second alternative, a variety of contingencies were made available to entire classes depending on the number of tokens earned.[95]   Other investigators have divided classes in half; the half of the class that receives the fewest chalk marks on the board for undesirable behavior is given such positive reinforcements as extra recess time.[96]   The technique has also been used in work with retardates with whom the goal was to reduce the rate of obscene gestures made in class.[97]   In this application, one of ten cards was flipped over each time any child made a gesture, indicating a loss of one minute of recess time for the entire class.   The daily rate of occurrence of the gesture was reduced from sixteen to two within two weeks.

The full range of Lindsley's procedures has not yet been reported in the literature, although it seems most likely that their effectiveness will soon be demonstrated.   The advantage of group reinforcement is that it gives the teacher allies among the students.   Without group reinforcement, the misbehavior of selected children in the class might provide an entertaining diversion for the remaining students, leading them both to stimulate and try to maintain the problem behavior.   When some cost, whether in the form of a delay or loss of reinforcement, is imposed, every child in the class has a stake in the good behavior of the problem child and all will assist the teacher in control efforts if the reinforcement has a value greater than relief from monotonous routine.

The third technique for increasing the effectiveness of token systems has been termed "contingency contracting" by Homme.[98]   The approach begins by development of a reinforcing menu that contains a potpourri of the things students are most likely to do when they are permitted to do whatever they want.[99]   The second step is to limit access to these events so as to increase their value.   Then a series of task cards is prepared that contains assignments such as reading a

---

[94] Op. cit.

[95] Bushell, Wrober, and Michaelis, op. cit.

[96] Barrish, Saunders, and Wolf, op. cit.

[97] S. I. Sulzbucker and J. E. House, "A Tactic to Eliminate Disruptive Behaviors in the Classroom: Group Contingent Consequences," *American Journal of Mental Deficiency,* Vol. 73, No. 1 (July 1968), pp. 88–90.

[98] Op. cit.

[99] Addison and Homme, op. cit.

number of pages in a schoolbook and answering questions about the reading. The student may select cards containing assignments that interest him or contingencies that he especially desires (naturally, interesting assignments will carry less reinforcement value than undesirable assignments). This enables the student to work at his own pace. By keeping track of the contracts completed by each child in a master record, the teacher has access to instant information about the educational status of every student in the class while also ensuring the maximum output of each student.[100]

Negative reinforcement. In the foregoing section it was shown that responses can be accelerated through positive reinforcement using several techniques. It is also possible to accelerate the rate of responses by removing an aversive event following a desired response. This is termed negative reinforcement. Laboratory demonstrations of its effectiveness have generally been confined to the treatment of sexual abnormalities, but teachers have often taken such action as keeping problem students after school until they publicly repent.

There is a problem in the use of negative reinforcement that is common to aversive strategies in general. The person attempting to manage behavior may acquire such an undesirable image that his subject will not be influenced by his disapproval.

Punishment. A punishing consequence is any stimulus that reduces the rate of responses that produce it. This is a functional definition, empirically defined. Punishment is typically associated with such "unpleasant" events as spanking or electric shock. These associations are often quite misleading, however. For example, penny arcades have for years offered electric shocks as reinforcers in games that people pay to play.

There are at least two broad classes of punishment: corporal and programmatic events. The use of corporal punishment in public schools had had an episodic history in which there has been a tendency to advance its use following each step in the "liberalization" of education. While punishments such as spanking have been used as an adjunct to a variety of effective therapeutic procedures with children demonstrating extreme behavioral problems, its use with schoolchildren has not been studied extensively.[101]

---

[100] D. M. Brethower, "Classroom Management: A 'Total Management System' for a Classroom." Unpublished paper, Reading Improvement Service, University of Michigan, 1969.

Apart from the legal ramifications that must be considered, there are several reasons for seriously questioning the use of punishment in such settings:

1. Many of the conditions that Azrin and Holz describe as necessary prerequisites for the use of punishment are often not met in natural settings.[102] For example, it is frequently impossible to punish problem responses immediately, severely, consistently, and without associating punishment with certain socially desirable consequences such as attention.

2. It has been shown that while punishment may lead to immediate suppression of a problem response, it is also true that when the conditions associated with punishment have been removed, the problem response is likely to recur.[103]

3. The delivery of a punishment is typically a fairly aggressive response. When a person in authority acts as a punisher, he models the use of aggressive interpersonal strategies that may then be imitated by the person being punished.

4. Further, the use of punishment is likely to disrupt the learning situation markedly because of the child's physical and emotional response to that punishment or because of the high probability that he will reflexively attack either the punisher or innocent bystanders.

Program may be used in preference to corporal punishment as a decelerative event, as has been suggested by Lindsley.[104] As an illustration, teachers have sought to use repetition of arduous tasks such as writing sentences a specified number of times as a means of decelerating the rate of a child's problem behavior. While this use of program has certain advantages over corporal punishment, it shares the disadvantages of reducing the attractiveness (and potential influence) of the teacher and it also may lend an unpleasant quality to the programmatic task.

---

[101] See, for example, J. S. Birnbauer, "Generalization of Punishment Effects— A Case Study," *Journal of Applied Behavior Analysis*, Vol. 1, No. 3 (Fall 1968), pp. 201–211; O. I. Lovass and J. Q. Simmons, "Manipulation of Self-destruction in Three Retarded Children," *Journal of Applied Behavior Analysis*, Vol. 2, No. 3 (Fall 1969), pp. 143–157; B. G. Tate and G. S. Baroff, "Aversive Control of Self-Injurious Behavior in a Psychotic Boy," *Behavior Research and Therapy*, Vol. 4, No. 4 (November 1966), pp. 281–287.

[102] N. H. Azrin and W. C. Holz, "Punishment," in Werner K. Honig, ed., *Operant Behavior: Areas of Research and Application* (New York: Appleton-Century-Crofts, 1966), pp. 380–447.

[103] Risley, op. cit.

[104] Lindsley, "Procedures in Common Described by a Common Language."

In place of repetitive tasks the teacher might require the student to emit an above-average number of less negative but more productive responses such as solutions to several set-theory problems or the writing of fiction.

Time out. If a desirable response is being maintained by an accelerative consequence, then time out from the opportunity to earn that consequence may be an effective way of decelerating the rate of any undesirable response that may become associated with the desirable response. For example, Baer demonstrated that once nursery school children were positively reinforced by being allowed to watch cartoons, temporary interruption of the cartoons contingent on thumb-sucking could reduce the rate of the latter behavior.[105] The same procedure has been used to modify the tantrum behavior of young children, the gross antisocial behavior of adolescents in institutional settings, and the disruptive behavior of schoolchildren.[106] Brown and Shields demonstrated that children sent home from school following specific rule violations—termed "systematic exclusion"— showed a radical decrease in the rate of these violations over a period of several months.[107]

The use of time-out procedures is a complex process. First, some of the child's behavior, such as playing with others in a group, must be maintained by a positive consequence. Second, a disruptive response must occur, such as hitting another child. Third, the positive consequence must be withheld for a definite time, such as removing the child from the group.

Patterson and White suggest that the time out must be mildly aversive.[108] This is brought about by (1) making certain that the individual has no access to reinforcing stimuli while undergoing time

[105] D. M. Baer, "Laboratory Control of Thumb-Sucking by Withdrawal and Representation of Reinforcement," *Journal of Experimental Analysis of Behavior*, Vol. 5 (1962), pp. 143–159.

[106] *See* Montrose Wolf, T. R. Risley, and Hayden Mees, "Application of Operant Conditioning Procedures to the Behavior Problems of an Autistic Child," *Behavior Research and Therapy*, Vol. 1, No. 4 (March 1964), pp. 305–312; E. R. Brown and Eloise Shields, "Results with Systematic Suspension: A Guidance Technique to Help Children Develop Self-control in Public School Classrooms," *Journal of Special Education*, Vol. 1, No. 4 (Summer 1967), pp. 425–437.

[107] Op. cit.

[108] G. R. Patterson and G. D. White, "It's a Small World: The Application of 'Time Out from Positive Reinforcement.' " Unpublished paper, Oregon Research Institute, undated. (Mimeographed.)

out, which is possible only when supervision is available during that time, and (2) prolonging time out as a consequence of disruptive behavior that takes place during the time-out period. As Baer has suggested, this removal of a positive reinforcer is in effect a decelerative consequence following disruptive behavior.[109] Further, positive reinforcement is restored when the child behaves as desired in the group setting.

The use of time out offers some decided advantages over extinction and punishment in that the behavior modifier can avoid the negative cast associated with the latter two strategies. In addition, negative interpersonal responses are not modeled and there is minimal disruption of the teaching-learning environment.

In school settings it is essential to apply consequences in a manner governed by rules rather than allowing them to be applied arbitrarily by the teacher. It is also essential to make certain that the environment in which the child is placed is not rich with reinforcement. The principal's office, where the child can overhear the school's administrative business, and the hall, where he can speak with his friends, are obviously positive rather than aversive environments. On the other hand, placement behind a screen in the classroom or in a special room designated for the purpose may be highly effective.

It has been shown that the broad classes of informational and material consequences available in all social situations may be divided into techniques that can accelerate or decelerate the rate of occurrence of the responses that produce them. It has also been shown that accelerative techniques offer distinct operational advantages over decelerative techniques, although the two are frequently used in combination. Two questions that have not been discussed pertain to the broader consequences of the use of behavior modification in the classroom: maintenance and generalization of behavioral effects.

Maintenance A behavior that has been therapeutically or experimentally manipulated is said to be maintained if its rate does not appreciably diminish following termination of the interventive procedure. Conventionally determined through an evaluation of the follow-up procedures, virtually all of the studies cited in this paper include such considerations.

---

[109] D. M. Baer, "Effect of Withdrawal of Positive Reinforcement on an Extinguishing Response in Young Children," *Child Development*, Vol. 32, No. 1 (March 1961), pp. 64–74.

The critical issues in follow-up evaluations are unfortunately somewhat arbitrary. For example, the amount of "drift" in the response rate that is tolerable within the "success" class is defined by the individual researcher and varies from study to study. The amount of time that must elapse before a response can be said to have been maintained is also arbitrary. Patterson has noted that many behavioral changes disappear six months after the termination of treatment.[110] This would suggest the need to use somewhat longer intervals.

The maintenance of behavioral change is never coincidental. In one set of behavioral therapy techniques, the patient or others in his immediate social environment is "instigated" to modify his behavior.[111] If the patient is the subject of instigation, he is responsible for reprogramming others with whom he interacts to reinforce him positively for a new set of positive responses. This is frequently difficult because, for example, a teacher is likely to have a negative set toward a troublesome child and is therefore unlikely to attend to his positive responses; the result is that these may be extinguished. On the other hand, if the teacher is instigated to change his behavior vis-à-vis the child, the child's environment can be reprogrammed to strengthen the desired responses.[112] In this case the behavior is more likely to be maintained. This reasoning affords a strong argument for the use of consultative services with teachers in place of direct services to children.

When direct treatment is used, the patient is placed in a "prosthetic environment" that intensifies the conditions conducive to the learning of new responses. For example, the behavioral therapist might carefully cue verbal responses and immediately reinforce these responses in much the same manner that the psychotherapist encourages reflective discussion of selected issues and reinforces a given class of verbal responses. When treatment is approaching the point of termination, the therapist must seek to weaken the client's dependence while strengthening the behavioral control found in the natural environment. This is achieved through the process of "fading."

In effect fading seeks to replace one set of controlling conditions with another. The procedure has been described in the following terms:

[110] G. R. Patterson, "Parents As Behavior Modifiers in the Classroom."

[111] F. H. Kanfer and J. S. Phillips, "A Survey of Current Behavior Therapies and a Proposed Classification," in Cyril M. Franks, ed., *Behavior Therapy Appraisal and Status* (New York: McGraw-Hill Book Co., 1969), pp. 445–475.

[112] G. R. Patterson, Nancy Hawkins, Shirley McNeal, and Richard Phelps, "Reprogramming the Social Environment," *Journal of Child Psychology and Psychiatry*, Vol. 8, No. 3–4 (March 1968), pp. 181–196.

Fading is used to develop new discriminations, i.e., to change the discriminative stimulus conditions controlling the behavior. Initially the behavior is maintained with reinforcement in those stimulus conditions where the behavior is already highly probable. Gradually, at a rate which produces no disruption in performance, the desired changes are introduced in these stimulus conditions (the behavior will come under the control of these new discriminative stimuli).[113]

Risley and Baer have described fading as a two-way procedure.[114] They describe the efforts of a therapist to reinforce imitative vocal responses in a retarded child who had already imitated the experimenter's motor responses. The therapist first faded in vocalizations by gradually associating vocal responses with motor responses; he then faded out the motor responses, leaving only vocal imitations, by reducing the complexity of the stimuli used to prompt the child. This left the child with a set of responses that more closely resembled those of "normal" children, thereby increasing the probability that the adults he will encounter outside of the experimental situation will respond to him as if he were normal. That in turn will increase the likelihood that he will receive positive reinforcement in these encounters.

The same goal—gradually reducing the special qualities of intervention procedures so as to make them more comparable to natural controlling conditions—can be achieved through fading other aspects of the intervention procedure. For example, Kale and his associates trained schizophrenic patients to greet an experimenter, reinforcing greetings with cigarettes.[115] They then increased the interval between the cueing and reinforcement of greetings, fading the temporal proximity of the two events. Gratifications rarely follow social responses immediately; by training their subjects to expect a delay, the experimenters enhanced the social repertoires of their patients.

In addition to fading the complexity of stimuli or their temporal association, behavior modifiers can also fade the intensity of reinforcement. When responses are initially induced to occur they are typically

[113] Sherman and Baer, op. cit., p. 196.

[114] T. R. Risley and D. M. Baer, "Operant Conditioning: 'Develop' Is a Transitive, Active Verb" (Lawrence: University of Kansas, undated), pp. 27–30. (Mimeographed.) See also D. M. Baer, R. F. Peterson, and J. A. Sherman, "The Development of Imitation by Reinforcing Behavioral Similarity to a Model," Journal of the Experimental Analysis of Behavior, Vol. 10, No. 5 (September 1967), pp. 405–416.

[115] R. J. Kale, J. H. Kaye, P. A. Whelan, and B. L. Hopkins, "The Effect of Reinforcement on the Modification, Maintenance, and Generalization of Social Responses of Mental Patients," Journal of Applied Behavior Analysis, Vol. 1, No. 4 (Winter 1968), pp. 307–314.

richly rewarded. For example, a first-grade teacher may reinforce every response approximating a correct approach to a given problem. Over time, the teacher may offer these reinforcements only following more work or may offer less reinforcement. By so doing the teacher "thins" the schedule or quality of reinforcement. Most social and task responses are cumulatively reinforced—that is, they are reinforced after increasing numbers have been accumulated. To expect reinforcement following every response would be to invite disappointment: to be prepared to work for reinforcements earned over time is to display some of the equipment needed for social survival.

Ackerman suggests that when social responses are desired, the rate at which these are reinforced should never fall below the rate at which deviant responses were previously reinforced.[116] This is a sound recommendation, since it accentuates the behavior modifier's control over positive responses. Ackerman also offers as a guideline for instituting a thinning of schedules ten successive intervals of constructive behavior at a criterion level. While this is an arbitrary determination, it appears to be reasonable.

Behavioral therapy that neglects the problem of fading may result in a schoolchild who has been changed in the treatment situation but who is underequipped to deal effectively with the normal stresses and strains of classroom life. To the extent that behavior modification techniques are behavioral prostheses, they must be faded to bring the individual under the control of those events that comprise his normal social environment. A child who learns to talk reasonably only to his therapist may have accumulated an isolated positive experience, but he has not developed social survival skills.

Generalization If maintenance is concerned with the problem of sustaining a response under conditions closely related to the original learning situation, generalization is concerned with accelerating the rate of the response under conditions related to, although not identical with, conditions under which it originally occurred. For example, the concept of roundness may be learned in association with small, perfect circles printed in black ink. Larger, less perfect, and differently colored circles will also be identified as round through the process of abstraction that is one illustration of generalization. The social worker who assists a teacher in changing the behavior of a child in one class may quite properly be concerned with the likelihood that this change will be

---

[116] Op. cit.

carried over to other classes as well.   Studies that have attended to
this issue have given strong indication that this may reliably occur.[117]

A certain amount of generalization will occur naturally.   For example, a child might greet a substitute teacher as he greets his regular
teacher.   If he is reinforced positively for this, the response will recur
and generalization from one teacher to another may be said to have
taken place.   This same effect may be deliberately achieved.   Several
investigators have sought to promote generalization of positive behavior through use of peers and parents as primary or adjunctive forces
in treatment.[118]   The value of such therapeutic allies lies in the fact that
their presence may set the occasion for desired responses and these
responses may then occur in a variety of environments.

In addition to concern with the range of environments in which a
client emits a desired behavior, a behavior modifier might also be interested in tracking the effect on other individuals of his efforts to modify
the behavior of one person.   This has been studied in classrooms as the
"ripple effect." [119]   Some evidence suggests that favorable consequences may be observed when other children watch the positive reinforcement of one of their peers.[120]   On the other hand, data collected
by Patterson, Ebner, and Shaw for other purposes suggests that the
behavioral change efforts directed toward one child may be essentially
unrelated to the responses of another.[121]   Definitive evaluations of the
ripple effect have not been published, but the question remains one
of great importance.

[117] *See,* for example, Buell, Stoddard, Harris, and Baer, op. cit.; Surratt,
Ulrich, and Hawkins, op. cit.; H. M. Walker and N. K. Buckley, "The Use of
Positive Reinforcement in Conditioning Attending Behavior," *Journal of Applied
Behavior Analysis,* Vol. 1, No. 3 (Fall 1968), pp. 245–250.

[118] *See* G. W. Evans and G. L. Oswalt, "Acceleration of Academic Progress
Through the Manipulation of Peer Influence," *Parsons Research Center Working
Paper,* No. 155 (1967); W. W. Hartup, "Friendship Status and the Effectiveness
of Peers as Reinforcing Agents," *Journal of Experimental Child Psychology,*
Vol. 1, No. 1 (January 1964), pp. 73–76; Patterson, "Parents as Behavior
Modifiers in the Classroom"; G. R. Patterson, D. A. Ebner, and M. J. Shaw,
"Teachers, Peers and Parents as Agents of Change," in Benson, ed., op. cit.,
pp. 13–47; Patterson, Jones, Whittier, and Wright, op. cit.; Susan Tiktin and
W. W. Hartup, "Sociometric Status and the Reinforcing Effectiveness of
Children's Peers," *Journal of Experimental Child Psychology,* Vol. 2, No. 2
(June 1965), pp. 306–315.

[119] J. S. Kounin and P. V. Gump, "The Ripple Effect in Discipline," *Elementary School Journal,* Vol. 59, No. 3 (December 1958), pp. 158–162.

[120] *See* H. M. Boudin, "Behavior Modification Techniques in the Ripple
Effect," unpublished master's thesis, University of Toronto, 1967; W. J. Gnagey,

Summary The process of behavioral change is orderly. It begins with specification of a response or identification of an objective positive response that occurs at a comparatively high rate. The rate of occurrence of the response is measured and recorded, and a decision is made about whether to attempt to modify the rate.[122]

If a decision is made to go further, the antecedent conditions that set the occasion for the response are identified as a second step. Falling into four classes—instructional (rules), facilitating (tools and skills), potentiating (increasing the value of the consequences), and discriminative (indicating the probability of certain consequences)— certain antecedent events set the occasion for positive responses (A+) while other antecedents set the occasion for problem behaviors (A—). An effort is naturally made to strengthen the A+ conditions and to weaken the A— conditions.

As a third step, the consequent conditions that ultimately determine the rate of the response are examined. Consequences may be informational or material, may be applied contingently or noncontingently, and may accelerate or decelerate the rate of the response. In summary fashion, accelerative consequences may be identified as C+ conditions, decelerative consequences as C— events. Again the behavior modifier's goal would be to strengthen the conditions conducive to positive response while weakening those conducive to problem behaviors.

The fourth step is complex. It calls for the fading of the prosthetic techniques while seeking to generalize their effects. Fading implies the systematic removal of therapeutic techniques and is achieved, for example, through reducing the schedule of reinforcement from extremely high response to reinforcement ratios to much lower ratios. Generalization refers to the efforts to make certain that the desired behavior occurs in the natural environment as well as the therapeutic environment. In many instances the processes of fading and generalization rival the complexity of the original response induction procedures and failure in these efforts may vitiate the effectiveness of the entire behavioral change process.

"Effects on Classmates of a Deviant Student's Power and Response to a Teacher-Exerted Control Technique," *Journal of Educational Psychology*, Vol. 51, No. 1 (February 1960), pp. 1–9; J. J. Ryan, "Factors Associated with Pupil-Audience Reaction to Teacher Management of Deviancy in the Classroom," *American Psychologist*, Vol. 7, No. 7 (July 1959), p. 378.

[121] Op. cit.

[122] A sample form for recording the rates of appropriate, inappropriate, and unacceptable behaviors may be obtained from the author.

Plans for Action

The foregoing account summarizes many aspects of behavior modification theory and practice as it pertains to the management of children in school settings. When the techniques are applied in individual classrooms, procedures should be selected according to whether they (1) result in minimal disruption of the normal classroom routines, (2) require a minimum of the teacher's time or that of other personnel, (3) draw maximally on students' capacities, (4) are likely to be maintained following the termination of intervention, and (5) provide the teacher and administrator with some measure of the effectiveness of the procedures.[123]

Many of the procedures described meet all of these criteria. Their acceptance, however, depends on the manner in which they are introduced. For example, Flanders suggests that only approximately half of the teachers are likely immediately to respond positively to the introduction of a feedback system.[124] He suggests that access to the remaining teachers should be gained through obtaining the cooperation of school administrators and other teachers.

In seeking to involve a teacher in a behavior modification plan, it is necessary to draw on every appropriate tactic of interpersonal influence because the success or failure of all behavioral maintenance and change plans in the classroom depends on the teacher's thoughtful cooperation. To achieve this cooperation three things must be done. First, it is essential to participate with the teacher in defining the categories of appropriate, inappropriate, and unacceptable behavior and the nature of the intervention to be used. Second, it is essential to clarify with the teacher the precise methodology to be used and the logic underlying decisions at choice points in the execution of the program. Third, it is essential to strive toward philosophical consensus with the teacher in order to ensure consistency in the application of the procedures.

Some teachers may readily accept the basic philosophy of contingency management—the notion that behavior is under environmental control and will be accelerated or decelerated in direct proportion to the presence or absence of appropriate controlling conditions. Others,

---

[123] *See* Patterson, Ebner, and Shaw, op. cit.

[124] "Some Relationships Among Teacher Influence, Pupil Attitudes, and Achievement," p. 237.

however, may offer philosophical disagreements premised on one or more of the following views, which may be discussed on the basis of the sample responses offered:

Philosophical Position	Counterargument
The control of behavior is coercive.	All behavior is under social control—even client responses emitted in client-centered (nondirective) therapy. One cannot control behavior.
The control of behavior is unethical.	Behavior may be controlled in the service of ethical or unethical goals. Behavior modification at least affords some protection through insistence that the goals be made explicit.
The use of positive reinforcement is a form of bribery.	Since bribery involves considerations given or promised for corrupt behavior, the performance reinforced in classroom settings cannot be so labeled.
Learning should be its own intrinsic reward.	The logical law of identity proscribes the use of one term for two distinct referents; therefore the response cannot also be the consequence. Moreover there is no evidence that operant responses recur without producing environmental change, so that responses relevant to learning must be positively reinforced through some external events—at least through the opportunity to make valid predictions.
A given child is "sick" and cannot be expected to conform.	Considerable evidence exists in support of the notion that situational factors account for even psychotic behavior. It behooves the teacher to define all relevant behavior as falling within his control, since only then could this behavior fall under appropriate social control in the classroom.
Behavior modification procedures directed toward one child will give rise to demands for like treatment from others.	There is little evidence to support this assumption. However, it may in fact be quite advantageous for the teacher to extend the procedures that have been effective with difficult children to all students as a means of achieving more positive control.

131

Philosophical Position	*Counterargument*
Behavior modification techniques are in some way harmful to the child.	The behavior modification techniques advocated in this paper have stressed the management of positive contingencies. It is hard to see how the selective use of such contingencies could be detrimental. Conversely it is easy to speculate that prolonged academic and social problems may culminate in the total disruption of the child's education.

If the teacher is invited to participate in the assessment and planning process and if the behavior modifier takes pains to explain the logic of the procedure and discuss its philosophical implications, then it is likely that the teacher's cooperation can be obtained.

The next objective is the identification of a behavioral change target and the selection of means to reach behavioral change objectives. Whereas one teacher might wish to stimulate self-expression by a student, another might regard that same behavior as "overintrusiveness." In the final analysis it must be the teacher who decides the target. The behavior modifier is faced with the need to make a value decision whether to (1) accept the decision outright, (2) accept the decision as a means of establishing a basis of collaboration with the ultimate goal of modifying the teacher's subsequent decisions, or (3) reject the target and terminate the interaction. Selection of the second alternative may constrain the behavior modifier to work toward the attainment of suboptimal goals, while selection of the third may preclude the possibility of change in the behavior of a teacher.

When agreement has been reached about the target and change procedures, the next step is to execute these procedures. If the behavior modification process is conceived in an experimental vein, data are generated at each step that permit evaluation of the direction and rate of change. Unlike many other less-precise techniques in which outcome or effect may not become apparent for months, the consequences of behavior modification should become evident the day it is initiated. The two virtues of this fact are that the student is protected from possible iatrogenic consequences of inappropriate action and the teacher may try several techniques in rapid succession and make empirically based decisions about which technique to use as a general strategy over time. The former advantage protects the teacher from the danger of mismanagement, while the latter protects the students from the risks of erroneous bias on the part of the teacher.

If the dependent variable in a given situation is task behavior and the teacher routinely counts the number of problems correctly solved, for example, additional data should be collected in an effort to monitor the effect of this intervention on the student's social behavior. Of course the measurement of secondary change in task responses is desirable when the primary target is social behavioral change. Furthermore, it is wise to evaluate the effect of the behavioral change process on the actions of one or more other children in the class in an effort to attend to unexpected changes in others.

When changes have been produced in the behavior of one or more students, these are a reflection of the modification of the teacher's behavior. Student change is a partial reinforcement for these new responses of the teacher. It is also important, however, to add to the salience of this reinforcement by calling to the attention of school administrators the efforts expended by each teacher. This can be done by sending a letter of appreciation to the teacher early in the behavioral change effort, with copies to the department head, principal, and school superintendent. To further compensate the teacher, an advertisement might be purchased in the local newspaper praising the teachers who have cooperated in the behavioral change program, or Lindsley's technique of giving teachers "precision teaching awards" for their participation might be adopted.[125] This is necessary in order to compensate for the deficits of the school systems, which are better adapted to identifying teacher failure—through elaborate means of reporting student difficulties—than to identifying teacher excellence.

Finally, the child's parents should be brought into the program at an early point. The parents should above all be aware of the school experience of their children. Beyond this, however, the parent may be instrumental in helping the teacher to identify what events function as accelerators for his child and may also be of inestimable help by working out means of generalizing school-mediated intervention programs to the home.

Conclusion

Beginning with a critique of traditional conceptions of school social work, this paper has proposed an innovative model of intervention in

---

[125] Lindsley, "Procedures in Common Described by a Common Language."

which social workers would function as educational technologists. In such a role they would seek to use behavior modification techniques to increase or redirect the teacher's influence within the classroom and would replace the notion of sickness in the child with the notion of a less-than-optimal teaching/learning environment.[126] Use of this procedure offers five distinct advantages over current approaches:

1. Behavior modification techniques draw on testable assumptions and have been subjected to extensive experimental and practical validation.

2. The procedures permit immediate and continuous evaluation so that the teacher, student, and social worker may be appropriately guided in their actions.

3. The elements of behavioral control in this conceptalization are found within the classroom. Therefore the solution of classroom behavioral problems may be worked out using the resources that already exist in the classroom environment.

4. The principles of contingency management may readily be taught to teachers who have the skill to apply the same techniques as similar instances occur over time. This serves both as a preventive device and as a means of providing the teacher with means to limit deterioration in the behavior of any and all children in present and future classes.

5. The technique greatly extends the potential influence of social workers from the present small caseloads to the entire school population.

Several major concerns have not been included in this presentation because each would require the same full treatment as has been accorded the problem of classroom management. The most important area omitted is the program, curriculum, or educational content. The first efforts in the management of the behavior of schoolchildren should be devoted to determining a curriculum that is relevant, of interest, and commensurate with the child's capabilities. Sophisticated proposals such as that advanced by Smith and Smith include close attention to educational content as well as to other important dimensions such as the physical resources of the classroom.[127] Going beyond behavioral and curriculum management of the classroom, molar concerns such as the location and architectural style of school buildings (such as

---

[126] See Estelle Fuchs, "How Teachers Learn to Help Children Fail," *Trans-Action*, Vol. 5, No. 9 (September 1968), pp. 45–49.

[127] J. M. Smith and D. E. Smith, *Classroom Management* (New York: Learning and Research Associates, 1970).

including the fewest possible load-bearing interior walls to permit maximum program flexibility), the nature and enforcement of school-wide disciplinary policies, and the use of modular scheduling are important issues that have not been discussed in this paper.

On the other hand, this paper has also neglected molecular aspects of the management of schoolchildren. For example, abundant literature describes intervention with the school-phobic child using systematic desensitization and operant conditioning techniques.[128]

If the management principles that have been described in this paper are applied in typical classroom settings, the amount of influence exercised by the teacher can be increased immeasurably. To the extent that the principles are used effectively, the need for ancillary services can be expected to diminish as fewer children will be seen to fall outside the perimeter of normal classroom control, and it is likely that fewer disruptions of classroom routine will occur, with a salutary effect on the educational experience of the child and the professional experience of the teacher.

---

[128] For desensitization techniques *see* W. P. Garvey and J. R. Hegrenes, "Desensitization Techniques in the Treatment of School Phobia," *American Journal of Orthopsychiatry,* Vol. 36, No. 1 (January 1966), pp. 147–152; A. A. Lazarus and A. S. Abramovitz, "The Use of 'Emotive Imagery' in the Treatment of Children's Phobia," *Journal of Mental Science,* Vol. 108 (1968), pp. 191–195; A. A. Lazarus, G. C. Davison, and D. A. Polefka, "Classic and Operant Factors in the Treatment of a School Phobia," *Journal of Abnormal Psychology,* Vol. 70, No. 3 (June 1965), pp. 225–229. For operant conditioning techniques *see* G. R. Patterson, "A Learning Theory Approach to the Treatment of the School Phobic Child," in Ullmann and Krasner, eds., op. cit., pp. 279–285.

Labeling Theory and
School Social Work

Edward J. Pawlak

For the most part school social work practice has relied on a view of deviance in which the maladaptive behavior is perceived as an intrinsic feature of the person.[1] The responsibility for the deviance is seen to rest with the individual, although it may be a consequence of his own or of his parents' personal characteristics or of family functioning.

One consequence of this perspective is the reliance of school social workers on individual methods of treatment that emphasize the student's emotional problems and his personal adjustment.[2] Another consequence is the failure to consider certain organizational factors as sources of deviance. Thus change efforts are not directed toward school structural arrangements or operating modes that may be a source of strain for the faculty as well as for the students.

---

[1] In this paper the term deviance will be used in a general way to include underachievement, misconduct, and emotional disturbance.

[2] For a detailed report of the tasks that school social workers deem important in their practice, *see* "An Analysis of the Tasks in School Social Work as a Basis for Improved Use of Staff: Final Report" (Washington, D.C.: U.S. Department of Health, Education & Welfare, Office of Education, Bureau of Research, February 28, 1968). (Mimeographed.)

In this paper a perspective of deviance will be discussed that takes such factors into account. This perspective—labeling theory—views deviance as a product and a process of interaction. This paper builds directly on the findings of social workers and social scientists who have examined and analyzed social problems and malperformance in the schools from a social interaction perspective.[3]

Labeling Theory

Labeling theory as such is not an actual theoretical framework. Rather, it is itself a denotation for one method of conceptualizing deviance, that is, the concept of deviance as a product and process of interaction. Under such a conception social organization is used to explain individual deviance. Specifically the labeling theorists focus on the manner by which people are categorized or labeled in organizational settings and on the consequences of such processing. Deviant statuses are seen as outcomes of organizational structures and operating modes— that is, deviance-labeling arises from norms, evaluative systems, and sanctioning systems—and the organization is structured to give selected responses to certain individuals. For example, students with inferior scores on standardized achievement tests are placed in a track for academically weak students and are exposed to a curriculum that matches their ability. Labeling serves the organizational function of defining, simplifying, and standardizing the way in which organizational functionaries are to act and react toward certain students. Organizational categorization or labeling may also shape how students relate to one another.

DIMENSIONS OF THE DEVIANT CAREER Given this perspective, attention is then directed to such dimensions as these: (1) the acquisition of deviant identities, that is, who applies the deviant label to whom and under what conditions, and what characteristics of an individual or his performance are salient to organizational screening processes, (2)

---

[3] *See* Howard S. Becker, "The Teacher in the Authority System of the Public School," in Amitai Etzioni, ed., *Complex Organizations: A Sociological Reader* (New York: Holt, Rinehart & Winston, 1961), pp. 243–251; Howard Becker, ed., *The Other Side: Perspectives on Deviance* (New York: Free Press of Glencoe, 1964); Harold Garfinkel, "Conditions of Successful Degradation Ceremonies," *American Journal of Sociology*, Vol. 61, No. 5 (March 1956), pp. 420–424.

the organizational maintenance of deviant identities, (3) the anticipated and unanticipated consequences of labeling, such as stigma, and (4) the transformation of deviant identities.

Within some of these dimensions are several subdimensions that may be used to refine our analyses of labeling processes: (1) early versus late versus no labeling—for example, identification of students who show signs of maladjustment in the primary grades versus doing this in the upper grades versus not doing it at all, (2) formal versus informal labeling, such as processing a student through psychological services versus having a teacher attempt to resolve the student's problem within the confines of the classroom, (3) public versus private labeling, and (4) partial versus total labeling—that is, whether the student's deviant identity is confined to one class or generalized to all school activities (does the "possession of one deviant trait have a generalized symbolic value so that people automatically assume that its bearer possesses other undesirable traits associated with it?").[4] When all of these dimensions are considered in a temporal context, then the gestalt is referred to as a deviant career.

The notion of career suggests that the organization's decision to categorize or label an individual is not a simple act, but rather a transitional process with identifiable stages. According to Erikson there are three related stages: (1) *confrontation* between the deviant suspect and the organization (a case conference), (2) the announcement of a *judgment* about the nature of his deviance (a diagnosis), and (3) an act of *social placement* that assigns the deviant to a special role or status (a special class or school).[5]

SHORTCOMINGS Labeling theory is not without its shortcomings. For the most part it has been conceptualized as and used to focus on the acquisition, maintenance, and transformation of negative labels. It also fails to make the detection of deviant behavior problematic; rather, labeling begins after detection. In addition, organizational labeling is viewed as an arbitrary and unfair process that has unpleasant consequences for the person labeled. The positive consequences of labeling or categorization are virtually ignored. The tone of moral

---

[4] Howard S. Becker, *Outsiders: Studies in the Sociology of Deviance* (New York: Free Press of Glencoe, 1963), pp. 32–33.

[5] Kai Erikson, "Notes on the Sociology of Deviance," in Becker, ed., *The Other Side: Perspectives on Deviance*, p. 16.

indignation that is frequently found in the writings of the labeling theorists has led to their being given the label "moral entrepreneurs." Notwithstanding the shortcomings of labeling theory, the concepts, dimensions, and perspectives identified here are useful in sensitizing us to easily overlooked organizational arrangements and processes that may have negative consequences for students.

Sources of Organizational Strain

Certain organizational arrangements and processes may maintain or even generate deviant identities. Focus here will be on tracking, the manner in which students are categorized or labeled in school settings, and the consequences of such processes.

TRACKING Children vary in their readiness for learning. As a consequence teachers vary their curricula and their teaching methods. However, the size of school populations, limitations in personnel, and demands for efficiency preclude individualized instructional arrangements. Consequently the school must routinize its services according to its assessments of the ability of the students. Tracking is in part a routinized formal public way of categorizing students according to their ability to learn. It is an organizational device for separating the academically weak from the academically strong, or for grouping students according to their vocational interests, for example, academic, commercial, or general curriculum. Several investigators have studied the process of tracking and its consequences for the students and the school as a whole.[6] Some of their findings will be synthesized here.

Curriculum placement decisions are made early in the student's career. Sarri and Vinter found that placement decisions were made in the eighth or ninth grade in two Michigan high schools. In a study of

---

[6] See David Hargreaves, *Social Relations in a Secondary School: A Case Study of a Secondary Modern School for Boys* (London, England: Routledge & Kegan Paul, 1967); Brian Jackson, *Streaming: An Educational System in Miniature* (London, England: Routledge & Kegan Paul, 1964); Aaron Cicourel and John Kitsuse, *The Educational Decision-Makers* (New York: Bobbs-Merrill Co., 1963); Rosemary C. Sarri and Robert D. Vinter, "School Goals, Social Class, and Pupil Careers," paper presented at the 44th Annual Meeting of the American Orthopsychiatric Association, Washington, D.C., March 1967; Walter Schafer, "Student Careers in Two Public High Schools: A Comparative Cohort Analysis," unpublished Ph.D. dissertation, University of Michigan, 1965.

English schools, Jackson found that 74 percent of the 660 schools he studied were "streamed" (tracked) by the time the student was 7 years old. By age 10 streaming was almost universal. Cicourel and Kitsuse also testify to early placement in the school they studied.[7]

In American school systems, in contrast to those of many European and Asian countries, tracking was not formally planned, but has occurred nonetheless. In fact the conception of the comprehensive secondary school initially was that of a system where tracking would be minimized. Only recently have school administrators and educators recognized the unanticipated consequences of elaborate tracking systems that begin at the early elementary level.

Middle-class students have a greater probability of being tracked into a college curriculum than working-class students. Even within the same IQ levels working-class students have less chance of entering the college track. Although there are certain routine criteria for placement, there is variation within and between schools, and the decisive determinant may be an arbitrary decision on the part of a counselor or teacher, ability and achievement notwithstanding. Once a student is placed on a given track, his chances of changing his formal status are slim. Thus early track placements are critical decisions that can affect the student's future life chances.

Tracking is a form of social as well as academic selection. Students in noncollege tracks experience status deprivation. For example, college-track students frequently dominate leadership positions and other extracurricular activities; non-college-track students or those performing poorly are frequently denied access to status-bearing school offices.

Hargreaves reports that higher track students condemn lower track students for being "unintelligent, academically lazy, 'messers,' and untidy"; lower track students despise higher track students for being "academically oriented, hard working, cowardly, and teacher's favourites." [8] (It is interesting that both teachers and students describe the tracks in terms such as lower and upper.) Hargreaves found that interstream relations between students were infrequent, that the stereotyped attitudes of students in different tracks were based on hearsay

---

[7] See Sarri and Vinter, cp. cit.; Jackson, op. cit.; and Cicourel and Kitsuse, op. cit.

[8] Op. cit., p. 71.

or superficial observation rather than on personal experience, and that there was mutual fear and distrust between students in different tracks.

Hargreaves discovered one especially striking unanticipated consequence of tracking. He found that students in a given track evaluate themselves and students in other tracks in terms of their own dominant values—that is, membership in and the values of a track other than one's own are viewed negatively. While the high-track students desire to remain there and this acts as an incentive toward academic achievement, low-track students have no such impetus toward achievement.

> The informal pressures within the low streams tend to work directly against the assumption of the teachers that the boys will regard promotion into higher streams as a desirable goal. Boys from low streams were very reluctant to ascend into higher streams because their stereotyping of A and B (upper) streams were defined in terms of values alien to their own and because promotion would mean rejection by their lower stream pals. Teachers were unaware that this unwillingness to be promoted to a higher status led the high informal status boys to depress their performance in examinations. This fear of promotion adds to our list of factors leading to the formation of anti-academic attitudes in low stream boys.[9]

Hargreaves also found that low-stream boys see themselves as less adequate than high-stream boys and think that teachers view them negatively. Tracking also leads to preferential treatment: upper track students have better teachers and grading practices favor the upper track students.

These findings show that tracking—early formal public categorization—contributes to the acquisition of a deviant identity. Stigma and status deprivation are frequently attached to membership in lower tracks. Tracking leads to the formation of an informal structure among lower track students that competes with rather than supports the academic goals of the school. Since there is little shifting between tracks, students become locked into a status. There appear to be no organizational mechanisms designed to help the student transform his identity. Furthermore, the preferential treatment and differential reinforcement of college-track students make it difficult for general- or vocational-track students to acquire more positive and acceptable identities.

The tracking system may be functional for certain students and for

---

[9] Ibid., p. 77.

the school as an organization, but it is an imperfect system and one that has unpleasant consequences for other students. Students with insufficient ability are often placed in college tracks and students with sufficient ability are often placed in noncollege tracks. In a national study Ramsoy found that about 25 percent of graduating seniors go on to college even though they did not take college preparatory courses.[10] This suggests that certain organizational modifications or interventions are in order. In the final section of this paper certain proposals in that direction will be made.

LOCALIZATION OF RESPONSES TO DEVIANCE   In his study of two Michigan high schools Schafer found that teachers in one school had more influence over the students in dealing with their serious problems, whereas in the other school where there was a cadre of specialized personnel to handle disciplinary problems, the teachers were less involved and had less influence over the disposition of the student's problem.[11] This finding led Schafer to speculate about the effects on student careers of differences in localization of responses to deviance. He speculated that if discipline is localized with the teacher, this has positive consequences for the student because sanctioning is confined to a given classroom. Thus alternative opportunities for positive assessment may remain unaffected. On the other hand, if teachers send students to a disciplinarian, it is more likely that this action will affect the student's identity throughout the school. This last hypothesis is based on the assumption that being sent to the office or to a counselor is a stronger and more public reaction.

It is important to recognize that these are hypotheses, not findings. However, these speculations do lead us to examine certain easily overlooked negative effects of referral to special services departments in public schools. For example, social workers who provide group treatment in schools have reported that teachers and students refer to the group as "the bad boys' group"; some students refuse referrals to group treatment because they do not wish to be identified with "the group for crazy kids."

Schafer's hypotheses also suggest that prior to making referrals to

[10] N. R. Ramsoy, "College Recruitment and High School Curricula," *Sociology of Education*, Vol. 38, No. 4 (Summer 1965), pp. 297–309.

[11] Op. cit.

special services school social workers and counselors should try to work discreetly with teachers to help them resolve student problems in the classroom. On the other hand, Schafer indicates that such practices may have negative consequences. Teachers may have to devote more time to controlling than to teaching, and students may not receive the specialized help they need. In any case, Schafer's speculations are worth consideration even without empirical confirmation or rejection.

SUSTAINING DEVIANT IDENTITIES As indicated earlier, certain organizational practices may unwittingly sustain a deviant identity, or certain policies may make it difficult for the student to acquire a more acceptable identity. School files or record-keeping systems are examples of such practices. Negative entries in the student's official school record may make it difficult for him to shed his reputation if the record is accessible to all teachers or if it follows the student from grade to grade. Study findings show that records frequently emphasize negative entries and that positive entries or changes in behavior are seldom noted.

In one school system the students knew that negative comments about their performance were recorded on "yellow sheets" and that these sheets followed them from grade to grade. The students judged each other's characters by glimpses they were able to catch of these sheets. If the sheet was filled they knew the student was bad; when the sheet was empty or contained but a few entries, it was something to boast about. Occasionally student messengers were used to take yellow sheets to the office; in the process they acquired valuable information.

Teachers also used the yellow sheets in an attempt to control classroom behavior by threatening to "take out" the student's sheet if his behavior persisted. In describing the seriousness of a student's problem a teacher might remark: "He has quite a yellow sheet." Thus the school record may become an organizational weapon to manage and manipulate students, or it may unwittingly sustain a student's deviant identity.

Deviant identities may also be sustained by the nature of the sanctions used by the school. Frequently malperforming students are given double penalties. Not only do they receive a low grade or a reprimand, but in addition they are frequently denied certain prestigious assignments and participation in school activities.

The limitations of this paper do not permit an extensive review of the sources of organizational strain for students from a labeling perspective. However, the introductory theoretical discussion of labeling theory and the sources of strain identified are compelling enough to suggest that labeling should become a part of the diagnostic perspectives of school social workers, teachers, and especially school administrators.

OTHER ISSUES There are two important issues that have not yet been covered and that deserve at least a passing mention. First, the properties of labels such as slow learner, brain damaged, and dull-normal and their use by teachers and social workers have been neglected. In a thorough and cogent review of the harmful effects of labels Stuart suggests that they may be both unreliable and invalid:

> The major danger inherent in low reliability is arbitrariness in the use of categories, while the major danger inherent in low validity is the formulation of unproductive treatment decisions.[12]

Stuart argues for the use of highly specific behavioral assessments and against the use of dispositional diagnoses in which an individual ". . . receives a negative label owing to the pathological character of the clinical nosology." [13]

Second, a discussion of the transformation of deviant identities has been omitted. It seems that this dimension is often neglected by human service organizations, such as courts, prisons, clinics, and hospitals. More often than not organizational resources are primarily deployed in the application of labels (diagnosis), but virtually no resources are directed toward certifying recovery, change, health, or innocence. It is necessary to examine why this is so and to devise means of conveying a reform identity in behalf of our student clients.

New Roles and Strategies

It is apparent that, given the sources of organizational strain identified, conventional school social work roles and strategies, with their emphasis on the personal adjustment of the student, need to be supplemented by roles and strategies designed to modify organizational variables. In this section two major strategies of intervention will be

---

[12] Richard B. Stuart, *Trick or Treatment: How or When Psychotherapy Fails* (Champaign, Ill.: Research Press, 1970), p. 103.

[13] Ibid.

suggested that may provide practitioners with some leverage over organizational factors that maintain or generate deviance—modification of record-keeping practices and ombudsmanship or advocacy.

MODIFICATION OF RECORD-KEEPING PRACTICES   Several modifications in school record-keeping practices can be implemented to mitigate the negative effects of these practices identified earlier.   First, school policies could require the entering of positive information about students into the record on a systematic basis.   Second, greater emphasis could be placed on areas of improvement and on the specific management and instructional practices that are especially productive.   Third, emphasis could also be placed on specification of the conditions under which the student's maladaptive behavior manifests itself.   Fourth, recording forms might be developed to shape teachers' recording practices and to avoid unsystematic anecdotal entries.   Finally, teachers might be required to participate in a brief training period with respect to their recording practices.[14]

A policy followed by police youth bureaus and juvenile courts regarding juvenile offense records can be adapted for use in the schools. Frequently youth bureau officers maintain an unofficial record of a child's first few minor offenses without filing a petition to the juvenile court.   Juvenile courts have been known to destroy juvenile offense records and to restrict accessibility to the court record.   Perhaps teachers and school social workers could also maintain unofficial cases and private records.   If a student reforms, perhaps the negative entries can be stricken from his school records, especially when he moves on to another school or class.

OMBUDSMANSHIP AND ADVOCACY   As schools grow in size, complexity, and bureaucratization, students may feel increasingly alienated because the system may not be sufficiently responsive to their interests. Certain structural features of the educational system itself compound this unresponsiveness and thereby increase the students' alienation.

The relationship between the students and the school personnel is quite asymmetrical.   The preponderance of power and authority rests with the school personnel.   The students' means of redress are quite

---

[14] Eugene Litwak et al., "A Design for Utilization of Special Services in the Detroit Public Schools," pp. 9–10.   Unpublished paper, University of Michigan School of Social Work, May 1965.   (Mimeographed.)

limited, making students at all levels vulnerable to the teacher's use of authority.[15] The findings of a few investigators concerning teacher-student authority relations suggest that there are potentials for the abuse of this inequality in authority relationships and, although there are professional norms among teachers that call for a just use of authority, teachers do err.[16]

Furthermore, certain bureaucratic features of the school (degree of formalization, centralization, standardization) may be sources of strain independent of the norms or sense of justice among the teachers. In addition, teachers may be highly committed to certain organizational practices that are seen by the students as imperfect and unfair and that in reality work against the goals of the school. For example, Jackson reports that an overwhelming majority of teachers in the school he studied wanted streaming, which, according to the teachers, made teaching less arduous while at the same time served the needs of all children.[17]

The result is a seemingly increasing rigidity of the school system while student demands for increased participation and flexibility are growing. This writer would argue, in the face of increased activism and protest among high school students, that there is a definite need for someone who is less committed to certain educational and administrative practices and who therefore could assume an advocacy role in behalf of student rights and interests.

School social workers may be in a position to serve in this ombuds-man-advocate role. However, a recent study of school social workers showed that they may not have the training or the temperament to function in such an activist capacity. In a government-sponsored study, school social workers rated as least important the work related to leadership and policy-making that includes student welfare policies.[18]

---

[15] Dan C. Lortie, "The Teachers' Shame: Anger and the Normative Commitments of Classroom Teachers," *School Review*, Vol. 75, No. 2 (Summer 1967), pp. 155–171.

[16] *See* R. Jean Hills, "The Representative Function: A Neglected Dimension of Leadership Behavior," *Administrative Science Quarterly*, Vol. 8, No. 1 (June 1963), pp. 83–101; Neal Gross and Robert Herriott, *Staff Leadership in Public Schools: A Sociological Inquiry* (New York: John Wiley & Sons, 1965); Becker, "The Teacher in the Authority System of the Public School"; Lortie, op. cit., p. 159.

[17] Op. cit., p. 44.

[18] "An Analysis of the Task in School Social Work."

In any case it would be desirable for school social workers to experiment with an advocacy role.[19] A person in such a role could conduct a regular and systematic audit of marginal students in particular, perhaps with the result of advising their transfer into "higher" tracks. School social workers could also intercede in behalf of malperforming students to acquire "equal opportunities" for prestigious positions in school government, athletics, and so on. Practitioners could also petition for a "striking of the record" or serve as advocates in disputes between student groups and the administration. In short, practitioners should attempt to modify school policies that prevent students from acquiring positive identities.

The adoption of such roles and strategies of intervention would undoubtedly challenge existing status and power relationships in the school.[20] However, with increased demands for community controls and for student participation in decision-making on the high school level, it appears that changes in status and power will be forthcoming whether individual administrators or teachers want them or not.[21] The involvement of parents and students in decisions about school practices may improve the schools, and student and community commitment to the school may be strengthened. In any case the roles and strategies identified here may provide for planned change and constructive disruption.

---

[19] For a review of advocacy roles and issues *see* the following articles in *Social Work,* Vol. 14, No. 2 (April 1969), pp. 5–32: Harry Specht, "Disruptive Tactics"; the Ad Hoc Committee on Advocacy, "The Social Worker As Advocate: Champion of Social Victims"; and David Wineman and Adrienne James, "The Advocacy Challenge to Schools of Social Work."

[20] Specht, op. cit., pp. 5–15.

[21] Wallace Roberts, "The Battle for Urban Schools," *Saturday Review of Literature,* November 16, 1968, pp. 97–117.

PART II

Innovative Strategies and Practice Applications

Breaking Out of the Bind in School Social Work Practice

Helen R. Nieberl

If school social workers are going to make a greater impact on the problems and needs of school systems and move into the role of change agent, a new model of field instruction and practice is needed. This article presents a model that is problem centered rather than method centered. It is believed that it offers a means by which school social work practice can break out of the bind resulting from the traditional definition of its practice in terms of method. Education for problem-centered practice in the schools appears to be the soundest way of ensuring that school social workers become able to relate to the various needs of the school as a system and to address themselves to school-community problems effectively and intelligently.

A Problem-Centered Approach

The critical issues in education and in society in the 1970s make it imperative that social work in the schools take a broad focus in order

Much of the inspiration for and content of the school-community study assignment came from an unpublished memorandum (1967) of Betty Walsh, now Associate Professor, School of Social Work, Wayne State University, Detroit, Michigan, for which the author is greatly indebted.

to provide services and leadership in relating education to present-day realities.

> These critical issues and changing conditions require of school social workers an awareness of the revolutionary changes which are occurring, a commitment to innovation, a willingness to plan every action in relation to the sum total of the parts (system thinking), and keeping abreast of new knowledge.[1]

The social work student who makes an early choice of the narrow specialty of a method is not especially well served for his future professional development. Coughlin observes that such an early choice may largely "fail to develop the flexibility of mind and the professional scope needed to deal with the important issues that he will some day face but which at the time of his education do not yet exist."[2] The literature of the 1960s and the early '70s reflected these same concerns.[3]

In the fall of 1968 the writer introduced to her students the idea of problem-centered practice of social work in the schools—practice that was neither casework, group work, nor community organization.[4] The shift was from the microcosm of the individual schoolchild to the wider world of the school community, to include the child and his

---

[1] Committee on Certification, Preface, "Interim Procedures for Certification of School Social Workers" (Seattle: Washington Association of School Social Workers, June 21, 1971), p. 5. (Duplicated)

[2] Bernard J. Coughlin, "Reconceptualizing the Theoretical Base of Social Work Practice," in Lilian Ripple, ed., *Innovations in Teaching Social Work Practice* (New York: Council on Social Work Education, 1970), p. 59.

[3] *See*, for example, Scott Briar, "The Casework Predicament," *Social Work*, Vol. 13, No. 1 (January 1968), pp. 5–11; Herbert Aptekar's review of *Theory for Social Work Practice* by Ruth Smalley in *Journal of Education for Social Work*, Vol. 3, No. 2 (Fall 1967), pp. 99–105; David A. Goslin, "The School in a Changing Society," *American Journal of Orthopsychiatry*, Vol. 37, No. 5 (October 1967), pp. 843–858; Gordon Hearn, ed., *The General Systems Approach: Contributions toward an Holistic Conception of Social Work* (New York: Council on Social Work Education, 1969); Carrel B. Germain, "Social Study: Past and Future," *Social Casework*, Vol. 49, No. 7 (July 1968), pp. 403–409; Sister Mary Paul Janchill, "Systems Concepts in Casework Theory and Practice," *Social Casework*, Vol. 51, No. 8 (October 1970), pp. 467–474; Michael Kami, "Planning for Change," *Social Casework*, Vol. 51, No. 4 (April 1970), pp. 209–210.,

[4] The problem-centered approach has much in common with the model of practice described by Kurt Spitzer and Betty Welsh in "A Problem Focused Model of Practice," *Social Casework*, Vol. 50, No. 6 (June 1969), pp. 323–329. The main point of difference is the emphasis in the present writer's model on the social systems model as a conceptual framework that shifts attention from characteristics of the individual to concepts of interaction and interrelatedness.

relationships as integral parts of a whole system. It was an attempt to conceptualize the tasks of the social worker in the schools in terms of his mediating the interaction between individuals and social systems.

The problem-centered approach requires of the social worker the same complete identification with the basic value system of the social work profession, the same emphasis on the inherent worth of each individual, as does the traditional method-centered approach. In problem-centered practice the social worker requires knowledge of the types of systems in relation to which he carried out his role and knowledge of the phases of planned change or problem-solving process that he goes through in performing his role. He also needs the analytical and interactional skills to be used in data collection, data analysis, and intervention.[5]

The plan that the writer evolved directed the student to begin his fieldwork placement by trying to understand the core problems of the school and its neighborhood. It was planned that this grasp of basic needs would serve as background knowledge while the student was engaging with the system representative (usually the school principal) in the process of identifying specific problems. The various roles that the student might play in the process of giving service were identified as need and/or problem-identifier, social systems analyst, change-planner, implementer, and change-evaluator.[6] Although these roles are listed in logical order in terms of a frame of reference for problem-solving, it was recognized that they are not necessarily sequential, that they may occur simultaneously, and that they may alternate in various patterns. The aim was to enable the student to see the problem as a totality before either managing it or devising ways to deal with it.

To provide the student with needed direction, he was given an instrument called the "school-community study assignment." Details of the assignment follow. Examples drawn from the work of a student will be given to illustrate both the understanding of the problems of a school and a school community that were gained and how this understanding served to underpin the social service roles carried by the student.

---

[5] Allen Pincus and Anne Minahan, "Toward a Model for Teaching a Basic First-Year Course in Methods of Social Work Practice," in Ripple, ed., op. cit., pp. 34–57.

[6] "Definitions of Roles and Performance Criteria," in "Interim Procedures for Certification of School Social Workers," p. 9.

The School-Community Study Assignment

At the beginning of the fieldwork placement, the student was assigned to an elementary school in Seattle, Washington. At the same time he was provided with a copy of the "school-community study assignment." This is that assignment:

TOPIC: A study of your assigned school community leading toward a problem-focused stance for social work in the schools. Think of of this study process as beginning with your first contact with the school and continuing throughout the second year.

I. Gather and examine all pertinent data about the school and its community to determine the various factors affecting learning.

A. The school

1. The staff (age, education, specialization, assignment, special functions, special abilities)
2. The program (number of classes, class composition, class size, special programs)
3. The student population (geographic location, grade equivalent, mental ability, failures, stability, age-grade distribution, educational intentions, racial distribution)
4. School practices (in relation to behavioral control and to the voice of teachers, students, and parents in school affairs)

B. The community

1. What groups exist?
2. What people are active? What are their interests and talents?
3. What "feel" of the neighborhood or school community do you get? What are the strengths of the school community? the weaknesses? the resources?
4. What are community practices in relation to the integration of minority group members?
5. What community resources of a social welfare nature exist?
6. What critical conditions exist in the community?

II. Identify problems that the school, community, and students are facing.

III. Speculate creatively on what a social worker might do to help solve these problems.

IV. Plan ways of evaluating the effectiveness of your problem-solving ideas. What procedures will you use? (Just as you think of the study process as continuous, also think of evaluation as a continuous process.)

The preceding outline provides a framework for systematically collecting data, analyzing it, and drawing conclusions concerning the problems that the school, community, and students are facing.

It is important that the principal of the school be supportive of the social work student's efforts to gain an understanding of the factors affecting children's learning. The contribution of the principal's knowledge and experience is indispensable. Gaining the principal's support is accomplished through discussion between the field instructor and the principal of the student's assignment prior to his placement and through ongoing communication during the placement period. Rejection by and resistance from an occasional staff member, such as a teacher, are experienced infrequently; when they do occur, they are overcome for the most part by focusing on common concerns "to facilitate the learning process and to maximize the functioning of pupils by dealing with potential or actual dysfunctions existing" within the social systems that make up the school.[7]

The social work student being discussed obtained data through formal and informal conferences with school personnel, interviews with those persons in the community who had special responsibilities or concerns (such as officials of the parent-teacher association, the president of the community council, and the like), published data, his own observations, and so on. The interviewer's status as a student was openly shared with all those interviewed, school and community personnel alike. The purpose of the data collection—to gain an understanding of the factors affecting children's learning—was also clearly stated. This openness resulted in greater cooperation rather than in refusals.

DATA-COLLECTION AND ANALYSIS The student began by collecting facts about the school, which included the number and composition of the staff, the network of informal relations and unofficial norms among the staff, the school's program and practices, and the makeup of the student population. Specific information about the community—its strengths, weaknesses, and resources—was also gathered.

At the same time that the student gathered data, he also had periodic conferences—both formal and informal—with the principal (sometimes jointly with the field instructor), at which time there was a mutual sharing of system needs and problems. Out of such conferences came the identification of an issue as having priority and the planning of how to resolve that issue.

[7] "Interim Procedures for Certification of School Social Workers," p. 8.

Following his data-collection, the student was asked to analyze the data, speculate creatively with it, and identify problems that he saw the school, community, and students as facing. The skill of analyzing data is basically that of being able to use theories and concepts to make sense out of the data gathered. Learning to think about what one has observed, read, and heard is an important goal of student behavior; the ability to connect actual situations with the realm of theory is what is desired.

The main issues the student under discussion saw related first, to the problem of the large number of non-English-speaking students in the school and second, to an increasing number of behavioral and disciplinary problems among the student population. The school's population of 700 is heavily Oriental in ethnicity—31 percent Chinese, 16 percent Japanese, and 7 percent Filipino—with the remainder 20 percent Caucasian, 18 percent black, 7 percent Spanish-speaking, and 1 percent American Indian. A recent immigration of Chinese families had introduced twenty-four non-English-speaking children into the school in one term. The factor of transiency in the community had great bearing, the student felt, on the behavioral problems being manifested. The student also saw the school's projected move into new quarters, with a concurrent changeover to team teaching and ungraded class assignments, as placing strains on the school personnel.

Speculating on how he thought social work service could help in relation to the problems just mentioned, the student wrote:

For the matter of the changing nature of the community and the movements in and out of it, a social worker in the schools could help the community to organize services for newly arrived people such as "official greeter or orientation sessions" at which new arrivals could be informed of the various services available to them within the community if needed. . . . community activities would be a logical arena of service for a school social worker, especially in areas where the usual social services are nonexistent or overburdened with other matters.

Turning to the problems to be anticipated in moving to a new building and a new organization of teaching, a social worker could be of help by organizing discussion groups for pupils, parents, or teaching staff to deal with the fears and concerns or other problems which may be experienced because of such a move.

Alleviating the disciplinary or behavior problems exhibited by individuals or groups of pupils could be an important area of service for the social worker. Direct service via group work or the casework method could be helpful to the pupil involved, to his parents, and in reducing tension in the classroom or the school.

Finally, in the area of the need for an expanded and coordinated program of help for the non-English-speaking pupils, the social worker can be very useful in mobilizing resources and coordinating activities.

MEETING THE IDENTIFIED NEED   It was agreed that the student would take on the responsibility of mobilizing additional resources to meet the need for tutoring non-English-speaking children.   From the point of view of the field instructor, accepting this service need fitted well with the aim of providing experience for the student in using a problem-centered approach: identifying a need, analyzing the systems, developing change plans, implementing them, and evaluating the changes.

The student's plan was to determine the ways that adjacent schools had developed to deal with similar problems and to learn what tutoring resources were available in the immediate community.   He visited several schools and interviewed their administrators, interviewed leaders in local church-sponsored language classes, and talked with leaders in local ethnic organizations as well as in the school's PTA.

The student also planned to learn whether the school could draw on tutoring resources that were currently in use elsewhere in the city. To follow through on this he got in touch with the director of community services in the Seattle schools, a department that had been organized the previous year to coordinate the placement of volunteer reading and mathematics tutors in cooperating schools.   The director was interested in the problem the student described and arranged a meeting that was attended by the director of foreign languages for the district.   The latter agreed to help in the training of volunteers, to gather a library on teaching English as a foreign language, and to meet with volunteers in workshops to orient them to such a program. The community services director and the foreign languages director envisioned the planned program as a pilot project that might well yield useful knowledge to guide future tutoring programs in English as a foreign language.

After initial fruitless efforts to locate volunteers, appeals through the local news media resulted in an overwhelming response—fifty-five volunteers followed up telephone inquiries by attending a meeting at the school.   Because of the large turnout, some of the volunteers were directed to other schools that had expressed a need for help.   After a few technical problems were overcome, the tutoring program functioned smoothly.

EVALUATING CHANGE As part of the original plan to obtain feedback from the volunteers in the pilot project, meetings were scheduled to obtain information from the tutors as to what had and had not worked well and the general problems or frustrations they had encountered. At the final meeting of the year the operation of the pilot project was summarized and plans were made for the following year that included several day-long areawide workshops to induct new volunteers into the program and to make use of the experience that had been gained. The student conducted a survey of the participating teachers, who responded in an overwhelmingly favorable way toward the project.

For the most part principals have been supportive of the efforts of social work students to gain an understanding of the factors affecting learning. Not all students make the same use of this tool; sometimes the identified need or problem is so global that it is impossible to work with. In that case the student is helped to break the problem into its subparts and to begin to work toward a realistically attainable goal. In other instances the school-community study serves the purpose of enabling the student to be more knowledgeable in his consultative activities with teachers and in his work with parents and children.

Relation to Past Efforts

One may take an analysis of the tasks and goals of school social work that was made by Costin in the 1960s as indicative of past efforts:

> The study showed that most of the tasks and goals of school social work were not attuned to the urgent problems of children and youth. Professionals were relying on a definition of their work that was focused primarily upon casework with the individual child, dealing with his emotional problems and his personal adjustment; the problems of the child in school were viewed as arising mostly from his personal characteristics or those of his parents. The impact that school policies or community conditions had on pupils had gone almost unrecognized. School social workers had minimized the importance of their responsibilities for leadership in modifying school and community conditions. They also were reluctant to delegate tasks to persons with less than their professional social work status. These findings provide impetus to school social workers to reexamine their goals and their staffing patterns.[8]

The innovative aspects of the problem-centered practice being

---

[8] Lela B. Costin, "School Social Work," *Encyclopedia of Social Work* (New York: National Association of Social Workers, 1971), p. 1150.

described seem to be consistent with the trends noted by Costin in the beginning of the 1970s. The social work student was helped to identify and master new tasks and functions, to move away from the traditional, almost-exclusive reliance on casework and to think about other social work methods and approaches within those methods, to perceive the possibilities of contributing to the policy structure of the school, and to experience on a small scale the role of change agent in the school.

The school-community study is a tool that enables the student to become sufficiently knowledgeable to engage with the client system at any level in a consideration of dysfunctional aspects. The focus of concern is on the individual and the social system. The orientation is both immediate—the presenting problem and crisis situation—and on the near-future—preventive and developmental—and it is a practice that attempts to be "synchronized with the changing social conditions of people and systems." [9]

Problem-centered practice appears to move a little closer to this ideal. In the situation described earlier, the provision of traditional casework or group work services would have been inadequate. Involvement of the principal and other members of the school staff, the school community, the director of community services, and the director of foreign languages was essential to the success of the intervention. The most important aspects of the intervention were its preventive features: the children received the help they needed and it appeared that successive generations of children would also benefit. The student was enabled to perceive and to practice several of the roles identified by Costin as responsibilities of the school social worker:

Identification of children in need. . . . This identification may come about through study of the characteristics of a particular school, its school population, the community and neighborhood it serves, and through consultation with school administrators, teachers, and specialized personnel. *Work with school personnel.* . . . The range of tasks carried out with other school personnel in behalf of children may include . . . consulting with administrators in an examination of symptoms and causes of pupil problems in the school system, and in the formulation of policies that directly affect the welfare of pupils.[10]

---

[9] Jack Stumpf, "Teaching an Integrated Approach to Social Work Practice," in Ripple, ed., op. cit., p. 24.

[10] Op. cit., pp. 1150–1151.

Further Questions

An obvious question is related to the critical state of current practice in school social work: Does this approach deal adequately with the dilemma brought about by the methods approach, which has tended to predetermine where strategic entry is made on the basis of the social worker's expertise? Another issue relates to the lack of fit between the theory of social work practice that the student is learning in academic classes and the theory that underlies this specific school social work practice. Obviously these differences place strain on the student. Students respond in individual ways to the demands placed on them in the problem-centered approach, of course. It has been the writer's observation that the vast majority find this approach to be both realistic and relevant.

School Suspension:
Help or Hindrance?

John J. Stretch
Phillip E. Crunk

What happens when a typical child in the public school system receives an indefinite suspension? [1] The three-year research study reported here was conducted in an attempt to answer this question. The study's findings serve to increase both the theoretical knowledge base and professional practice understanding of the problem. In the New Orleans public school system the number of children in the ninth grade or below who were recorded as indefinitely suspended rose dramatically from 1967 to 1969. In 1967, 803 pupils were so recorded out of a population of 86,127, in 1968, 917 out of 87,588; and in 1969, 1,075 out of 88,317. Of those who were indefinitely suspended, the

Grateful acknowledgment is made to Dr. Julianna Boudreaux and Eloise LeBauve for their guidance and support of this project. Additional support was provided through Title I of the Elementary and Secondary Education Act.

[1] The term "indefinite suspension" refers to an official administrative act by the district superintendent whereby a child is enjoined from attending any class in any school of the system until officially reinstated by action of the district superintendent.

number who were referred for social service was as follows: in 1967, 283; in 1968, 341; and in 1969, 434.

Although indefinite suspension from school has been a time-honored prerogative of the school, there has been little theoretical analysis and much less solid empirical documentation about its effect on the child and his family. Facts are needed in several areas, for instance: What are the characteristics of indefinitely suspended students? Does suspension have any therapeutic value? How is suspension perceived by teachers and principals? What is its impact on the child's family?

While fully recognizing the importance of the school's environment and the influence of the teacher and principal in the suspension, the social science researchers and social work practitioners who developed this study purposely limited its scope and data sources to facts contained in official school records and to direct confidential reports from the child's family in order to assess the major characteristics of the child and the degree of detrimental impact of the suspension on the child and his family.

The detrimental impact of indefinite suspension was explored for the following reasons: (1) Whereas assumed benefits are often cited in individual situations, parents, educators, and social work practitioners have reported nonsystematically on its undesirable consequences. (2) The focus is appropriate for a social service-directed study because school social work is primarily charged with the responsibility of removing or working around detrimental social influences that hinder the maximum educational development of a child. The limitation in focus should not, however, be taken as justification for excluding the professional judgments and pertinent observations of other school personnel or the assessment of putative positive results of suspension. Limitations of time, research personnel, and funds made choices necessary, but they are considered far from desirable.

The current therapeutic intervention role of a school social worker in the New Orleans public schools is to restructure or, if that is not possible, to lessen detrimental psychological and social forces that act on the child. A major way to accomplish this goal is to strengthen the interaction between the family system and the school system. Because both the home and the school systems are significant socializing influences on the normal growth and development of the child, the school social worker—equipped through professional training and experience and obliged by law (Act 109 of the 1964 and Acts 194 and 306 of the 1970 Legislature of the State of Louisiana) to intervene to maintain a positive home-school relationship—helps the child to function better at home and in the educational setting.

Specifically the research described here tested the major hypothesis that indefinitely suspending a child from school results in counterproductive negative judgments, feelings, and behavior on the part of his family toward the suspending school in particular and toward the school system in general. Suspension, by completely separating the child from school, has the immediate effect of isolating his household from the educational system until such time as the school is ready to readmit him. In such a situation the parent sees that he has little leverage to influence, let alone control to any appreciable degree, the major decisions of the school relative to his child's suspension.

What connotes appropriate behavior in school is established by the school at its discretion. When his child is suspended, therefore, a parent can develop feelings of normlessness, since the rules of the school may appear foreign to him—if not designed to help only those children who present no problems for the school. The result of this combination of powerlessness, normlessness, and social isolation has been presented in the social science literature as *alienation*, which involves estrangement of the person from his environment and is often characterized by an inability to cope.[2] In addition to defining the salient characteristics of the suspended child, the investigation had as its major subject matter determining the presence and extent of the determinants of alienation and measuring their detrimental effects on the suspended child's family.

One assumption of the study is that consistent positive interaction between home and school will materially aid a child to achieve his educational potential, eventually decreasing the rate, duration, and negative consequences of suspension. When indefinite suspension is shown to be statistically associated with alienation of the family, this suggests (1) that school and home are not maximally engaged as mutually cooperative agents in the education and socialization of the child and (2) inasmuch as professional help is available through the school system, immediate remedial action is necessary.

---

[2] Frank P. Besag, *Alienation and Education: An Empirical Approach* (Buffalo, N.Y.: Hertillon Press, 1966); Besag, "Deviant Student Behavior and the Role of the School," *Urban Education Quarterly*, Vol. 2, No. 1 (September 1966), pp. 27–35; Dwight Dean, "Alienation: Its Meaning and Measurement," *American Sociological Review*, Vol. 26 (1961), pp. 753–758; Arthur Stinchcombe, *Rebellion in a High School* (Chicago: Quadrangle Books, 1964).

Study Population

The main study population was composed of three groups: (1) 150 students who had been indefinitely suspended from school but were not referred for social work service, (2) 150 students who had been indefinitely suspended from school but who had been referred for social work service, and (3) a comparison group of 100 students who had neither been suspended nor referred for social work service.

From a research design standpoint, an immediate consideration was to minimize the possibility that a child's suspension might have been affected by already-existing alienation in his home. To guard against this, procedures were instituted to measure the degree of dependence between suspension and alienation factors through (1) selection of a nonsuspended group for purposes of statistical comparison and (2) control matching of a subsample (reported elsewhere in the study) on selected factors (age, grade, sex, race, and family income) thought to be influential. These factors were conceived as partial controls for the presence of prior alienation in the child's household.[3] Subgroup matching on the variables of age, grade, sex, and race was accomplished through utilizing existing school records.

With respect to the variable of family income, it was decided to select children from low-income schools designated by Title I of the Elementary and Secondary Education Act and match them with children from schools not so designated. In this way there would be an approximate control on the influence of poverty between the suspended and nonsuspended groups. Since the researchers did not find existing statis-

---

[3] A note on the mixed sampling design must be interjected at this point. On five descriptive variables—age, sex, race, grade, and poverty-nonpoverty school—matching controls were instituted in a selected subsample of 100 suspended and 100 nonsuspended children to ensure that these factors would not unduly influence a refined analysis of basic theoretical issues concerning the impact of the suspension on certain critical outcome variables (alienation scores and child adjustment and school knowledge scores) selected to be studied. (*See* Phillip E. Crunk, "A Social-Epidemiological Inquiry into Indefinite Disciplinary Suspension and Alienation of the Maternal Household Head." Ph.D. dissertation, Tulane University, 1970. A copy may be obtained from University Microfilms, Ann Arbor, Mich.) Consequently, for the comparison group these factors were not allowed to vary independently in the subsample analysis reported later. However, independence of variation among these factors was assured by the random sampling design for the two experimental subgroups (VT and NVT). Therefore, when subsamples are combined, although significance levels are reported, generalizations with respect to these five factors should probably be limited to the suspended child population and not include the nonsuspended comparison group.

tical evidence in the literature regarding sources of significant variation on both suspension and alienation factors, and because of the control factors built into the study for purposes of both design and analysis, it is thought that the study findings contain sufficient evidence for partially assessing the impact of indefinite suspension on the child and his family.

The phrase "partially assessing the impact" is chosen to sensitize the reader to the fact that one cannot rule out the prior existence of alienation in the home and that alienation and its associated factors are causative in the suspension of the child, rather than the suspension itself causing increased alienation and associated factors in the home. One suggested way to untangle the relationship of suspension, alienation, and other factors studied would be a cohort analysis of a sufficiently large sample of children admitted to the school system with before-and-after measurements of alienation and associated factors as various sub-samples of the children were indefinitely suspended. This would be a costly and time-consuming enterprise, but it would tend to answer some basic issues posed by this research, which does show a statistically significant differential association between alienation and associated factors and indefinite suspension of a child from school. Further, there may exist a yet-to-be-discovered third factor correlated both with alienation and suspension that would serve to explain their mutual association. The findings of this research point the way for additional refinements to answer causal associations.

The study population is limited to students in the ninth grade and below, since it is these children who form the clientele of the New Orleans school social worker (called in that city a visiting teacher). Children in the first two study groups—(1) suspended but not referred to a visiting teacher (hereafter referred to as the NVT group) and (2) suspended and referred to a visiting teacher (hereafter referred to as the VT group)—were selected to represent, proportionately, the four administrative subdistricts of the Orleans Parish School System, according to the total number of students in the junior high and elementary school population. Within the sampling design just noted, final selection within each district was by random procedures.

Criteria for including students within the suspended population were as follows: (1) separation from school must have been legally specified by the district superintendent as an indefinite suspension (four days or more) and (2) the suspension must have occurred in the two academic school years studied (1967 and 1968).

Children in the comparison group (hereafter referred to as the NS group) were drawn from four schools: two poverty schools—one elementary and one junior high—and two nonpoverty schools—one elementary and one junior high.

Data Sources

There were two data sources for the study, official school records and reports by the children's mothers. Official records containing suspension information as well as information about age, grade, sex, race, and family income were obtained from either the district superintendent's office (suspended groups) or the child's local school (nonsuspended group). The data source for each interview was the maternal head of the household in which each child resided. The mother was selected as a data source on the assumption that she would have more contacts with the school than the father and would therefore be in more of a position to communicate information about attitudes, feelings, and behavior. The child's natural mother was the respondent in over 85 percent of the cases. In the other cases the respondent was the person who was the household's maternal figure.

Information for the full sample and subsample about age, grade, sex, race, poverty, and pertinent facts about suspension were obtained by the social work staff from school records. A letter from the assistant superintendent for pupil personnel stating that a skilled interviewer would be contacting the maternal head of the household for information was sent to each household before the home interview. The collection of interview data by specially trained personnel was completed within a month.

A pretest of the interview schedule was conducted by the senior research associates on a small sample of representative respondents. In addition each interviewer conducted a minimum of two interviews for training purposes. Interviewing time per household did not usually exceed forty-five minutes.

To ensure and maintain consistent quality and administrative control and uniformity in the collection of data, weekly group meetings were held with the interviewers to discuss progress and report difficulties. Although there were some refusals (less than 1 percent), interviewers consistently reported excellent cooperation by the respondents.

A coding system was developed whereby all collected data could be analyzed by computer. Data were tested for statistical significance at the .01 and .05 levels with some trends toward significance when appropriate at the .10 level noted in selected areas.

Analysis of the Data

This research concerns New Orleans public school children who had been indefinitely suspended during either the 1967–68 or 1968–69 school years. The report to follow is a blend of an initial descriptive study reported on fully in a previous monograph based entirely on school records on the same problem during the 1967–68 school year, hereafter called Study I.[4] This first study was based entirely on school records and a random sample of 400 cases (200 VT, 200 NVT).

The second study, reported fully here and hereafter called Study II, is based on data collected by personally administered in-depth interviews with a child's mother or mother substitute and on information abstracted from the child's official school records. With the exception noted later, the sample referred to in this report consists of 400 families, of which 150 had children who were suspended but not referred to a social worker, 150 had children who were suspended and referred to a social worker, and 100 had children who had not been suspended but were matched on a group basis as closely as possible with those suspended so that they could serve as a comparison group.

The analysis that follows makes statistical comparisons of these data on two levels: (1) a selective comparison of descriptive characteristics of suspended children between Study I and Study II to ascertain if there were any significant changes during the school year in population characteristics of suspended children studied and (2) a clinical comparison confined to Study II that measures the degree of detrimental impact associated with indefinite suspension between (a) VT and NVT children and (b) the suspended children by VT and NVT category and the comparison (NS) group.

In most cases when the findings are statistically significant, an appropriate supporting statistical table will be shown. For the most part data were analyzed by computing the significance of the difference

---

[4] John J. Stretch and Phillip E. Crunk, "An Exploratory Study of Major Characteristics of the Indefinitely Suspended Child: A Comparison of Statistically Significant Differences Between Children Referred and Children Not Referred to the Visiting Teacher Service of the Orleans Parish School System, 1967–1968, with Suggestions for Improvement" (New Orleans: Visiting Teaching and Attendance Section, Orleans Parish Public Schools, 1969). (Mimeographed.)

between two percentages pertaining to the NVT group, the VT group, and/or the NS group.[5] Two additional statistical tests, the test for analysis of variance and the T-test, were used when appropriate.

THE CHILDREN In this section a profile of the suspended child categorized by whether he was referred for service is presented and highlighted by comparisons with the nonsuspended group. It answers the questions of whether there are significant differences between suspended and nonsuspended children and whether the suspended children who were referred for social work services are different from suspended children who were not referred for service in a number of characteristics of interest. Occasional reference is made to Study I when warranted by an apparent trend in the data for the two time periods studied.

At the bottom of each table information is provided as to whether the observed differences are statistically significant. A comparison is made in order to ascertain differences in characteristics of children and their reaction to suspension by their referral status. A further comparison is made in terms of those who were suspended, by referral status, and those who were not suspended. Thus in the tabular presentations the following comparisons appear:

1. NVT/VT=comparison of children within the suspended category of those not referred and those referred.

2. NVT/NS=comparison of those children in the suspended category who were not referred and children who were not suspended.

3. VT/NS=comparison of those children in the suspended category who were referred and children who were not suspended.

The accepted level for reporting statistical significance for the study is the .05 level. However, in some cases when statistical trends are indicated, the .10 level of significance is noted. In all tables percentages given refer to the total population of interest. In some cases not all information is reported when such data are irrelevant to the issue under consideration. Further, in some cases cumulative percentages may be slightly over or under 100 percent because percentages within categories were rounded off in computer analysis to the nearest significant whole digit.

Age. There are no marked differences among the three groups with

---

[5] Details of this method may be found in Vernon Davies, *A Rapid Method for Determining the Significance of the Difference Between Two Percentages* (Seattle: University of Washington, 1962).

Table 1

Suspended and Nonsuspended Children, by Age (*percentage*)

Age	Suspended		Nonsuspended
	NVT	VT	
Latency (5–10)	15	38	26
Adolescence (11–17)	82	56	74

NVT/VT is significant at the .01 level; NVT/NS is significant at the .05 level; VT/NS is significant at the .10 level.

Table 2

Suspended and Nonsuspended Children, by Sex (*percentage*)

Sex	Suspended		Nonsuspended
	NVT	VT	
Male	80	91	84
Female	20	9	16

NVT/VT is significant at the .01 level; NVT/NS and VT/NS are not significant.

respect to age. Adolescents form the major part of each group. Within the suspended group, however, more latency-age children than adolescent children were referred for social service. This is consistent with the results of Study I. Table 1 shows the pertinent data distribution. Social service referral was more prevalent for young children than older children.

Sex. There is no statistically significant difference between the NVT and NS groups as far as the sex of the child is concerned. Males make up over 80 percent of all groups. However, within the suspended group one difference becomes quite apparent: nine out of ten VT children are males, whereas only eight out of ten NVT children are males. This finding is in keeping with those of Study I. (See Table 2.)

Race. Race does make a difference in determining whether a child is referred for social work service. Table 3 shows that although most of the suspended children are black and comprise the bulk of referrals within both suspended groups, proportionately more white children are referred. This finding does not differ from that presented in Study I, although the proportion of NVT blacks has increased in Study II by about 16 percent over Study I.

Grade at suspension. The majority of VT children are in elementary

169

Table 3

Suspended and Nonsuspended Children, by Race (*percentage*)

| | Suspended | | |
Race	NVT	VT	Nonsuspended
White	18	33	20
Black	81	67	80

NVT/VT is significant at the .01 level; NVT/NS is not significant; VT/NS is significant at the .05 level.

Table 4

Suspended and Nonsuspended Students, by Grade at Suspension (*percentage*)

| | Suspended | | |
Grade	NVT	VT	Nonsuspended
Elementary	36	63	48
Junior High	55	21	52

NVT/VT is significant at the .01 level; NVT/NS and VT/NS are significant at the .05 level.

school, whereas the majority of NVT children are junior high students. Again, the findings shown in Table 4 tend to be similar to those of Study I—those referred come disproportionately from the elementary school level.

IQ. Sufficient IQ data for comparative purposes were not available because of incomplete school records. When data exist they tend to show differences in the predicted direction—that is, more of the NS children have a reported IQ above 80, whereas more of those suspended have an IQ under 80. This finding must be considered tentative, since there were not enough data available in official school records to support the finding in any convincing statistical manner. Study I showed a trend supported by the tentative data of Study II that more VT children had an IQ under 80, whereas more of those in the NVT group had an IQ over 80.

Health. A broad subjective evaluation was made of physical illnesses and emotional difficulties reported by the maternal head of the household for each child in the study to approximate whether recent illness—physical or emotional—might have a bearing on suspension. The information revealed that most of the children had been judged physi-

Table 5

Suspended and Nonsuspended Children, by Illness During Preceding Twelve Months (*percentage*)

Type of Illness	Suspended		Nonsuspended
	NVT	VT	
No operations	99	99	98
No severe illness	99	99	95
No physical injuries	98	97	95
No major emotional difficulties	99	97	97
No other major physical illness	98	99	100
No continuing chronic physical illness	96	94	95
No continuing chronic emotional illness	99	97	97

NVT/VT, NVT/NS, and VT/NS are not significant.

Table 6

Suspended and Nonsuspended Children, by Marital Status of the Respondent (*percentage*)

Marital Status	Suspended		Nonsuspended
	NVT	VT	
Married	62	52	71
Separated	22	24	17
Divorced	5	7	7
Widowed or other	11	16	7

NVT/VT and NVT/NS are significant at the .10 level; VT/NS is significant at the .01 level.

cally and emotionally healthy during the preceding twelve months. If the reported assessment of health is generally valid, it may indicate that other factors—such as stresses of the home environment, parental perception of education, or parental support of the school and its goals—might have a more important bearing on suspension than the immediate past physical and emotional health of the child. There is no statistically significant difference between either the NVT or VT and the NS groups nor between the VT and NVT groups in terms of the mothers' reports of the children's recent physical or emotional illness. (See Table 5.)

THE MATERNAL RESPONDENTS This section will present a number of the family social background characteristics of the interviewed maternal respondents.

Marital status. Reported data show that children tend to come from homes in which the parents have been legally married. Upon inspection of the data, one fact becomes apparent—namely, that suspended children tend to come from broken families far more than NS children. (By broken family is meant one in which there has been divorce, separation, or widowhood.) Within the suspended group, more VT children were from a broken family. (See Table 6.)

Religion. As far as the religious affiliation of respondents is concerned, there is a trend in terms of denominational difference between those suspended and those not suspended, despite the fact that both groups tend to be predominately Protestant. However, more VT children than NS children are Roman Catholic. The difference is more pronounced in the VT/NVT and VT/NS group comparisons, with a significant number of Roman Catholic children being referred for social work service. (See Table 7.)

Education. As can be seen from Table 8, the educational level of the parents of NS children is significantly higher than that of parents whose children were suspended. More parents of NS children graduated from high school or had some college experience than did parents of those in the suspended group. The difference between the NVT and NS groups is statistically quite striking.

The difference between the VT and NVT parents does not reveal such a marked contrast. Although the latter difference was not as statistically significant, a slight association emerges between education and

Table 7

Suspended and Nonsuspended Children, by Religious Affiliation of the Respondent (*percentage*)

Religion	Suspended		Nonsuspended
	NVT	VT	
Protestant	74	61	75
Roman Catholic	23	35	23
Other	3	4	2

NVT/VT is significant at the .01 level; NVT/NS is not significant; VT/NS is significant at the .01 level.

Table 8

Suspended and Nonsuspended Children, by Education of the
Mother (*percentage*)

	Suspended		
Educational Level	NVT	VT	Nonsuspended
Some college	2	5	13
High school graduate	10	17	22
Did not graduate from high school	87	78	64

NVT/VT is significant at the .05 level; NVT/NS is significant at the .01 level; VT/NS is significant at the .05 level.

Table 9

Suspended and Nonsuspended Children, by Occupation of the
Breadwinner (*percentage*)

	Suspended		
Occupation	NVT	VT	Nonsuspended
White collar	9	9	20
Blue collar	63	57	59
Not employed	18	22	14

NVT/VT is not significant; NVT/NS is significant at the .01 level; VT/NS is significant at the .05 level.

referral. The better educated respondents were somewhat more likely to have their children referred.

Occupation. The occupations reported by respondents have been collected into two traditional categories: white collar and blue collar. The data show that the majority of the sampled parents hold blue-collar jobs. Table 9 shows that the occupational difference between the parents of children who were suspended is not as striking as the difference between those suspended by referral category and those not suspended. The NS group is characterized by a larger proportion of breadwinners who hold white-collar occupations.

Social class position. The Hollingshead two-factor index of social position, which incorporates two measures as an index of the social class position, education, and occupation of the main breadwinner, was used to rate families in the present study.[6] Hollingshead has sug-

---

[6] *See* August B. Hollingshead, *Two-Factor Index of Social Position* (New Haven, Conn.: published by the author, 1957).

173

Table 10

Suspended and Nonsuspended Children, by Social Class Position
(*percentage*)

	Suspended		
Social Class	NVT	VT	Nonsuspended
I–III	8	7	19
IV	25	26	22
V	40	34	35
Indeterminate	26	28	24

NVT/VT is not significant; NVT/NS is significant at the .05 level; VT/NS is significant at the .01 level.

Table 11

Suspended and Nonsuspended Children, by Illness Record of Parent
During the Preceding Twelve Months (*percentage*)

	Suspended		
Selective Illness Record	NVT	VT	Nonsuspended
No operations	93	93	90
No severe illnesses	99	99	93
No physical illness	99	100	99
No emotional illness	98	99	98

NVT/VT, NVT/NS, and VT/NS are not significant.

gested five categories, I–V, that represent ranges of social position. Category V corresponds to the lowest end of the social stratification ladder, Category I, to the highest. Table 10 reveals that the majority of families who reported data tend to be at the lower end of the social class index. In addition it can be seen that there are at least twice as many families of NS children in the upper categories. The difference between both the NVT and VT groups and the NS group is quite significant; no such difference emerges between the NVT and VT groups.

Health. A subjective and broadly judged medical history of the preceding twelve months was obtained from respondents. Although a few parents had undergone an operation or had chronic illnesses, nine out of ten mothers reported that they had been relatively healthy. No significant differences were revealed by the data for the suspended and NS groups. (See Table 11.)

SUMMARY From a combined analysis of general descriptive characteristics and social backgrounds of all the children in this study there emerges a basic picture of the suspension experience. The typical NVT child is a black adolescent boy, somewhat less academically bright than his school peers, whose social background is characterized by greater family disorganization. He has undergone few major emotional or physical upsets during the twelve months prior to suspension. In addition the NVT child comes from a family in which the main breadwinner tends to be rather poorly educated and consequently holds a manual job of some kind. A combination of these demographic factors reveal that the family and social background of the NVT child is at the lower end of the social ladder.

A comparison of the children in Study II suspended during the 1968–69 school year and those in Study I who were suspended during the 1967–68 school year shows a consistent difference between those referred to a social worker and those who were not referred. As in the first study, more males than females were referred for social work services. A further similarity between the two years studied is that there are proportionately fewer adolescents and more latency-age children in the VT than in the NVT group.

The VT child shares the same characteristics as the NVT child with the following notable differences: The VT group contains a larger percentage of younger latency-age, white, elementary-grade, Roman Catholic children from less stable homes, although with better educated parents.

Given these demographic characteristics of the study children, we will now turn to an analysis of the effects of the suspension experience, including the major reasons for the suspension and its disposition.

The Suspension Experience

In this section comparisons will be made between Study II and Study I and between the VT and NVT children in Study II. The NS group is not included here, since these children did not undergo suspension.

PREVIOUS SUSPENSION RECORD In both studies officially recorded information for previous suspensions is incomplete. Data are lacking for 76 percent of the NVT group and 42 percent of the VT group. It thus becomes difficult to make statistically valid generalizations

Table 12

Previous Indefinite Suspension, by Referral Category (*percentage*)

Previous Suspension	NVT	VT
Yes	2	15
No	22	42
No data	76	42

NVT/VT is significant at the .01 level.

Table 13

Number of Three-Day Suspensions, by Referral Category (*percentage*)

Number of Suspensions	NVT	VT
None	19	32
One or more	17	22
No data	75	44

NVT/VT is significant at the .01 level.

about previous suspensions by referral categories. Tables 12 and 13 show the percentage distributions for two administrative categories of suspension, indefinite and for three days. A three-day suspension is by intent a less severe removal from the school than an indefinite suspension. However, although it is limited to no more than three days in duration, administratively, there is no fixed upper limit on the number of separate three-day suspensions. There are no systematic data available systemwide about the number, reasons for, extent of, and effects of this practice. In general, if data on previous suspensions are available, more data are available for the VT group than the NVT group. Also when additional VT data were obtained, they revealed that more children were suspended previously, irrespective of the reason for suspension.

DATE OF SUSPENSION Table 14 reveals a trend toward more suspensions in the first half of the school year than in the second half. This finding is consistent with Study I, although percentage differences between the two halves of the school year in the previous study are much larger. Thus the data suggest that variability in the number of indefinite suspensions and referrals tends partly to be a function of the academic calendar.

176

LENGTH OF SUSPENSION Of striking statistical significance as far as length of suspension is concerned are the differences between children who are and are not readmitted during the same school year. Table 15 reveals a number of interesting points:

1. The majority of suspended children are readmitted.

2. A child is more likely to be readmitted if he has *not* been referred for social work services.

3. When suspensions do occur, they tend to endure for less than one month in the majority of NVT cases. Conversely, for VT cases suspensions tend to endure longer than one month. Why these differences occur is a critical question that requires further investigation. The phenomenon may be partly accounted for by referring to Table 17, which reveals the amount of outside referral activity by the social work staff in directing suspended children to community agencies dealing with physical and emotional difficulties. These two findings suggest that a suspended child referred for social work services may have problems that require more intensive professional help to resolve.

The direction of this distribution is similar to that of Study I. In Study II more children were readmitted (NVT 82 percent, VT 72 percent) than in Study I (NVT 76 percent, VT 50 percent). Important to note is the statistic revealing that the percentage of VT children who

Table 14

Date of Suspension, by Referral Category (*percentage*)

Date	NVT	VT
September–January	54	60
February–May	47	37

NVT/VT is significant at the .10 level.

Table 15

Length of Suspension, by Referral Category (*percentage*)

Length of Suspension	NVT	VT
More than four days but less than one month	80	39
Over one month	2	33
Not readmitted during the current school year	12	24

NVT/VT is significant at the .01 level.

Table 16

Reasons for Suspension, by Referral Category, by Major and Contributing Reasons [a] (*percentage*)

Behavioral Problem [b]	NVT Major reason [c]	NVT Contributing reason [d]	VT Major reason	VT Contributing reason	Total [e] Major reason	Total [e] Contributing reason
Aggressive behavior						
Fighting	19	7	11	31	15	19
Disrespect of superiors	18	23	10	26	14	25
Habitual rule violation	15	12	11	13	13	13
Attention-getting behavior	5	5	18	28	12	17
Conduct injurious to peers	7	3	7	17	7	10
Threatening peers or teachers	6	7	3	16	5	12
Defacing school property	6	1	3	5	5	3
Theft	3	1	1	3	2	2
Carrying implements usable as weapons	1	6	1	5	1	6
Profane language	1	9	0	14	1	12
Use of tobacco or alcohol	0	3	0	3	0	3
Passive behavior						
Truancy	7	9	3	13	5	11
Leaving school without permission	0	4	2	17	1	11
Withdrawn behavior	1	0	1	6	1	3
Habitually tardy	1	3	0	3	1	3
Mixed behavior						
Academically behind	1	0	3	21	2	11

[a] A percentage difference greater than five between VT and NVT is significant beyond the .05 level.

[b] Ranked according to incidence of major reason in each category.

[c] This represents behavior judged as the primary basis for a specific suspension decision.

[d] This represents behavior judged as secondary to the suspension decision but that nevertheless had occurred and was considered in that decision.

[e] Since the reasons for both groups are combined, this column gives an indication of the overall incidence of each behavioral problem for the study period.

failed to be readmitted during the 1968–69 school year was double that of NVT children (24 percent versus 12 percent).

REASONS FOR SUSPENSION   The most frequently cited official reasons for suspending a child have been grouped into three major classifications (1) aggressive, acting-out behavior, such as fighting, use of profane language, or disrespect toward superiors, (2) passive, introverted behavior typified by a withdrawal from interaction, such as truancy or failure to interact with peers or teachers, and (3) mixed behavior, such as being behind academically or being unable to perform classroom work.   Of all the reasons given for suspending a child, those that show statistically significant differences between the VT and NVT groups fall predominantely in the first category.   Suspension for conduct injurious to peers, threatening peers or teachers, attention-getting behavior in the classroom, and being behind academically resulting in an inability to perform classroom work show statistically significant differences between the VT and NVT groups.

It will be noted that available data indicate that when there are statistically significant differences between the two groups, in the majority of cases the NVT group shows a larger percentage of children manifesting the behavioral problem than does the VT group.   Table 16 shows the major and contributing reasons given for suspension and their percentage frequency.

From an inspection of the data it can be seen that VT children are much more likely than NVT children to be referred to outside professional resources.   It is also apparent that most VT children are referred for psychiatric evaluation within the school system (43 percent).   The second most frequent referral activity is to public treatment facilities, principally the local public hospital.   Table 17 shows the usual types of services to which suspended children are referred.

These data support the findings of Study I although the percentage differences between the NVT and VT groups with reference to psychiatric evaluation and placement in special classes are more pronounced in Study II.   Study II also reveals that the VT child is more likely to be referred for a broader range of services today than he was a year ago if he had been referred to a school social worker.

TREATMENT ACTIVITY   If the school social worker has a direct focus, once the VT child has been referred, does he focus his activities on

Table 17

Type of Referral, by Referral Category (*percentage*)

Type of Referral	NVT	VT
Outside the school system		
Private hospital	3	19
Public facility	3	26
Inside the school system		
Psychiatric evaluation	1	43
Special class	1	14

All NVT/VT comparisons are significant at the .01 level.

Table 18

Treatment Activity with Referred Children (*percentage*)

Focus of Treatment Activity	VT
Work primarily with child	50
Work primarily with child's teacher	30

Table 19

Disposition Activity, by Referral Category (*percentage*)

Disposition Activity	NVT	VT
To be readmitted in 1969–70 [a]	5	8
Transferred to a special class [b]	1	5
Transferred to a different school [c]	42	26
Returned to the same class [d]	35	17

[a] NVT/VT is not significant.
[b] NVT/VT is significant at the .10 level.
[c] NVT/VT is significant at the .01 level.
[d] NVT/VT is significant at the .01 level.

the child or on the teacher? Table 18 shows that direct work with the child is the focus for half of the VT cases. Work on behalf of the child with the child's teacher comprises almost one-third of the treatment focus. This item reflects a stated primary treatment focus. In some cases, of course, a combination of activities with parents, teachers, administrators, other professionals, and the child comprises the treatment regimen.

SUSPENSION DISPOSITION Any child who was suspended during the school year usually experienced one of the following administrative dispositions (1) suspension lifted without change of status, (2) suspension sustained, or (3) a change of status.

Suspension lifted without change of status. As Table 19 shows, when the suspension was lifted, the VT child was less likely than the NVT child to be transferred to a different school. In addition, the NVT children were twice as likely to be returned to the same class as the VT children.

Comparing the figures in Table 19 with Study I shows the results of Study I to be sustained: More NVT children than VT children were transferred to a different school and twice as many NVT children than VT children were allowed to return to the same class. Similarly the Study I findings concerning the children's return to school and transfer to a special class are almost identical with the Study II data.

Suspension sustained. When a suspension is sustained, a child remains in no-man's-land, waiting for some academic or administrative decision to be made on his case. Some are waiting for direct therapeutic help. Few children, however, were waiting for testing and evaluation (14 percent) or placement in a special class (3 percent). These results are also in keeping with the findings of Study I.

Change of the child's status. Only a few children—approximately 5 percent of all cases—were officially recorded as having dropped out of school. (Since the study sample was by design largely limited to students 16 years of age and below and since Louisiana has compulsory school attendance to age 16, this category would be influenced by those two factors.) Placements in correctional or treatment institutions were rare. The data also show a tendency for more NVT children that VT children to drop out of school (NVT 7 percent, VT 2 percent). (See Table 20.) The information from the present study shows a slight change from Study I in that more VT children were institutionalized in the Study II group.

SUMMARY Most indefinite suspensions take place within the first half of the school year and the majority of students are suspended for aggressive, insubordinate behavior. A student suspended in September through January is more likely to be referred for social work services than a student suspended in February through May. Most students are usually readmitted within a few weeks; however, those referred are not likely to be readmitted as early as the others.

Table 20

Change of Status, by Referral Category (*percentage*)

Status Change	NVT	VT
Dropped out of school [a]	7	2
Placed in correctional institution [b]	1	3

[a] NVT/VT is significant at the .10 level.
[b] NVT/VT is not significant.

A child may be further referred for specialized treatment—most probably if he has already been referred—to an agency outside the school or a special class within the educational system. When a direct focus is appropriate, the school social work service tends to focus treatment by working either with the suspended child or with the child's teacher. A small percentage of suspended children are officially recorded as having dropped out of school. Of these, however, a lower percentage come from the VT group.

Effects of Suspension

In this section major aspects of the detrimental effects of suspension on the child and his family are discussed.[7] Such detrimental effects are manifested in a number of ways. A comparison of those children who were suspended with those who were not suspended is made in order to measure the distribution of the detrimental effects researched in this study.

IMPACT ON THE CHILD   Parental reports of the children's emotional health and social behavior both at home and in school during the preceding school year were examined to determine what relationship, if any, these factors had to suspension and referral. The maternal respondents were asked how they rated their child's general adjustment at school and at home, especially in terms of his ability to gain satisfaction by interacting with other children.

Adjustment at home. Table 21 shows that statistically significant differences do exist between both the NVT and VT groups and the NS group with respect to the adequacy of their interaction with others in

---

[7] For a more detailed and systematic documentation of the impact of indefinite suspension on the child's family, *see* Crunk, op. cit.

Table 21

Suspended and Nonsuspended Children by Ability To Get Along with Others at Home (*percentage*)

Ability To Get Along at Home	Suspended		Nonsuspended
	NVT	VT	
Well	43	26	32
Average	40	43	59
Not well	17	32	9

NVT/VT, NVT/NS, and VT/NS are all significant at the .01 level.

Table 22

Suspended and Nonsuspended Children, by Child's Emotional State at Home (*percentage*)

Emotional State at Home	Suspended		Nonsuspended
	NVT	VT	
Happy	80	79	95
Sad	12	16	4

NVT/VT is not significant; NVT/NS and VT/NS are significant at the .01 level.

the home. On the whole, NS children were perceived as interacting more adequately (91 percent in the well and average categories grouped together) than the suspended children (NVT 83 percent, VT 79 percent). The data also show a significant difference within the suspended category, with an inverse relation between the quality of interaction in the home environment and VT status. Almost twice as many children who were referred for social work services were perceived as unable to relate well to others at home.

Table 22 reveals that in seven out of ten cases the suspended children were perceived as happy and that no statistically significant difference exists within the suspended group as a whole. More NS children were perceived as happy (95 percent), however, than either category of suspended children (79 percent for both NVT and VT).

Briefly, suspended children were characterized by the maternal respondents as having greater feelings of sadness in the home than those who were not suspended. One might infer that their reported inability to interact adequately with others as well as their academic disappointments would be manifested in a generalized sadness.

Table 23

Suspended and Nonsuspended Children, by Child's Emotional
State at School (*percentage*)

| | Suspended | | |
Emotional State at School	NVT	VT	Nonsuspended
Happy	56	40	91
Sad	30	48	5

NVT/VT, NVT/NS, and VT/NS are all significant at the .01 level.

Table 24

Suspended and Nonsuspended Children, by Ability To Get Along
with Others at School (*percentage*)

| | Suspended | | |
Ability To Get Along at School	NVT	VT	Nonsuspended
Well	25	19	31
Average	39	30	59
Not well	36	51	10

NVT/VT, NVT/NS, and VT/NS are all significant at the .01 level.

Adjustment at school. Another area investigated was the child's
general perception of the school environment. Again, it might be
suggested that suspension is closely related to a child's emotional
well-being and his continued adequate social interaction. Therefore
the maternal respondents were asked how they perceived the child's
happiness at school in terms of how he got along with other schoolchildren. In general NS children were judged to be much happier at
school. Table 23 reveals that more NVT children tend to be happy
at school (56 percent) than VT children (40 percent), while the NS
group shows the largest percentage (91 percent).

From these data one must infer that a large proportion—nearly
half—of the VT group were perceived as unhappy at school. If,
however, these children were perceived as unhappy at school, does this
necessarily mean that as a group they are also having problems in
getting along with others? The answer from the data is emphatically
yes. It can be seen from combining the distribution of children who
got along well and average with others at school (Table 24) that nine
out of ten children who were not suspended (90 percent) were perceived as getting along with others, while only 64 percent of the NVT
and 49 percent of the VT children were rated similarly. Furthermore, a

statistically significant difference is revealed within the suspended category since half of the VT group (51 percent) is shown to interact with others rather poorly, as opposed to a little better than a third (36 percent) of the NVT group.

By way of summary the following points should be noted:

1. As expected, children who were not suspended are reported to be much happier and able to get along better with others both at home and in school than those who were suspended regardless of referral status.

2. Of the children who had been suspended, those who were seen as less happy and less able to interact well with others in school and at home were those who had been referred for school social work services.

3. A combined adjustment score (a summation of all adjustment ratings at home and in school) revealed a statistically significant difference in home-school adjustment between the suspended and non-suspended groups, with the suspended group again showing less adjustment regardless of referral status.

4. Suspension is indeed related to reported emotional instability and problem social interaction, irrespective of social environment as these terms have been operationalized in this study. The cause-and-effect relationship between home-school adjustment and suspension is, however, not necessarily established by these data. These data do establish the necessity and potential fruitfulness of additional research in this area to rule out or more firmly establish causal connections.

IMPACT ON THE FAMILY Maximizing a child's education is at least the partial product of a positive growth-inducing interaction between two important environments—home and school. The way a family relates to the school is important. An emotionally secure and supportive environment conducive to the more formal learning situation of

Table 25

Maternal Respondents' Judgments of Treatment at School, by Suspension Categories (*percentage*)

Satisfaction with Treatment	Suspended		Nonsuspended
	NVT	VT	
Satisfied	36	36	87
Dissatisfied	40	48	3

NVT/VT is not significant; NVT/NS and VT/NS are significant at the .01 level.

the school should be maintained by the family. Suspension affects a family in a detrimental manner because it engenders and tends to reinforce in the family distortions of the school system. Also it increases the family's state of powerlessness, normlessness, and social isolation, which leads to strains and breakdowns in the mutual support system needed by the child.

Perceptions of education and the school. This section of the analysis begins by focusing first on parental perceptions of the school and the effects of suspension and then on the educational experience as a whole. In other words, it will proceed from the specific to the general effects.

The way in which a child is handled by school personnel is important to a family. Research studies in social psychology have repeatedly shown that the manner in which someone is perceived and treated affects his self-image and consequent behavior. Maternal respondents were therefore asked whether they were satisfied with the way their child was treated by teachers and other school officials. Table 25 reveals that mothers' feelings tend to run in a generally expected direction. Mothers of suspended children, regardless of the child's referral status, reported more dissatisfaction than did mothers of NS children. In fact, over four out of ten of the mothers of suspended children in both subcategories were dissatisfied with their child's treatment, whereas nearly nine out of ten mothers of NS children were satisfied with the school's treatment of their child. Referral status seems to have no effect on the rate of satisfaction among the mothers of suspended children.

It was further suspected that suspension would be related not only to satisfaction with the school's general treatment of the child, but also with judgments of the fairness of disciplinary measures. It could thus be argued that parents whose children were suspended would be dissatisfied with that form of discipline and judge that their child had been unjustly punished, whereas parents of NS children would judge that discipline at the school was fair. Table 26 shows that a statistically significant difference in the expected direction does exist between the groups compared. Over eight out of ten mothers of NS children, as compared to over four out of ten mothers of suspended children, rated discipline at the school as fair. Referral status in the suspended groups is not related to judgments of disciplinary fairness or unfairness.

Considering the negative judgments of fairness associated with suspension regardless of referral status, it may be said that suspension has a detrimental effect on a child by undermining his parent's faith in the fairness of the system. Furthermore, mothers of suspended

Table 26

Maternal Respondents' Judgments of School Discipline, by Suspension Categories (*percentage*)

	Suspended		
Fairness of School Discipline	NVT	VT	Nonsuspended
Fair	46	45	83
Unfair	28	28	4

NVT/VT is not significant; NVT/NS and VT/NS are significant at the .01 level.

Table 27

Perceived Effects of Suspension, by Suspension Categories (*percentage*)

	Parent in Agreement		
	Suspended		
Effects of Suspension	NVT	VT	Nonsuspended
Child is branded a troublemaker [a]	66	66	33
Door to future educational opportunities is closed [b]	53	50	41

[a] NVT/VT is not significant; NVT/NS and VT/NS are significant at the .01 level.
[b] NVT/VT is not significant; NVT/NS is significant at the .10 level; VT/NS is not significant.

children indicate on the whole that suspension brands the child as a troublemaker and tends to limit his future advancement.[8] When asked to give their opinions about the statement "Once a person is suspended from school and then returns to school, he will always be looked upon as a troublemaker," mothers tended to respond in predictable directions. That is, only one-third (33 percent) of the mothers of NS children agreed that there is a permanent detrimental stigma attached to suspension, whereas two-thirds (66 percent) of the mothers of suspended children made that judgment. (See Table 27.)

A corollary question about whether suspension actually closes the door to further educational opportunities did not reveal as great a difference between the compared groups as did the previous question, although one can see a faint direction emerging. With the exception of a slight difference in the NVT/NS groups, there was no significant dif-

---

[8] For a theoretical discussion of how limited access, coupled with pressures to achieve, results in deviant behavior, *see* Richard A. Cloward and Lloyd E. Ohlin, *Delinquency and Opportunity: A Theory of Delinquent Gangs* (Glencoe, Ill.: Free Press, 1960).

ference in response to this question by suspension status. Slightly fewer mothers of NS children agreed with the statements than mothers of suspended children. In summary, almost half of all the mothers judged that suspension would cause future educational doors to close.

In view of the fact that up to now the data reveal that parents of suspended children do not rate the schools as positively disposed toward their children and their problems and agree that their children have somehow been stigmatized, it remains to be seen whether these families are generally clear about the goals and aims of education. Crunk suggests that associated with their child's suspension, or because of it, these families are estranged from one of society's major social institutions—education—and therefore that significant differences would emerge between families whose children were and were not suspended.[9]

To obtain data on this issue, four statements were combined to form an index called the School Confusion Scale. The four statements were (1) "The education of children is too complicated to be understood by anyone but experts," (2) "I don't know who deserves the credit when things go well in the school system," (3) "Nobody really has any very good answers for the problems that face education today," and (4) "Experts disagree, so how can the average person decide what is best for the school?" The agreement or disagreement of the respondents with these statements is shown in Table 28.

The data do not reveal a significant difference within the suspended groups between the VT and NVT groups with respect to the first statement. They do reveal a state of high confusion about the enterprise of education regardless of referral status between the mothers of suspended and NS children.

It can be seen from Table 28 that over two-thirds (67 percent) of the mothers of NS children feel that in general they can understand the educational process and thus do not feel overwhelmed by its complexity. On the other hand, within both VT and NVT categories only one-half of the mothers of suspended children judge themselves able to understand education. Referral status does not reveal itself to be statistically differentiating within the suspended category.

The ability to feel minimally comfortable with the institution of education and its complexity and, more particularly, to understand the machinery of the school system was determined by asking respondents whether they felt capable of attributing credit for things accomplished in education to the correct people. It can be seen from Table 28 that

---

[9] Crunk, op. cit., p. 94.

Table 28

Agreement and Disagreement with the Statements in the School
Confusion Scale, by Suspension Categories (*percentage*)

Agreement	Suspended		Nonsuspended
	NVT	VT	
Statement 1 [a]			
Disagree	52	50	67
Agree	44	46	29
Statement 2 [b]			
Disagree	60	65	68
Agree	28	23	18
Statement 3 [c]			
Disagree	36	40	58
Agree	52	54	37
Statement 4 [d]			
Disagree	28	39	51
Agree	60	50	39

[a] NVT/VT is not significant; NVT/NS and VT/NS are significant at the .05 level.
[b] NVT/VT, NVT/NS, and VT/NS are not significant.
[c] NVT/VT is not significant; NVT/NS and VT/NS are significant at the .01 level.
[d] NVT/VT is significant at the .05 level; NVT/NS is significant at the .01 level; VT/NS is significant at the .10 level.

a trend does not exist for Statement 2 between the suspended and NS categories. Also, differences between the VT and NVT groups are not statistically significant. As might be expected, these data still show parents of NS children to have a slightly more positive perception of and attitudes toward the educational system. These parents also indicate faith that the educational system has answers for the issues it faces, as shown by the positive responses of mothers of NS children to Statements 3 and 4.

By way of summary, the data show that the parents of suspended children, irrespective of referral status, have confused attitudes toward the school as measured by all four items of the School Confusion Scale. They judge that their children have been inadequately handled by school personnel, especially when discipline is concerned, and that the suspension process is unfair and prejudicial to their children's future educational chances. The sense of frustration and futility felt about their children vis-à-vis the school diffuses toward the institution of education as a whole. Thus the suspended child's family shows not only a lack of knowledge about but also an inability to grasp and feel comfortable with the educational process in society. In short, the same parents who as a group report their children to have adjustment problems at home and at school further report themselves to be confused about and passively oriented toward the educational process.

Family crisis. The suspension of a child from school often creates a state of crisis for the family in two ways: (1) the household is effectively cut off from the educational system until the school is ready to allow or in most cases even to consider readmission of the child and (2) the child is for a time totally isolated from the maturational influences of school and peers. It has already been noted that the suspended child's family has little understanding of and reports general confusion about the educational process. Moreover it can also be reasoned that the parent of a suspended child basically views himself as powerless because he not only lacks control over what happens in the school situation, but, more important, he has no control over and little influence on the final disposition of the suspension.

Therefore it is not surprising that these same parents judge the norms and rules of education as at least inadequate, if not unfair, because they seem to them biased toward helping nonsuspended children achieve their educational potential. It is not unreasonable to suggest that, given a position on the lower rungs of the social ladder and the very fact of their child's suspension, these parents may become characterized by increased feelings of inadequacy and impotence. Alienation—the term conceptualized to describe such a pervasive generalized orientation—is composed of three subdimensions studied in this research: powerlessness, social isolation, and normlessness.

The first subdimension—powerlessness—reveals a social orientation characterized by personal ineffectiveness and social vulnerability on the part of the respondent. Its extent is measured by agreement with statements in the following vein: "Sometimes I have the feeling that other people are using me," and "We're so regimented today that there's not much room for choice even in personal matters."

The second subdimension—social isolation—is characterized by feelings of being left out of things and of being estranged from others. Agreement with the following types of statements indicates this facet of alienation: "There are few dependable ties between people anymore," and "Sometimes I feel all alone in the world."

The third subdimension—normlessness—is measured by a lack of social stability and roots, manifested in feelings that the rules of the game of life are constantly shifting. This dimension is manifested by agreement with such statements as "People's ideas change so much that

I wonder if we'll ever have anything to depend on," and "The only thing we can be sure of today is that we can be sure of nothing."

The data in Table 29 show that the suspension of a child, regardless of referral status, is a significantly differentiating factor in the degree of general alienation and its major dimensions present in the suspended and nonsuspended child's household. The table further reveals that while there is some variation between the VT and NVT groups, the most consistently significant difference is between suspended and non-suspended groups in the area of powerlessness. When powerlessness, social isolation, and normlessness are combined and considered as a whole, a strong statistical difference emerges between the suspended and nonsuspended groups. This bears out a major hypothesis of Crunk's study—that alienation significantly differentiates the families of suspended and nonsuspended children.[10]

Of major concern to the project, however, was not only an investigation of the impact of indefinite suspension of a child from school on the child's family and the family's relationship to the school system, but also the development of an area of sound practice theory to guide school social work intervention. As previously stated, a basic assumption of school social work is that for a child's education to be maximized there must be a positive mutually reinforcing relationship—a non-alienating relationship—between the home environment and the school environment.

In examining the impact of suspension on the child's family, it was theorized that indefinite suspension from school provokes a crisis situation in the household. Suspension completely separates the child from the school and its maturing influence. The household is in effect completely isolated from the benefits of the educational system until the school is unilaterally ready and willing to readmit the child. The parent becomes powerless, since he cannot control what happens at school for his child's benefit. Additionally he must recognize and accept that appropriate school behavior is established totally at the school's discretion. Hence a normless orientation often develops in that the rules of the school appear designed to help other children obtain an education—-but not his suspended child. The multiple frustrations generated by these perceptions are conceptualized in the social science literature as alienation.[11] If the households of suspended children are significantly more alienated than those of nonsuspended students, it is an inference of this study that the school and the home are not

---

[10] Crunk, op. cit., pp. 35–44.
[11] Dean, op. cit.

Table 29

Maternal Respondents' Alienation, by Suspension Categories (*percentage*) [a]

Statement and Dimension Measured	Agreement with Statement	NVT	VT	Nonsuspended
Powerlessness				
"I worry about the future of to-day's children."	Agree	93	94	79
"Sometimes I have the feeling that other people are using me."	Agree	61	50	59
"It is frightening to be responsible for the development of a little child."	Agree	47	50	56
"There is little or nothing I can do toward preventing a major 'shooting' war."	Agree	90	92	84
"There are so many decisions that have to be made today that sometimes I could just 'blow up.'"	Agree	74	69	65
"There is little chance for promotion on the job unless a man gets a break."	Agree	66	54	53
"We're so regimented today that there's not much room for choice even in personal matters."	Agree	52	47	33
"We are just so many cogs in the machinery of life."	Agree	62	70	52
"The future looks very dismal."	Agree	50	44	40
Social Isolation				
"Sometimes I feel all alone in the world."	Agree	60	53	43
"I don't get invited out by friends as often as I'd really like to."	Agree	42	33	40
"Most people today seldom feel lonely."	Disagree	59	64	59

Table 29 (continued)

Statement and Dimension Measured	Agreement with Statement	NVT	VT	Nonsuspended
Social Isolation (cont.)				
"Real friends are as easy as ever to find."	Disagree	17	27	36
"One can always find friends if he shows himself friendly."	Disagree	80	84	82
"The world in which we live is basically a friendly place."	Disagree	58	64	61
"There are few dependable ties between people any more."	Agree	64	65	47
"People are just naturally friendly and helpful."	Disagree	34	38	46
"I don't get to visit friends as often as I'd like."	Agree	74	64	68
Normlessness				
"The end often justifies the means."	Agree	19	28	25
"People's ideas change so much that I wonder if we'll ever have anything to depend on."	Agree	67	64	56
"Everything is relative, and there just aren't any definite rules to live by."	Agree	36	32	28
"I often wonder what the meaning of life really is."	Agree	67	66	60
"The only thing we can be sure of today is that we can be sure of nothing."	Agree	58	46	36
"With so many religions abroad, one doesn't really know which to believe."	Agree	56	61	75

[a] All variables are presented according to the percentage response signifying alienation. A percentage difference greater than twelve between VT/NVT, NVT/NS, and VT/NS is significant beyond the .05 level.

Table 30

Alienation Scores, by Suspension Category; Means, Standard Deviation, T-Test Values, and Significance Levels

| | Suspension Category | | | | | |
| | Suspended (n=100) | | Nonsuspended (n=100) | | | |
Measure of Alienation	Means	Standard Deviation	Means	Standard Deviation	T-Test Values	Level of Significance
Total alienation score	54.74	11.00	48.29	11.94	3.96	.001
Powerlessness	22.13	5.28	19.89	5.42	2.96	.005
Social isolation	20.22	3.94	17.80	4.67	3.94	.001
Normlessness	12.40	4.31	10.62	4.35	2.89	.005

functioning fully as mutually cooperative agents in the education and socialization of the child.

To control for the possible confounding influence of age, sex, income, race, and grade, a matched subsample of 100 suspended and 100 non-suspended children was obtained. This matched subsample showed that parents of indefinitely suspended children interpret the social situation between themselves and the school as being beyond their control (powerlessness), that the rules established by the school are designed to help others (normlessness), and since their child has been "thrown out" of school, these parents also experience a sense of separation from the school (isolation). Parents of suspended children also view suspension as stigmatizing the child as a troublemaker and limiting his opportunity for future educational advancement.

Regardless of whether the higher incidence of alienation in the households of suspended children than of nonsuspended children is viewed as a cause or a result of indefinite suspension, suspension itself is a potentially damaging factor in the maintenance of a positive home-school relationship. For example, if alienation is seen as a cause of indefinite suspension, denial of school attendance would tend to increase rather than resolve the problem. On the other hand, if alienation is a result of indefinite suspension, then the question is raised as to its ultimate positive value considering the negative judgments and feelings it provokes in parents. Table 30 statistically illustrates this conclusion strongly.

While part of school officials' assumed rationale for suspensions is to motivate the parents or directly involve them in resolving the child's difficulties in school, the opposite in fact appears to occur. That is, rather than becoming more motivated to become involved with the school on behalf of the child, parents of suspended children become more negatively disposed toward the school. Suspension is not viewed as positive, but as punitive in intent and results.

Summary and Implications

It can be seen from the data that parents of suspended children are not positively oriented toward the school; they exhibit marked confusion concerning the educational system and its main goals. Their judgments of the school system are associated with a pervasive orientation characterized by alienation, an estrangement from and uncertainty about the mainstream of life and the ability to cope with and influence it.

These findings would suggest a number of implications for possible remedial action.[12] First, the very fact of the existence of a school social work service does create a link, albeit at times tenuous, between the educational system and the family. Second, although it often takes time and additional school and community resources, the suspended child can be helped by the social work service to return to school and attain his educational potential. Third, the fact that positive communication between the school system and the family to resolve the child's suspension problem is established by school social workers should lead to changes in both attitudes and behavior of parents of suspended children. In turn, increased parental understanding of the goals and resources of the educational system should enhance the probability of a mutual adjustment of child and school so that the child's basic needs for education and socialization will be met.

As a consequence of this research, a school-community demonstration project to test the validity of these practice-based hypotheses is currently being undertaken. This is one of the results of the cooperation and support of a steering group representative of all major departments of the Orleans Parish School System that deal with suspension problems. This group of concerned administrators, educators, principals, school social workers, and teachers came into being as a result of cooperative efforts and mutual concerns that made this research possible. The successful implementation and utilization of the knowledge generated in the research study is now in their hands.

___

[12] Further policy and practice implications for social work in school settings are discussed in Crunk, op. cit.

Systems Analysis
Applied to
School Social Work

Linda P. Wassenich

Social workers in a school system have an opportunity to observe the vast array of influences on the schools and to intervene in different areas according to the determined need for change. Since the school is a complex organization, the school social worker potentially can achieve greater effectiveness if he understands its organizational structure, what influences it, what its goals are, and how he fits into the total scheme. What is needed by the social worker is an organizing theory with which he can examine a complex organization and also take account of the interaction between the individual and his social and physical environment.

This paper presents systems theory as a problem-solving technique for social workers. It is useful for setting social work goals, making a diagnosis of or assessing the situation, planning intervention, and evaluating outcome. These processes compare to output, input, throughput, and feedback in the systems approach.

Systems theory is applicable in numerous settings in which social

The author expresses her appreciation to Drs. Maeda J. Galinsky and Albert Johnson of the University of North Carolina School of Social Work for their valuable help in preparing this article.

workers provide service. A system may be an individual, a family, a group, a complex organization, or a community. This paper will illustrate the use of systems theory by the social worker in a complex organization—the school. The school was selected for this illustration because it deals basically with social competence rather than pathology.

It is essential first to establish that the school is a complex organization and then to indicate the reasons for using systems theory to analyze it. Complex organizations are defined as having the following characteristics:

> (1) stable patterns of interaction, (2) among coalitions of groups having a collective identity (e.g. a name and location(s)), (3) pursuing interests and accomplishing given tasks, and (4) coordinated by power and authority structures.[1]

Applying this definition to the school, one notes that (1) the primary pattern of interaction is the daily meeting, (2) in the classroom between students and teachers, who form the main coalitions of groups, (3) who pursue educational and socialization goals, and (4) who are coordinated by the principal, the administrative offices, the school board, and even the community as a whole.

Systems analysis presents a broad and comprehensive framework within which to view a complex organization. Using the systems approach one can look at the organization as a whole and examine changes in and outcomes of the institution as well as the institution's effect on the environment. In order for the social worker to work effectively in the school system, he should have a conceptual understanding of the school in its totality. It is important that the social worker understand the school as a complex organization in order to set objectives for his work, to know the system's goals and its constraints, and to plan appropriate interventions to accomplish his purposes and contribute to the system's goals.

Characteristics of an Open System

Systems theory is relevant to the social worker for the purpose of organizing his knowledge and insight about a system and then planning his actions.

The systems approach is, then, a problem-solving technique with a scientific basis. The four stages of the technique are:

[1] Ronald G. Corwin, "Education: The Sociology of Complex Organizations," in Donald H. Hansen and Joel E. Gerstl, eds., *On Education—Sociological Perspectives* (New York: John Wiley & Sons, 1967), p. 161.

1. Determine the objectives to be achieved.

2. Analyze the situation to find the variations affecting the solution of the problem and the restrictions under which the systems must operate.

3. Define the alternative ways of relating the most important variables to achieve the most efficient system.

4. Establish feedback and control subsystems and test the system according to the achievement of the objectives.[2]

These four stages are comparable to the first four characteristics of an open system—output, input, throughput, and feedback. The problem that the school social worker attempts to solve is to help the school to state and achieve its goals—the desired output. Then the school social worker looks at the input variables that affect the achievement of those desired outputs. These input variables may be subclassified as determiners, which are outside the control of the actual school system but affect it tremendously, and components, which are more modifiable within the school system. The school social worker is regarded as one of the agents in the throughput who relates the input variables in different ways so as to maximize the output. He needs to identify his role within a subsystem of the organization in order to find his part in the total throughput of the system. Finally, the school social worker uses feedback to measure the school's actual output and to evaluate the degree to which the school achieves its goals as well as to evaluate his own practice as the throughput. Figure 1 presents an analytical model of the school that focuses on these four characteristics that provide the skeletal structure of the model.

The systems theory utilized in this paper describes open systems. Viewing the school as an open system is useful in understanding how it exists, functions, grows, and changes interdependently with other systems in the environment. The schools interact as open systems with other elements of the community, such as its agencies, the political structure, and families. Open systems have nine common characteristics, the first four of which exist in all open systems models and are considered by the writer to have the most utility for the social worker.[3] These nine characteristics are as follows:

1. *Input.* The system is stimulated—or energized—by other people, institutions, or the environment. Examples of inputs into the school system are family and community characteristics, students, teachers,

---

[2] Janet G. Donald and John F. Flowers, "The Systems Approach in Education," *Ontario Journal of Educational Research,* Vol. 8, No. 2 (Winter 1965–66), p. 152.

[3] *See* Daniel Katz and Robert L. Kahn, *The Social Psychology of Organizations* (New York: John Wiley & Sons, 1966), pp. 8–12 and 19–26.

principals, school programs and their characteristics, administrators, and financial resources. The school social worker also becomes an input in the school system when he participates in it. The subdivision of inputs into the two classes of determiners and components is shown in Figure 1. The inputs of family and community characteristics, which are outside the control of the school system but highly influential on it, are shown as determiners. The other inputs are described as component inputs because they are more directly subject to reorganization within the school system.

The school social worker must be highly aware of the inputs, for these are the material with which he works. Knowing what the inputs are also provides him with some idea of the constraints on the system, which define not only what influences the school system but also what limits it. By delineating which inputs are determiners and which are components, the school social worker will have a more realistic idea of the potential outcome of his interventions. Thus he could expect less immediate change in the school's output if he were to focus on the determiners, even though they have much influence on the school system and its functioning, because they are less accessible to change by traditional methods. Using the school social worker as a community action agent with families and the community may be one way of affecting the determiners.[4]

When the social worker considers the system's inputs, he needs to be as specific as possible in order to organize his observations and to be sure that he is not overlooking pertinent influences on the system in question. For example, in describing the inputs of school programs he should note what kinds of academic, nonacademic, and vocational classes are offered, what kinds of extracurricular activities are available, what the policy is with respect to participation in extracurricular activities (bearing in mind that some students feel further alienated from the school when they are excluded from extracurricular activities because of their grades), and so on. This type of specificity aids later in analyzing any changes brought about through the system. When possible, inputs should be delineated in measurable terms so that the

---

[4] James S. Coleman, in *Equality of Educational Opportunity* (Washington, D.C.: U.S. Government Printing Office, 1966), and Jesse Burkhead, in *Input and Output in Large-City High Schools* (Syracuse, N.Y.: Syracuse University Press, 1967), both discuss a number of inputs in the school system and their relative effect on the school's output. They both conclude that the influence of family and community characteristics have the most important effect (in relation to the other inputs) on the educational outputs of the schools studied.

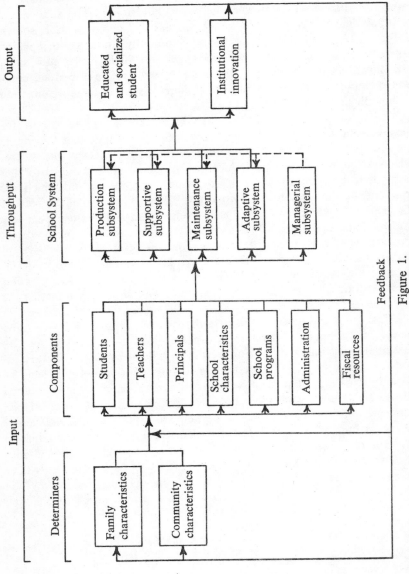

Figure 1.
An Analytical Model of the School System

change can be verified. Generally speaking, when the social worker becomes more specific in defining the inputs and the outcomes he hopes to achieve, he has already begun to use the systems approach for more effective problem-solving.

2. *Output.* The paramount product of the school is the student. Determining what kind of student is desired is part of setting the goals of the school. The schools are essentially aimed at producing educated and socialized students. An educated student may be further described as one who demonstrates some skills in reasoning, judgment, and creativity; who has completed or will complete a certain level of schooling; and who has the skills required for further education or employment. The socialized student is one who accepts society's norms and values, who has some skill in social relationships, and who maintains adequate physical and mental health. In order to produce this kind of student, the school itself sometimes changes. This means that an innovative or changing school may also be an output.

The school social worker must not only know what the school's goals are but also what its actual outputs are. Recognizing that the school is not the only means of achieving the goal of an educated and socialized youth, the school social worker must be aware of what other influences there are—such as the family and community—on the goals set by the school. His role is to help the school reach its goals; he also sets his own specific goals for school social work that are part of the school's overall goals. For example, in working with students toward the generalized goal of becoming educated and socialized, the school social worker may set as his goal a program aimed at potential dropouts. Thus the school social worker is working to meet the system's goals and also expanding the nature of those goals through his own endeavors.

3. *Throughput.* The process of taking the inputs and converting them into the outputs is known as throughput. The work of teachers, principals, administrators, and school social workers may be regarded as part of the throughput that is directed toward producing educated and socialized students as well as necessary innovations in the school. Just as the school social worker is not the only means of throughput, one social worker cannot perform all the interventions necessary to make the desired transformations in the output. The social worker's role in throughput depends on his place in and relationship to the subsystems of the school, which will be discussed later.

4. *Information input, negative feedback, and the coding process.* Information input, communication, and feedback may be regarded as

synonymous. Feedback consists of taking information about the output
of a system and putting it back into the system as new input in order to
help the system reach the desired output. The feedback loop is
illustrated in Figure 1. The open system gets information input or
communication in part through negative feedback or criticism. The
sources of feedback in the school are numerous: students, parents,
teachers, the community, and so on.

In order to determine whether the school is meeting its goals, the
school social worker will want to utilize various sources of data, such
as psychological and intelligence tests, school dropout rates, unemployment rates among youths, data on juvenile delinquency, and data on
physical and mental illness among youths. Attitudinal surveys in the
community and analysis of voting patterns may provide feedback from
the community. These kinds of data will vary in their availability and
degree of applicability for the school social worker. By utilizing feedback based on such data, the social worker avoids the pitfall of over-
generalizing from a few clinical examples. His observations may be
replicated by others, and he is not so subject to his own biases.

5. *Systems as cycles of events*. "The product exported into the
environment furnishes the sources of energy for the repetition of the
cycle of activities." [5] Former students get jobs that provide income
from which they pay taxes to support the schools. They send their
children to school. Some return as employees of the school system.
Collectively they form the community attitudes that influence the school.
It is easy to see that the school social worker's work—as it affects the
students directly or indirectly—will have a cyclical effect on the school.
For example, if one student's attitude toward school is improved
because of the treatment rendered to him or because of modification of
the school system, he may later help to influence the community's
attitude or his own child's attitude, which will come back into the
school system as inputs.

6. *Negative entropy*. Open systems import more energy from their
environment than they expend. Thus they have negative entropy in
that they survive and continue. In contrast, closed systems have insufficient energy coming into them and ultimately move toward disorganization and cessation. Open systems are necessarily interrelated
with their environment in order to import energy. The concept of
negative entropy serves to illustrate the interdependence of the school

---

[5] Katz and Kahn, op. cit., p. 20.

system with other institutions. The school system imports energy from these other sources, just as its output may provide input energy to other systems. The school social worker must be politically sensitive to these connections as he seeks to intervene in certain areas if his efforts are to be accepted and effective.

For example, when a social work program is to be established in a school system, the principals and teachers must first be prepared so that they will accept the social worker in a nondefensive way. This preparation should include an explanation of the role of the social worker in the school and an exploration of educational and social goals with which the schools must deal. The social worker may also meet with the parent-teacher association, the student council, and the faculty, and he may hold collaborative meetings with persons from other agencies. He may further strive to learn about special interest groups in the community: the nature of their influence—whether it is innovative, supportive, or critical—and whether they are related horizontally to other groups in the community or vertically to state and national organizations in terms of their interaction with the schools and his interaction with them.[6] In this manner the social worker strives to maintain the energy input from other sources by attempting to clarify roles and goals and to prevent possible misunderstanding.

7. *The steady state and dynamic homeostasis.*

The importation of energy to arrest entropy operates to maintain some constancy in energy exchange, so that open systems which survive are characterized by a steady state. A steady state is not motionless or a true equilibrium. There is a continuous inflow of energy from the external environment and a continuous export of the products of the system, but the character of the system, the ratio of the energy exchanges and the relations between parts, remains the same. . . . Thus, the steady state which at the simple level is one of homeostasis over time, at more complex levels becomes one of preserving the character of the system through growth and expansion.[7]

The school appears to be in a steady state when a given grade is examined year after year. Yet over the years the public school system has grown from elementary education alone to include secondary and higher education. This characteristic is important for helping the school social worker to determine at what level in the school system

---

[6] Marilyn Gittell and T. Edward Hollander, *Six Urban School Districts* (New York: Frederick A. Praeger, 1968), pp. 255–258.

[7] Katz and Kahn, op. cit., pp. 23–24.

he wishes to intervene. Working with individual students may affect the output in terms of those individuals, but it leaves the overall system relatively unchanged, except as the individuals treated may later affect the system. On the other hand, social work interventions at the school system level may cause the growth and expansion of services, programs, and curricula to meet the school's goals, which ultimately affect many students. The former intervention is important for meeting a student's immediate needs, while the latter addresses itself to meeting long-range needs of many students. Both are necessary and important.

8. *Differentiation.* "Social organizations move toward the multiplication and elaboration of roles with greater specialization of function." [8] One change in the schools has been a greater elaboration of courses with specialists to teach each one. Of special interest to the social worker is the elaboration of roles in the area of pupil personnel services—school social workers, guidance counselors, and school psychologists are involved in meeting students' needs. Traditionally the school social worker has worked with the parents of the student, while guidance counselors have dealt with emotional crises in the school and school psychologists have offered testing and evaluative services. The current trend seems to be toward greater merging of all three disciplines in a team approach.

9. *Equifinality.* The principle of equifinality states that "a system can reach the same final state from differing initial conditions and by a variety of paths." [9] After considering the wide variety of types of schools, teaching methods, and students' abilities, one realizes that the educational process through which a large number of students achieve the same final goal of a high school diploma must be described by this principle. It is also noted that considerable variation exists in the extent to which students are educated and socialized on graduation from high school. One student may be able to acquire considerably more maturity and education than another, depending on the type of inputs he brings with him.

The school social worker would do well to bear the principle of equifinality in mind in order to avoid rigidity with regard to strategies of intervention. He may direct his efforts toward specific segments of the community, the families of the students, various groups in the school system such as teachers or principals, program-planning in the

8 Ibid., p. 25.
9 Ibid.

school system, or he may work specifically with students. Any one or all of these interventions would still be directed at the same ultimate goals of benefiting the students and creating institutional innovations. Thus the principle of equifinality suggests that openness to new ideas and flexibility on the part of the school social worker in using techniques and skills from community organization, group work, and casework will enhance his ability to assist the system in reaching its goals, even when there are differing initial conditions and various methods being used in the schools.

These, then, are the nine characteristics of an open system. In order to clarify his observations of the outstanding features and processes of a system, the social worker may use the basic model of an open system and concentrate on the concepts of input, throughput, output, and feedback. He increases his understanding of the system as a whole and its relationship with its environment by studying the other five characteristics. He then moves toward planning interventive strategies based on his analysis of the system. The social worker's role in these interventions may be clarified by examining the five generic types of subsystems.

The Social Worker in the Subsystems

Thus far systems analysis has been presented as a theoretical orientation through which the social worker may provide some order to his examination of a given system. The systems approach aids in identification and classification of the inputs into a system and in definition of the goals and outputs of that system. Once the social worker begins to understand the overall structure of a complex organization through systems analysis, he needs to consider how he fits into that system. Subsystem analysis is crucial to an understanding of the internal workings of a complex organization. It is in the subsystems that the input is converted into the output. The social worker's role in throughput and his interventive strategies will depend on his place in and relation to the five generic types of subsystems—the production, maintenance, supportive, adaptive, and managerial subsystems.

Considering the scope of the inputs, the school social worker may feel overwhelmed by all the areas of possible intervention. However, if the social worker is clearly identified with a specific subsystem, many of the possible interventions will already be prescribed for him. For example, a social worker in the maintenance subsystem may direct his

interventions basically toward students who are identified as dysfunctional, while a social worker in the adaptive subsystem may work
primarily for institutional innovation. It may be difficult for the
worker to intervene in areas outside his own subsystem, but at least he
can know the relation that his area of work has to the rest of the
school by utilizing subsystem analysis.

If school social work is new to a school system or is in a school system where it may be applied flexibly, then the social worker may
participate in any one, or perhaps several, of the subsystems and can
thereby select from a broad range of possible interventions. He
may analyze the school system to ascertain at what points there are
major problems with the output—such as juvenile delinquency, drug
abuse, a high number of dropouts, or underachievement—and then
select certain inputs with which to intervene. Or he may simply intervene in certain areas in which he feels he has the most to offer.

The school social worker potentially has a role in each of the five
generic subsystems. However, one social worker's expertise probably
would not be simultaneously recognized in all five subsystems. Thus
the school social worker is likely to develop proficiency in a specific
area, but not throughout the entire system.

PRODUCTION SUBSYSTEM "The production subsystem is concerned
with the throughput, the energic or information transformation whose
cycles of activity comprise the major function of the system." [10] In
the school the main part of the production subsystem is the classroom,
where the major function of the school takes place: educating and
socializing students. The school social worker does not normally have
a direct function in the classroom. However, some schools are ex-
perimenting with classes variously titled "successful living," "mental
hygiene," and "emotional skills." Such classes could be taught by
social workers, or social workers could offer the same concepts to all
students in a school by means of extracurricular group experiences.
Thus when social work is viewed as part of the production subsystem,
its function is institutional. It serves the total institution and all the
people in it.

MAINTENANCE SUBSYSTEM On the other hand, when social work's
function is regarded as residual, its services are directed at selected
persons who have been identified as having failed in some way. Social
work as a residual function is part of the maintenance subsystem.

---

[10] Ibid., p. 39.

The maintenance subsystem is concerned with "tying people into their functional roles." [11] School social workers serving as consultants may help define teachers' and principals' functional roles. With regard to the student's role, the teacher has a large responsibility in defining it. However, the school social worker may be of importance when the student is not fulfilling his role adequately. He works with the student by focusing on treatment goals such as improved social relationships, alleviation of emotional stress, socialization to appropriate norms, improved attitudes toward education, and better study habits.

SUPPORTIVE SUBSYSTEM The school social worker would work directly in a school in the production and maintenance subsystems. In the supportive subsystem he would serve more of a boundary function between the school and the administrative offices or other agencies. Supportive subsystems are concerned with the work of the production subsystem in importing materials for it and exporting the finished product into the environment. They are also involved in "maintaining a favorable environment for the operation of the system." [12] The school social worker may work with the student's family or with the community to affect what inputs are brought into the school system; with certain groups of students, such as the Neighborhood Youth Corps, in a coordinating capacity between their school and their job; and with community groups and agencies to link the school and the community. In addition the school social worker has primary responsibility for relating to certain other systems such as the child welfare agency, the mental health center, the vocational rehabilitation agency, and the public health department to focus the services of these agencies on schoolchildren who need their help. Guidance counselors and school social workers aid the student's transition into the environment when he leaves school. The school board serves a boundary function of maintaining favorable relations with other systems in the environment in that it represents a liaison between the professional educators and community control of the schools.

ADAPTIVE SUBSYSTEM The adaptive subsystem ensures "organizational survival in a changing environment." [13] In the schools those who are responsible for research and curriculum development are in the forefront of adapting the school to meet the needs of the changing environment. The school social worker has an important feedback function as

[11] Ibid.
[12] Ibid., p. 40.
[13] Ibid., p. 42.

a part of the adaptive subsystem, since he is often in a position to know the students' and community's criticisms of the school and what studer.: needs are going unmet. He can use his awareness and knowledge to help develop institutional innovations that will meet the pressures for change coming from students and the community.

Since the role of the school social worker in a planning and research capacity is somewhat unusual, it seems pertinent to expand on the possible interventions he may attempt. There are several areas currently of social concern in which the schools have been involved. The schools are seen as a primary area of socialization to prepare students for their future lives. The problem of students dropping out of school before graduation thus becomes a major concern. Social workers have conducted studies to describe the characteristics of malperforming students, thereby identifying a potential dropout population on which the school can focus special programs and services.[14] Another possible intervention is to restructure certain parts of the curriculum so that teaching materials will be more relevant to the potential dropout's life experiences and vocational interests. The social worker may also work to facilitate the reentry of a dropout if he decides to return to school.

It has been pointed out in the general literature that some students might be more appropriately called school "pushouts" rather than dropouts because of the school's policies, attitudes, and actions.[15] The school social worker together with the school administrators may be able to bring about some changes in this area. When the traditional school concept fails to work for some students, the school social worker in the adaptive subsystem can work to develop alternatives such as student-run schools or storefront schools. Thus greater responsibility is placed on the student to define and pursue his own educational goals together with educators, social workers, and other community resources. One experiment of this type was described as humanizing the schools and at the same time it seemed to create opportunities for the students to pursue intellectual challenges.[16]

---

[14] *See,* for example, Robert D. Vinter and Rosemary C. Sarri, "Malperformance in the Public School: A Group Work Approach," in Edwin J. Thomas, ed., *Behavioral Science for Social Workers* (New York: Free Press, 1967).

[15] Two articles that illustrate this point are George H. Weber and Annabelle B. Motz, "School as Perceived by the Droupout," *Journal of Negro Education,* Vol. 37, No. 2 (Spring 1968), pp. 127–134; and Beatrice M. Hill and Nelson S. Burke, "Some Disadvantaged Youths Look at their Schools," *Journal of Negro Education,* Vol. 37, No. 2 (Spring 1968), pp. 135–139.

[16] William K. Stevens, "Oregon High School's Experiment in Free Study," in Neil Postman and Charles Weingartner, eds., *The Soft Revolution* (New York: Dell Publishing Co., 1971), pp. 76–78.

Social workers should also be involved in planning to facilitate school integration. Courses in minority group history and culture need to be offered. Small group experiences to enable person-to-person contact may be planned. Positive leadership is needed from various elements of the community; community meetings and parent groups may be used constructively by social workers.

Another example of the social worker's role in the adaptive subsystem relates to children who have been described as emotionally disturbed, mentally retarded, or educationally disadvantaged. Social workers in the maintenance subsystem may carry on direct treatment with these children and those in the supportive subsystem may deal with their families or with community agencies and institutions; those in the adaptive subsystem may participate in developing innovations within the school to deal with these children in regular classes. For example, behavioral problems of the special student are often the focus of consultation between social workers and teachers. Social workers may be able to suggest techniques based on learning theory and behavior modification. Grouping of children may be accomplished on the basis of the desired learning outputs rather than on the basis of labels derived from input chracteristics.

MANAGERIAL SUBSYSTEM The managerial subsystems "comprise the organized activities for controlling, coordinating, and directing the many subsystems of the structure." [17] There are many managers in the school system: principals, the superintendent and his staff, and the school board. School social workers may work with other managers toward establishing system goals and the responsibility for carrying them out. School social workers may serve a managerial function in directing social work services in the school system.

Since it has been pointed out that social work may have a function in each of the school's subsystems, it may be necessary to have a department of school social work to serve the entire school system in the ways that have been indicated, with a social worker to perform the managerial functions of controlling, coordinating, and directing the department. It is especially important for the social worker in a managerial subsystem to understand the school system in its entirety through systems analysis so that in directing the social work department he can help determine common goals within the school and the more specialized goals on which social workers would focus. As the manager of the social work department, he would set goals with the other social workers and review the results. He could further coordinate the social work

_____
[17] Katz and Kahn, op. cit., p. 42.

program in each of the subsystems to focus on a general concern from several different perspectives. That is to say, the social worker–manager would be involved in determining what the social worker in the school system has to offer and then in developing the strategies for pursuing those goals.

Management is seen as distinct from the activities it manages. Thus another role for the social worker in the managerial subsystem would be to apply group work skills in meetings of educators in which the social worker does not contribute to the content of the meeting but enables the group to function more effectively. Also, as the school system grows and becomes more complex, there may be management problems between or within departments. The organizational structure does not show personalities, yet the work of the system may be hindered by interpersonal problems. As a consultant, the social worker may be able to deal with interpersonal problems without dealing with functional roles as he would in the maintenance subsystem.

Conclusion

Systems theory provides a basic structure for understanding complex organizations. Applying this theory to the schools affords the social work practitioner a more comprehensive view of the system in which he works. Considering the desired output of the schools helps the school social worker to set goals for his work. Awareness of the determiners of the school system aids the social worker in knowing the constraints under which he works. Enumerating the component inputs is important in pinpointing areas of intervention. Analyzing the five subsystems assists in determining the social worker's role in relation to the total system.

No one social work practitioner could make all the interventions in the school system that are suggested in this paper. Using systems analysis, the school social worker may set priorities for his own work by selecting certain inputs to modify or he may delegate areas of responsibility within a school social work department. Traditionally much emphasis has been placed on treatment of individual students and families by school social workers. Increasingly school social workers are engaging in consultation with teachers and principals. An examination of the other inputs from the community, school characteristics and programs, administration, and finances suggests that more attention must be directed toward intervening in the total system to create institutional innovations.

The Mental Health Worker as a Systems Behavioral Engineer

Jerry W. Willis
Joan S. Willis

Critics of American education are charging that it fails to meet the needs of either society or its students. Many students do not learn even the most basic academic skills; others fail to learn the social skills required to live successfully in our complex society.

The mental health field also has its share of critics and reformers. Recent studies show that direct mental health services reach only 2 percent of those schoolchildren who need help.[1] Of those served, only half receive help that is of the kind, quality, and duration they need, and but one child in three seen at a child guidance clinic receives more than diagnostic and referral services.[2] It is obvious that the direct service model cannot meet the needs of even a minority of children with problems. Recognizing this, mental health professionals have in increasing numbers sought involvement with schools, juvenile

The authors would like to thank Erskine Banks, Mrs. Jeane Crowder, Tom Hobbs, Mrs. Doris Klopper, Mrs. Margaret McFerrin, George Park, Mrs. Montriel Pitts, Alethia Porter, Mrs. Karen Robinson, Mrs. Mildred Snipes, Mrs. Frances Todd, and Mrs. Avanelle Weldon for their help in preparing this article.

courts, welfare agencies, public health services, and other mental health agencies. Behind this move to community mental health is the assumption that the social worker, psychiatrist, and psychologist can, by collaborating with care-givers in the community, improve the outcome of efforts to help children with mental health problems.

Three Approaches

A number of approaches to consultation, systems change, or community linkage have been reported in the literature. Most fall into one of three categories depending on their base: (1) psychodynamic, (2) field theory or organizational development, and (3) behavior modification or applied behavioral analysis.

PSYCHODYNAMIC APPROACHES   Berlin describes dynamically based approaches, emphasizing "understanding of the consultee's troubles as being the result of the worker's intrapsychic conflicts, upon which the client's problems and behavior impinge." [3]   Caplan feels that the cornerstone of consultation is maintenance of the unconscious nature of the defensive displacement that "allows the consultant to discuss the theme upsetting the consultee by discussing the client." [4]

One of the most recent applications of this approach, which focuses on the feelings and attitudes of teachers, is Lawrence's Rockland County Project.[5] The goals of this six-year project included helping teachers to become aware of children's hidden feelings, strengths, and needs in addition to the nature of their development and to assist

[1] Nicholas Long, William Morse, and Ruth Newman, eds., *Conflict in the Classroom* (Belmont, Calif.: Wadsworth, 1965), p. vii.

[2] *Mental Health Services for Children,* Public Health Service Publication No. 1844 (Washington, D. C.: National Institute of Mental Health, 1968), p. 1.

[3] *See* I. N. Berlin, "Learning Mental Health Consultation History and Problems," *Mental Hygiene,* Vol. 48, No. 2 (April 1964), p. 258. The quotation is from Berlin, "Mental Health Consultation in Schools as a Means of Communicating Mental Health Principles," *Journal of Child Psychiatry,* Vol. 1, No. 3 (October 1962), pp. 671–679.

[4] Gerald Caplan, *Principles of Preventive Psychiatry* (New York: Basic Books, 1964), p. 244.

[5] *See* Margaret Lawrence, Irene Spanier, and Mildred Dubowy, "An Analysis of the Work of the School Mental Health Unit of a Community Mental Health Board," *American Journal of Orthopsychiatry,* Vol. 32, No. 1 (January 1962), pp. 99–108; Lawrence, *The Mental Health Team in the Schools* (New York: Behavioral Publications, 1971).

teachers in the discovery of their own strengths, feelings, and attitudes and the influence of these on the child's ability to learn.[6] The primary vehicle for changing school practice was the child study. Members of the mental health team observed and tested the child, spoke with school professionals, and then met with the school personnel in a seminar. Although the project has drawn considerable attention, Lawrence, like many of the psychodynamic group, presented no data on its effectiveness.

A similar program reported by Schmuck used staff trained by nationally recognized experts. Schmuck concluded that "cognitive and attitudinal changes did occur in the teachers, but that these were not also accompanied by behavioral changes in the group."[7]

ORGANIZATIONAL APPROACHES Working from a different frame of reference, the staff of the National Training Laboratory (NTL) has developed a systems approach to changing school practice.[8] NTL and its followers focus on an organization (the school system) or a major component (a school) as the unit to be changed. What is changed and the rate of change are determined by members of the organization to be changed "as a result of analysis and diagnosis which they make of their own operations and with the guidance of change agents."[9] Typically encounter group and T-group techniques are used with a major focus on developing flexible and communicative relationships among system members. Often intervention focuses on or includes top-level administrators. The desired outcomes are often not the inauguration of a specific new technique such as team teaching, but the development of better channels of communication, more open administrative styles, and attitudes that encourage innovation and experimentation.

An example is a program described by Williams that used Benne's

[6] Lawrence, Spanier, and Dubowy, op. cit.; Lawrence, op. cit.

[7] Richard Schmuck, "Helping Teachers Improve Classroom Group Processes," *Journal of Applied Behavioral Science,* Vol. 4, No. 4 (October 1968), p. 402.

[8] *See* Goodwin Watson, ed., *Concepts for Social Change* (Washington, D.C.: National Education Association, 1967); Watson, ed., *Change in School Systems* (Washington, D.C.: National Education Association, 1967); Robert Luke and Dorothy Mail, "An Emergent Interuniversity Consortium for Educational Change," *Journal of Applied Behavioral Science,* Vol. 7, No. 2 (April 1971), pp. 194–214.

[9] Paul Buchman, "The Concept of Organization Development, or Self-Renewal, As a Form of Planned Change," in Watson, ed., *Concepts for Social Change,* p. 2.

Problem Profile Technique as a focal point for group meetings.[10] Unfortunately no data were presented on the effectiveness of the program.

Brenner, however, does present some interesting data on a project that used self-directed T-groups to encourage innovation in elementary schoolteachers.[11] Six weekly meetings were held, each with a specific purpose. The first, for example, was designed to "encourage feelings of affiliation and . . . improve members' skills in obtaining data about their colleagues' work. . . ."[12] Succeeding sessions used the T-group experience to encourage innovation, information exchange, and positive contacts among teachers. Brenner found that the T-groups did not develop a norm favoring innovation, that only 33 percent of the teachers were positive about the experience (perhaps because the principals volunteered their school and made after-school attendance of teachers mandatory), and that two months after the program ended teachers "were trying fewer innovations and knew less about colleagues' ideas and innovations than they had before the project began."[13] The data also indicated that schools in which more actual knowledge of new approaches was exchanged in the T-groups had a significantly higher number of innovations introduced by teachers.

BEHAVIORAL APPROACHES Since 1955 over two thousand articles have described applications of a technique called behavior modification or applied behavioral analysis.[14] This technique is now being hotly debated in social work, but it is also one of the few approaches that has received original and scholarly contributions from social work.[15]

[10] Martha Williams, "The Problem Profile Technique in Consultation," *Social Work*, Vol. 16, No. 3 (July 1971), pp. 52–59.

[11] Avis Brenner, "Self Directed T Groups for Elementary Teachers: Impetus for Innovation," *Journal of Applied Behavioral Science*, Vol. 7, No. 3 (July 1971), pp. 327–341.

[12] Ibid., p. 331.

[13] Ibid.

[14] An excellent bibliography of behavior modification has been prepared by Daniel Brown, *A Bibliography of Behavior Modification* (Champaign, Ill.: Research Press, 1972). Also useful are John Shack and L. Walker Barnett, "An Annotated and Cross-Indexed Bibliography of Behavior Modification with Behavior Disorders in Childhood" (Chicago: Loyola University, Child Guidance Center, 1970) (mimeographed); and Carl Insalco and Richard Shea, "Behavior Modification: An Annotated Bibliography 1965–1969" (Columbia: University of South Carolina, 1970) (mimeographed).

[15] See Max Bruck, "Behavior Modification Theory and Practice: A Critical Review," *Social Work*, Vol. 13, No. 2 (April 1968), pp. 43–55; Shirley Krapman,

At the applied level Wadsworth has described the use of behavior modification in school social work.[16] Like most behavior modifiers Wadsworth used charts to measure the effect of treatment programs. Instead of taking children out of the environment in which the problems were occurring, the school social workers taught parents and teachers first to observe and record the target behavior and then to apply specific interventive techniques and observe their effects. Wadsworth reports that a team of social workers and a psychologist were able to train many school professionals and parents. He presents three successful case studies.

A similar training program was described by Willis.[17] Teachers in a ghetto school attended six training sessions on behavior modification principles. They pinpointed observable behaviors about which they were concerned and developed a reward system based on privileges, free time, or tangible rewards for improved behavior. Behavioral data collected over the school year indicated marked improvement.

Using a different approach, Hall and Copeland developed a "Responsive Teaching Model" as a means of changing the ways in which teachers deal with children.[18] Hall points out that workshops and regular college courses on principles of behavior modification often

"Stop Quibbling About Methods," Social Work, Vol. 16, No. 1 (January 1971), pp. 127–128; John Nebo, "School Social Work Report Is Premature," Social Work, Vol. 16, No. 1 (April 1971), pp. 104–107. Contributions to the field by social workers include the following: Richard B. Stuart, "Assessment and Change of the Communication Patterns of Juvenile Delinquents and their Parents," in R. D. Rubin, A. A. Lazarus, and C. M. Franks, eds., Advances in Behavior Therapy (New York: Academic Press, 1969); Eileen Gambrill, Edwin J. Thomas, and Robert Carter, "Procedure for Sociobehavioral Practice in Open Settings," Social Work, Vol. 16, No. 1 (January 1971), pp. 51–62; Robert Carter and Richard B. Stuart, "Behavior Modification Theory and Practice: A Reply," Social Work, Vol. 15, No. 1 (January 1970), pp. 37–50; Edwin J. Thomas, "Selected Sociobehavioral Techniques and Principles: An Approach to Interpersonal Helping," Social Work, Vol. 13, No. 1 (January 1968), pp. 12–26.

[16] H. G. Wadsworth, "Initiating a Preventive-Corrective Approach in an Elementary School System," Social Work, Vol. 15, No. 3 (July 1970), pp. 60–66.

[17] Jerry W. Willis, "School Consultation in an Urban Ghetto School," Mental Hygiene, Vol. 56, No. 1 (January 1972), pp. 31–38.

[18] R. Vance Hall and Rodney Copeland, "The Responsive Teaching Model: A First Step in Shaping School Personnel as Behavior Modification Specialists," in Frank Clark, David Evans, and Leo Hamerlynck, eds., Implementing Behavioral Programs for Schools and Clinics (Champaign, Ill. Research Press, 1972); Hall, "Training Teachers in Classroom Use of Contingency Management," Educational Technology, Vol. 11, No. 4 (April 1971), pp. 33–38; Hall, Marion Panyan, Delores Rabon, and Marcia Broden, "Instructing Beginning Teachers in Reinforcement Procedures Which Improved Classroom Control," Journal of Applied Behavior Analysis, Vol. 1, No. 4 (Winter 1968), pp. 315–322.

appear to be ineffective in changing the actual classroom behavior of teachers. In Hall's Responsive Teaching Model school professionals are taught the principles of behavior modification in groups that preferably comprise all the personnel of a school. Participants receive social praise and attention for planning and implementing behavioral change programs. They also receive three hours of college credit, with 60 percent of their grade based on their behavior modification project. Large group instruction, small group discussion and planning, and supervision in the school by other school professionals who had already taken the course were major components.

ADVANTAGES AND DISADVANTAGES Each of the three approaches described has its strengths and weaknesses. The psychodynamic orientation focuses on motivation for behavior that comes from within. The same observable behavior may be due to quite different reasons in different children, and an understanding of these reasons may help in correcting the problem. The psychodynamic approach, however, has generated little research that supports its tenets. It is difficult to measure feelings or intrapsychic events, and even more difficult to show that changes in these intrapsychic events are correlated with desired behavioral change. Yet the same problems that make research difficult make practice from a psychodynamic point of view difficult. Without objective ways of measuring their target behaviors, psychodynamic practitioners are likely to explain behavior in terms of their previous training.

An additional problem is the length of time required for psychodynamic consultation. Berlin says: "Since the process is an indirect one, it is also often a slow process. The results may not be evident for a long time and perhaps are recognized only in a reduced need for consultation." [19] One of the complaints of school principals concerning the Rockland County Project was that an individual child study might go on for many weeks—making demands on the time of school personnel—and still not provide teachers with any answers.[20]

Concern for involvement of administrators has been a hallmark of the training laboratory movement, which, more than any other approach, has pointed out that a teacher dealing with children in a classroom is behaving within a number of interacting social systems—among them the school, the school system, and the community. Each of these

---

[19] "Learning Mental Health Consultation History and Problems," p. 259.
[20] Lawrence, op. cit., p. 152.

systems influences and interacts with the others and helps to determine the behavior of system members.

Training laboratories tend, however, to focus primarily on attitudinal change and changes in relationships among system members. But a change in attitudes does not necessarily lead to a change in behavior. Haefner and Kirscht described a program to change attitudes toward health practices.[21] In an eight-month follow-up they found significant changes in attitudes but no actual behavioral changes in established patterns of behavior such as eating habits and exercise.

An ambitious study by Schmuck is an encouraging move by the training laboratory group.[22] Schmuck describes perhaps the most comprehensive approach to systems change reported in the literature. His "teacher development laboratory" had seven major training activities: (1) sensitivity training, (2) teaching research related to classroom behavior, (3) teaching classroom problem-solving techniques, (4) data-collection and analysis from the teacher's own classroom, (5) group discussions of techniques by teachers, (6) role-playing and practice of proposed changes, and (7) follow-up discussions during the school year. Schmuck presents a variety of data that show the laboratory was effective.

The third approach, behavior modification, has as its strongest point a research emphasis that insists on the accumulation of objective data on the effect of any intervention. Behavior modifiers also avoid wholesale labeling of children and the prescription of standard programs of remediation or treatment. Each case is a study in its own right. What has worked with one emotionally disturbed child may actually be detrimental to the next. However, behavior modifiers sometimes ignore the total environment so emphasized by the training laboratory group. The success or failure of work with an individual teacher may hinge on the administrative style of the principal, community response to the new project, or parental reactions. Almost all human behavior is multiply determined, and neglecting any of the many determiners of behavior may lead to failure.

Another problem sometimes seen in the application of behavior modification is a tendency to set up the programs in a mechanistic, autocratic manner. Carkhuff, commenting on the need to develop viable relationships between counselor and client, says: "An effective

---

[21] D. P. Haefner and J. P. Kirscht, "Motivational and Behavioral Effects of Modifying Health Beliefs," *Public Health Reports*, Vol. 85, No. 6 (August 1970), pp. 478–484.

[22] Op. cit.

relationship establishes the counselor as a potent reinforcer for the client so that the counselor may involve the client in programs that will influence the client constructively." [23] The change agent would also do well to consider what other rewards are available for the school professional as well as for the child. Rewards and support must be available to the innovators. One study of the effect of a comprehensive supervisory training program in a large company showed that those who participated were actually less effective than those who had not received the training because the principles they learned were incompatible with the expectations of their superiors.[24]

An additional criticism that has been leveled at mental health practitioners from all theoretical camps is that they are untrained and unprepared for community- or school-oriented work. Commenting on recruiting for an Arizona project, Libo says:

> Of the social workers and psychologists, too many, unfortunately, had no conception of prevention, consultation, community organization, or interagency coordination. They were familiar and comfortable only with diagnosis and/or treatment in a highly structured setting. Such "conservatism" was particularly strong in women.[25]

The combination of training for a wide range of target populations from casework with individuals to group work to community organization provides the social worker with potentially the broadest spectrum of skills available in the mental health field. Unfortunately, the current social work literature points to the conclusion that few social workers actually use this broad range of skills. Instead they concentrate on one area such as casework or community organization.

The Birmingham Model

This paper describes a school-focused community mental health project, the Birmingham School Consultation Project (BSCP). Funded by a grant from the Alabama State Department of Mental Health and the Jefferson County Department of Public Health, BSCP has a yearly

[23] Robert Carkhuff, "Training As a Preferred Mode of Treatment," *Journal of Counseling Psychology*, Vol. 18, No. 2 (March 1971), p. 129.

[24] E. A. Fleishman, "Leadership and Supervision in Industry: An Evaluation of a Supervisory Training Program" (Columbus, Ohio: Bureau of Educational Research, Ohio State University, 1955). (Mimeographed.)

[25] Lester Libo, "Multiple Functions for Psychologists in Community Consultation," *American Psychologist*, Vol. 21, No. 6 (June 1966), p. 533.

budget of about $30,000, a full-time director, two full-time parapro-
fessionals, and the opportunity to involve staff members of its parent
community mental health center (four social workers, three psychologists, a nurse, pharmacist, and psychiatrist) in community projects.

Before the project began the center was providing direct services
to children, with schools as the major source of referrals. Children
were processed through a typical intake and evaluation pattern. Contact
with school personnel, except through formal reports, was minimal.
Early in the planning for BSCP it was decided that a consultation and
linkage model would be used. Staff time would be spent primarily
with community care-givers and training, consultation, and planning of
cooperative ventures would be emphasized.

After considerable planning and discussion with school officials,
four schools in the two major Birmingham area school systems were
selected as target schools. Principals volunteered their schools and
it was understood that teacher and counselor participation would also
be voluntary. Mental health professionals were to spend days at
individual schools on a regularly scheduled basis. No concrete plans
for the use of the day were made in advance. Instead, through
faculty meetings and informal meetings with school staff, the program
model was explained.

Whenever any school professional recognized a problem for which
there was no resource within the school system, a referral could be
made to BSCP. The only additional requirement for referral was that
a school professional be willing either to carry out the intervention
program or to serve as a co-worker with the goal of becoming competent to set up a similar program independently in the future. In
return BSCP agreed to provide continuing and regular support to the
school professional and to help provide him with whatever equipment
and material were needed.

BSCP did not attempt to specify the type of relationship its staff
developed with schools. In some cases schools seemed ready only for
one-to-one contact on specific problems. Others soon asked for help
in developing more ambitious efforts to change school-wide practices
that involved many teachers. The problems referred by teachers
ranged from a shy child in the first grade to a group of underachieving,
disruptive junior high school students. Counselors asked for help with
individual children, groups of children, and parents and to find ways
of consulting with classroom teachers. Principals also referred problem children and in some cases asked for help in planning and

implementing school-wide change efforts. In addition, regular contact with central office school administrators brought requests for help in system-wide change efforts. Examples of BSCP projects will be given later.

BASIC ASSUMPTIONS Each effort was characterized by a number of basic assumptions. While these assumptions have a distinct learning theory base, they reflect influences from other theories as well.

1. *A focus on observable behavior in the natural setting.* Few will deny that unobservable internal events influence overt behavior. However, the tremendous amount of research generated by behavior modifiers indicates that changes in overt behavior can occur without a focus on internal change first and may even bring about greater change.[26] In addition, focusing on observable, measurable behavior allows the change agent and care-giver to collect objective data on the effect of interventive techniques.

2. *A two-stage model of change.* Any effort to change a system or one of its components generates many responses within the system. These may be viewed as respondent or operant behavior. Respondent behavior is elicited by stimuli that come before the response. Suggested changes, especially if they originate from outside the system, may arouse anxiety (respondent behavior) in system members. Emotions such as anxiety may hamper change efforts in two ways: (*a*) They may prevent a school professional from trying a new technique because of the anxiety its arouses. (*b*) In addition, if a sufficient amount of anxiety and feeling of threat is aroused by the change agent, school professionals may act to reduce anxiety—the easiest way to do this is to eliminate the source. At the beginning of the Rockland County project described previously, school officials expressed concern about the presence of an outside agency in the school, felt that this implied the schools were not doing their job, and were afraid that the problems of one school system would . be shared with others. When local school officials sought reassurance at the state level, the psychology section of the state department of education expressed anger over the perceived invasion of their territory.

---

[26] S. A. Batrawi, "The Differential Effects of Two Therapeutic Techniques on Selected Aspects of Client Behavior," unpublished doctoral dissertation, George Washington University, 1964; E. L. Phillips, "Parent-Child Psychotherapy: A Follow-Up Study Comparing Two Techniques," *Journal of Psychology*, Vol. 49, No. 2 (April 1960), pp. 195–202; Larry Greiner, "Antecedents of Planned Organization Change," *Journal of Applied Behavioral Science*, Vol. 3, No. 1 (January 1967), pp. 51–85.

Emotional responses to change efforts are often ignored by change agents, especially behavior modifiers. Even the laboratory training approach has been criticized because a trainer "frequently overlooks the historical preconditions which may determine the success or failure of such programs." [27]

Working with individual cases, behavior modifiers have developed a systematic procedure for dealing with respondent behavior.[28] Termed systematic desensitization, this procedure consists of associating a pleasant, relaxed state with gradually increasing degrees of the anxiety-producing stimulus. The ability of the stimulus to elicit anxiety gradually diminishes. In practice desensitization can be similar to the first stage of Lippitt's change process—sensitivity training "to create openness to seek, receive, and use nondefensively data about one's own performance. . . ." [29] Both appear designed to reduce emotional responses that interfere with further work. They may be especially useful when proposed changes appear to violate moral codes or long-established local practice.

Early in any change effort it may be necessary to develop *in vivo* desensitization procedures for system members. Regular, positive experiences with the social worker, encounter groups, positive workshop or in-service training experiences, positive recommendations from other systems, even the successful provision of direct services may help to eliminate negative emotional responses from system members. Once this has been accomplished, work with operant responses can proceed more effectively. Operant responses are controlled by stimuli that follow them. Most of man's behavior is operantly determined. If a response brings desirable changes, it will be repeated; if neutral or negative consequences occur, the probability of a repetition of the behavior decreases. Change efforts in school systems must take into consideration the probable consequences when teachers, counselors, and administrators change their behavior.

A teacher who departs from a lesson plan to meet individual needs may receive a feeling of satisfaction (positive reinforcement) if he is successful, but this departure may involve increased preparation time and some tedious work (negative reinforcement). The success of the

---

[27] Greiner, op. cit., p. 51.

[28] *See* Joseph Wolpe, *The Practice of Behavior Therapy* (New York: Pergamon Press, 1969).

[29] Ronald Lippitt, "The Use of Social Research to Improve Social Practice," in Watson, ed., *Concepts for Social Change*, p. 79.

effort may not be immediately evident (extinction). And even if the teacher's efforts are successful, he may be criticized by his principal because he is not following the prescribed instructional program (negative reinforcement) and by other teachers who do not agree with the new approach (negative reinforcement). If the teacher has previously attempted change efforts that have resulted in large amounts of negative reinforcement, he may refuse to attempt further changes (extinction).

Thus in the initial stages of change efforts considerable attention must be paid to the reinforcement given to those involved. Rewards such as social recognition (praise, a complimentary letter to superiors, positive publicity), a new position in the system, money (stipends for training), academic credit, or symbolic recognition (a certificate for participating in the program successfully) are all rewards that can be used to maintain new behavior until the natural rewards of a smoothly running, successful program take over.

3. *Focus on technique training.* It is obvious from the programs reviewed that the change process may be approached from many different angles. A change agent may try to help the consultee with unconscious feelings that interfere with his work; he may help members of the target system to communicate with each other, understand each other better, and feel freer to try out new approaches; or he may focus on training the target group in specific skills to handle specific problems. The question of which approach produces the greatest effect is an empirical one. In a review of "training as a preferred mode of treatment" Carkhuff has made an excellent case for using a systematic, planned approach to training target groups.[30] Considering the research evidence available to date, training approaches that pinpoint specific target behavior to be changed, develop systematic training programs, and collect objective data on their effect appear to be the most efficient means of changing behavior.

4. *Focus on rapid development of interventions to handle specific problems.* When a problem was referred, BSCP staff attempted to provide assistance in developing intervention plans quickly. Psychological examinations or other time-consuming diagnostic procedures that did not lead directly to specific behavioral recommendations were rarely used.

5. *A "filtering-up" rather than a "filtering-down" approach.* Changing a school system can begin at the top. Work with the superintendent

---

[30] Op. cit.

may convince him that an innovation is useful; he can sell his assistant superintendents; they can sell the principals, who then sell their teachers. BSCP took an alternative approach. Teachers and counselors who actually worked with children every day were trained in innovative approaches on the assumption that if these approaches were effective they would filter up through the system. In addition, the tendency for the more innovative and successful teachers to be promoted to administrative and supervisory positions also facilitates the filtering-up process. This does not mean that administrators and supervisors were ignored, however. Without consistent contact with administrators and clear feedback concerning change efforts, projects may be brought to a premature end by system administrators who are unfamiliar with what is happening. Indeed, because of his experience, training, and knowledge of the local situations, the administrator may often be a great asset to change efforts. If he supports them wholeheartedly, another source of reward and attention is provided for the teacher and counselor.

CHANGE EFFORT STEPS Gradually BSCP has developed a systematic series of steps in change efforts that are similar to a sequence developed by Gambrill, Thomas, and Carter at the University of Michigan School of Social Work.[31]

1. *Dealing with respondent behavior.* For those directly involved this is the initial step. For those not involved directly, but in positions that influence the outcome of change efforts, this step may continue over the course of the change sequence. Principals, for example, should always be aware of the work going on in their schools. Lack of communication may elicit suspicion that leads to lack of support.

2. *Cooperative problem identification.* The mental health staff and the school professional identify the problem of concern.

3. *Commitment.* Both sides must agree to regular—at least weekly —contact and to the work required to develop and implement changes.

4. *Pinpointing target behavior and identifying probable controlling conditions.* A specific, measurable behavior is selected and the environmental conditions controlling it (setting events, eliciting stimuli, and reinforcing stimuli) are tentatively identified, often through the use of classroom observation and anecdotal records taken by teachers, counselors, or parents.

5. *Base line.* Preintervention data are collected on the pinpointed behavior.

---

[31] Op. cit.

6. *Planning the intervention.* A behavioral goal is established; available managers, usable techniques, and potential reinforcers are considered and a behavioral change program developed. If necessary, school professionals are trained in behavioral change techniques.

7. *Implementation.* The change plan is implemented, data-collection continues, and if necessary the plan is modified as feedback is received.

8. *Fading to natural conditions and follow-up.* The change techniques are withdrawn as the natural environment gains control of the behavior, or the technique may become an accepted part of the regular environment. Regular checks are made to determine whether the behavioral change persists.

9. *Independent development of behavioral change programs.* Once the school professional gains experience, he is expected to function independently of the mental health professional when future problems of a similar nature arise.

In practice this sequence was not always followed, but the general progression will be obvious in the examples that follow. In some cases a full description of each step was omitted to conserve space. The examples were chosen to illustrate the wide range of involvement of the project staff.

PRACTICE EXAMPLES *One teacher—one student.* A third-grade teacher referred one of her students who "would just sit for hours without doing anything except staring into space." Attempts to get him to work had included verbal criticism and not permitting him to take a break. He often worked only when the teacher stood by his desk. The teacher agreed to carry out a behavior modification project and to evaluate the success of her efforts and chose to collect data on mathematics problems done correctly. Base-line data, taken before the behavior modification program was initiated, showed that the child averaged only one correct problem every ten minutes. The teacher read a text on classroom behavior modification and, after conferring with a member of the project staff, developed and implemented a behavioral change plan. Basically this involved paying attention to the student only after he had been working for a short period of time, allowing him to earn an extra break by acceptably completing work, and giving a generous amount of praise for successful work. The rate of correct problems increased dramatically. During the final week of data-collection the opportunity to earn an extra break was dropped while praise for completed work continued. The pinpointed behavior was maintained at an acceptable rate and formal data-collection was discontinued.

One counselor—group of children. The counselor in one of the target schools expressed an interest in helping a group of children who were disabled readers. In cooperation with the project staff she developed and undertook a remedial reading program for ten disabled readers in the fourth grade.[32] Eighth-grade student volunteers, who received about two hours of training as behavioral engineers, worked with the fourth-graders thirty minutes each day. The pinpointed behavior was reading sentences of five or more words correctly.

Each student was given a ten-minute reading test by the counselor and then presented with "high interest—low vocabulary reading material" especially selected for him. The volunteers were trained through modeling and role-playing to reward successful reading with praise and attention and to correct errors with a minimum of negative interchange. In addition, the reader received a green plastic chip each time he read a sentence correctly and a red chip for sentences with errors. At the end of each daily session the children counted and charted their green and red chips and again were praised for success. The charts were also used to reassign students to more or less difficult material when their rates of response showed that their assigned material was inappropriate. The volunteers showed unusual enthusiasm for their work. They too were regularly given praise and attention for good work and after several weeks received gold pins.

The results were dramatic. In seventy-five days of training the mean reading gain was 1.3 academic years. Through use of a simple procedure to test the significance of single-group applied research results described by Libau, Berres, and Coleman, the gains were shown to be significant at the .001 level.[33]

Several teachers—several children. Two sisters in the first and second grades were referred because of excessive absences. Linda was absent forty-one days during the first five months of the school year, and Mary had thirty-eight absences for the same period of time. A

[32] A more detailed description of this project may be found in Jerry W. Willis, Betty Morris, and Jeane Crowder, "A Remedial Reading Technique for Disabled Readers Using Students As Behavioral Engineers," *Psychology in the Schools,* Vol. 9, No. 1 (January 1972), pp. 67–70.

[33] Frieda Libau, Frances Berres, and James Coleman, "A New Method For Evaluating the Effectiveness of Treatment of Learning Difficulties," *Journal of Educational Research,* Vol. 55, No. 10 (August 1962), pp. 582–584.

school social worker had made many contacts with older children in this family for the same problem. Since school attendance was not rewarded in the home environment, a plan to increase the girls' school attendance was devised to be implemented in the school setting. Tangible rewards paired with social praise were used to motivate the girls.

During Phase 1 of the treatment plan, which lasted approximately eight weeks, the social worker made weekly contact with Linda and Mary to establish rapport and urge them to attend school. If the girls had been present for a complete week (except for verified illnesses), they earned a surprise on Friday such as candy, ice cream, or school supplies. Mary's monthly school attendance increased from 50 percent during the base line to over 90 percent during this first phase. Linda's improvement was similar.

For the next four weeks (Phase 2) verbal contracts were made with the girls and they were allowed to choose their own rewards (coloring books, sunglasses, slates). In the event the girls had unexcused absences during the week, smaller rewards were also decided on (candy, chewing gum, and the like).

As the school year drew to a close, Phase 3 was put into operation for three weeks. In order to fade the reinforcers back into the natural environment (the classroom), the teachers rewarded their entire classes with candy when Linda and Mary were present for a week. At this point peer approval and attention became a motivating factor. During the last two phases attendance remained above 90 percent.

This behavior modification program was highly successful in increasing school attendance. Linda and Mary were definitely motivated by small tangible rewards as well as by the praise and attention they received from the social worker, teachers, a reading specialist, and their peers.

Parental involvement. BSCP staff members served as consultants to an innovative Title I reading program in the Jefferson County School System. Children in the first three grades who were considered potential school failures were selected for intensive help. Parental involvement was achieved through child-management groups. In six county schools parents' groups were conducted for four weeks by two school social workers. The primary goal of these meetings was to teach specific techniques of handling problems with children. Approximately one hundred parents attended the group meetings. Techniques that proved effective in involving parents in the meetings included small group discussions and role-playing.

Parents were requested to pinpoint a specific problem of one of their children, observe and count this behavior, and attempt to implement change by systematic use of rewards. Rewards received by the parents included the opportunity for social interchange with other parents, refreshments, praise from group leaders for completing the steps to change a specific behavior, and certificates from the Board of Education signifying attendance at all four meetings.

A twenty-four-item test covering principles of child management was used as a pre- and post-test in three of the groups. The test was part of a cooperative research effort of the project, the school system, and the University of Alabama School of Nursing. A senior nursing student was a co-leader for one of the parents' groups to enable her to learn how to carry out similar groups on her own. Compared to a control group that received no training, the child-management group had a significantly higher gain ($p<.001$) using a Mann-Whitney U-test.

A more structured approach was taken to motivate active participation by the parents at the last series of meetings. Presentation of the certificates was based on points accumulated by attending meetings, reading designated text assignments, and counting pinpointed behavior each week. Other rewards were offered in the form of door prizes at each meeting and a large prize was earned by the person with the highest number of points. A more structured approach in the group meetings appeared to produce more intense involvement by the parents; a larger number carried out projects and a much larger percentage of the group received certificates.

An example of a behavior modification project by a parent in a child-management group is the case of a girl—Donna—who was taking as long as an hour to get dressed in the mornings. Her mother chose to try to decrease the time it took Donna to get ready for school. After a six-day base line, Donna was placed on a system whereby she earned points that could be exchanged for desirable items such as toys and clothing. During the first week of treatment Donna received specified points each day she dressed within forty-five minutes; during the second week points were awarded if she was dressed within thirty minutes. This plan proved effective.

Home-school behavioral change programs. Tommy, a second-grader, was described as "emotionally disturbed," "socially maladjusted," and "hyperactive." He rarely did his work and often disrupted the class by making noise and crawling on the floor. Episodes of stealing were frequent. Before referring him to the counselor, the teacher and her aide had decided to give him great amounts of attention noncontingently. They reported that this was ineffective. Project staff observed in the classroom and asked the teacher to take anecdotal records of disruptive events. The school counselor and a staff member saw the mother together and by collaborating with the teacher, counselor and parent developed a behavioral change plan.

Tommy's teacher, using an ordinary kitchen timer, would set it for short intervals at first and then for longer ones. If Tommy had been working acceptably when the bell rang, he was given a plastic token and praised. Initially the bell was used for about thirty minutes of the day and it rang approximately every three minutes. Gradually the period it covered was extended and the intervals between rings were lengthened. The teacher was instructed to ignore disruptive events if possible and to praise improved behavior and work habits. At home Tommy's tokens could be used to purchase time to play or watch television. In Tommy's case one token was worth ten minutes of time, and he could earn a total of twenty each day. If he earned sixty in a week, he was allowed to select an inexpensive toy on Saturday.

The first three weeks of data-collection indicated that Tommy's behavior had improved considerably, and the operation of the program was turned over to the counselor and teacher. Follow-up inquiries during the next four months indicated that the system was still being used and was effective.

Many teachers—many children. After a number of contacts with the University of Alabama in Birmingham, the project developed a three-semester-hour course for teachers in classroom behavioral change. Teachers could receive either graduate or undergraduate credit for the course. The class was similar to the one described by Hall and Copeland.[34] Half the student's grade was based on a behavioral change project. The ratio of staff time invested to results in terms of completed projects indicated that the course was the most efficient staff activity. The group interchange that occurred as each person described and planned his project was highly beneficial.

An example of a project from the class is the case of a disruptive 17-year-old high school dropout attending a remedial education class of the Neighborhood Youth Corps. He rarely finished assignments. The behavior pinpointed was the number of sentences he wrote legibly.

---

[34] Op. cit.

The behavioral change plan involved allowing the student to leave five minutes earlier for every twenty sentences he wrote that a classmate could read. Although this actually decreased the time available for work, the number of sentences written legibly increased remarkably. When the contingency was dropped (reversal), the behavior decreased also; when the contingency was reinstated, the number of legible sentences increased again.

External classroom involvement. In some instances the behavior pinpointed seemed so resistant to change that the initial steps of the change effort were done in artificial settings. Such was the case with a shy first-grade boy—John—who during the preintervention observations did not interact with peers in his classroom at all. John did not play with other children, rarely spoke with them, and mumbled when reading. He would answer a question if asked directly, but rarely made spontaneous verbal comments. His mother reported that his father had behaved the same way as a child.

The initial stage of the behavioral change plan involved bringing John and another classmate to the counselor's office to play a "game." The counselor explained that the idea was for John and the classmate to talk to each other. She set a kitchen timer for a short interval and if in that interval John had talked to his classmate *both* children received a plastic chip and praise. When they earned three chips they could spend them on ice cream or a trinket provided by John's mother, who cooperated in the project. In addition, if John reached a set weekly goal, he was permitted to watch a preferred television program on Sunday night.

The counselor reported that the effect of this project was "the most amazing thing I have seen since I have been teaching." John almost immediately began talking in the game sessions, and his teacher reported that he soon began talking in class as well. After John was allowed to choose a different classmate each day to play the game with him, his social status also improved. Systematic plans to facilitate generalization to the classroom were not necessary, and a follow-up classroom observation showed six verbal interactions in thirty minutes.

This case had other effects as well. The principal of the school was favorably impressed with the results and subsequently asked members of the project staff to help teachers develop a new approach to primary education in the school. Teachers were given released time to attend group sessions. The result of the group meetings, which used both training laboratory and learning theory principles, was a plan of team teaching and individualized instruction that included a number of innovative mental health practices.

Failures. Two examples of projects that must be considered failures will be presented. The first case was that of a disruptive first-grade boy. Daily fifteen-minute observations by the counselor indicated that the boy—Tim—spent no time in his seat and rarely paid attention to tasks set. After conferring with the project staff, the counselor decided to work on the behavior in an artificial setting outside the classroom first and then ask the teacher to use similar techniques in the classroom.

The intervention developed consisted of a biweekly thirty-minute training session. Tim spent the time working with enjoyable materials such as clay, puzzles, and parquetry blocks. He was permitted to invite a different friend to come each time. When a kitchen timer set at variable intervals rang, each of the children received a token if they (1) had remained seated and (2) were working with the assigned material. Each could earn a maximum of ten tokens per session. If a child earned five or more, he could choose from a variety of trinkets supplied by parents. If he earned ten tokens for the week, Tim was also rewarded at home by being allowed to stay up late and watch a favorite television show. After two weeks the number of tokens required for a reward was increased to seven for a trinket and fifteen for a television show. At the end of twelve sessions (six weeks), Tim was in his seat and attending to the task 100 percent of the time.

After six weeks the counselor attempted to begin a generalization program in the classroom with either Tim's teacher or the teacher's aide managing the program. The teacher refused to permit this, and follow-up observations showed that Tim's behavior in the classroom was again at base-line levels. He rarely paid attention or worked on assignments. Perhaps the most obvious problem in this case was the failure of members of the mental health team to familiarize the teacher with what was being done and to obtain a commitment to participate.

The work of the project was successful in three of the four target schools. Work in one school, however, must be considered a failure. The principal and staff were initially enthusiastic, but problems quickly arose. The first major problem was related to the presence of paraprofessionals in the classroom. After a first-grade teacher requested help in dealing with a number of children who had behavioral problems and moderate-to-severe deficits in social, language, and readiness skills, the mental health team proposed a comprehensive remedial and preventive program that included language stimulation, fine motor training, and behavior modification procedures. The project agreed to provide the equipment needed and a full-time paraprofessional to do the work. The teacher initially agreed to provide overall supervision and to become generally familiar with the new program. Soon afterward, however, she complained to the principal that learning about the new material would be too time consuming and that another person working in her classroom would be disruptive. The principal supported her, saying she had never allowed a student teacher in her classroom when she taught because she preferred to work alone.

As the year progressed the staff experienced continuing difficulty in getting into regular classrooms and in obtaining the participation of teachers. Teachers were reluctant to try anything new, sometimes because they were afraid the principal would disapprove. The principal's primary concern was with obtaining direct services for children she considered disturbed. Gradually the mental health team began to avoid the school, using that school's scheduled day, for example, to prepare a grant proposal, attend state meetings, or write research reports. Any chance of improving communication was thus lost. End-of-year evaluations by the project staff and the principal were mutually negative.

Summary and Overall Evaluation

At the end of the school year school professionals were asked to complete an anonymous evaluation of the project. The evaluations were quite positive. For example, 94 percent of those who returned questionnaires felt the project was "more useful than regular clinic services for children where they are referred to one of the local agencies."

The attitudes of the school professionals as well as the objective data collected indicate that the approach used in Birmingham is one effective means of changing the behavior of school systems. Before adapting the model to another setting, a mental health worker should be familiar with behavior modification principles and techniques, understand the basic concepts of the training laboratory approach, and, if possible, have some experience in using these techniques in school settings.

Some professionals may raise objections to this program, such as that it treats human beings as objects, manipulates teachers, and does not allow people to develop freedom of choice. As Kelman puts it:

The practitioner must remain alert to the possibility that he is imposing his own values on the client, that in the course of helping the client he is actually shaping his behavior in directions that he—the practitioner—has set for him.[35]

The present writers take the position that any change effort is a behavior-shaping process.   Change efforts by nondirective change agents lead to proposed alterations that are in accord with the agent's philosophy.   Groups run by behavior modifiers do not initiate psychoanalytic counseling as a solution to problems.   As Kelman says:

> The therapist cannot avoid introducing his own values into the therapeutic process. He cannot be helpful to the patient unless he deliberately tries to influence him in the direction of abandoning some behaviors and trying others.[36]

The staff of BSCP worked with this premise in mind.   However, it should be pointed out that teachers and counselors were given a valuable tool with which to evaluate their work.   If the daily behavioral data gathered on a project showed it was ineffective, the evidence was immediately available.   In a comprehensive NIMH review of mental health consultation to programs for children, the authors concluded:

> The need for systematic evaluation of every phase of mental health consultation is mentioned in almost every paper written in the field.   Without exception, these authorities place this need at the top of a list of priorities, before the need for more personnel or more facilities and even ahead of more training.   In spite of this, a search of the relevant literature reveals no research of sufficient exactitude to permit replication.[37]

An additional criticism often heard is that behavioral change procedures are mechanistic, that they do not include essential "tender loving care."   Scenes like an excited eighth-grader enthusiastically praising a beaming fourth-grader who is probably receiving more positive attention than in all of his previous school life, or a smiling teacher tenderly hugging a boy who has begun a tantrum and then checked himself, convinced the authors that the approach need not be mechanistic—that as Meacham has said, one can have "humanistic behaviorism." [38]

[35] Herbert Kelman, "Manipulation of Human Behavior: An Ethical Dilemma for the Social Scientist," in Warren Bennis, Kenneth Benne, and Robert Chin, eds., *The Planning of Change* (New York: Holt, Rinehart & Winston, 1969), p. 587.

[36] Ibid.

[37] Franklin McClung and Alastair Stunden, *Mental Health Consultation To Programs For Children,* Public Health Service Publication No. 2066 (Chevy Chase, Md.: National Institute of Mental Health, 1970), p. 20.

[38] Merle Meacham and Allen Wiesen, *Changing Classroom Behavior: A Manual for Precision Teaching* (Scranton, Pa.: International Textbook Co., 1969), p. v.

Changing
School-Community
Relations

Betty Deshler
John L. Erlich

A child cannot be educated adequately unless all the forces that act upon that child are considered. Taylor has referred to the "whole child" in discussing "education as a total process, in which the conditions of society deeply affect the child's mind, the level of his achievement, and the range of his possibilities." [1] Without substantial community support and involvement there is no "whole child" to educate. Hence the Great Cities Project—a four-year, Ford Foundation-sponsored project in the Detroit public schools—developed the role of school-community agent as a new and extended link between school and community, a catalyst for innovations, and an initiator of interchange.

Historical Development

In an effort to consider innovative approaches to improving the relationship of school and community, this paper will examine the ex-

---

[1] Harold Taylor, "The Whole Child: A Fresh Look," *Saturday Review,* December 10, 1961, p. 31.

periences of the school-community agent program in a large urban setting, Detroit, Michigan. To understand the role of school-community agent, its evolution in the Detroit public schools must be traced and then the functioning of the agent must be examined, with the aid of a conceptual model developed out of the experiences of agents themselves.

In the 1959–60 school year, Detroit conducted a pilot program in three inner-city schools (two elementary, one junior high) to test some new approaches to educating the disadvantaged child. It had been clearly demonstrated that children coming from the city's ghettos were falling by the educational wayside.[2] For example, the median reading scores of eighth-grade students in inner-city areas were four years behind those of children in other parts of the city. The proportion of culturally deprived students in the schools was rapidly rising; in 1960 it was estimated that every third child was disadvantaged. Attendance department figures for 1959–60 show that in the areas of absenteeism, truancy, voluntary dropout, juvenile offenses, and the like the inner city led all other areas of Detroit.[3]

The unsatisfactory (if not overtly hostile) relations between the school and the community it served were chosen as one critical area for intervention. An individual on the staff of each school was selected to function in a liaison capacity between school and community and was designated a community coordinator. Initially the basic criteria used in the selection of this person were a gregarious personality and demonstrated rapport with parents in the school community. The major interventive device used by the initial coordinators was to set up activities in the school building after regular school hours, with specific emphasis on adult education classes. This was the beginning of the community-school program.

On the basis of the results of that first experimental year, staff of the Detroit public schools went to the Ford Foundation in 1960 with a program proposal designed to strengthen this community-oriented approach. The foundation agreed to support a program expanded to seven inner-city schools for a four-year period. This launched the Great Cities Project, and the term school-community agent replaced community coordinator as the designation of the professional person assigned to each school in the community liaison role. It was also

---

[2] Carl L. Marburger, "Considerations for Educational Planning," in A. Harry Passow, ed., *Education in Depressed Areas* (New York: Teachers College, Columbia University, 1964), pp. 303–321.

[3] "1959–60 Statistical Report" (Detroit: Department of Attendance, Detroit Public Schools, 1960). (Mimeographed.)

decided that recruitment for these positions should not be conducted among the professional staff of the school system. This was done not only because it was felt that people trained in other disciplines, such as social work, might be better equipped for the job, but also because good teachers were in such short supply that the purposes of the project would be undermined if personnel were "stolen" from the classroom.

In the 1960–61 school year seven school-community agents, each assigned to one of the seven schools in the project, were hired as professional noncertified employees of the Board of Education. There was no job description or precedent; all agents were relatively free to develop the role as they determined. In keeping with the overall purposes of the Great Cities Project, the enhancement of the school's educational objectives was considered a primary goal by each agent. Agents were charged to build a durable connection between school and community. At the same time a healthy recognition was emerging—on a system-wide basis—of the need to involve the community in educational processes and the corresponding value of involving the school staff in the daily life of the community.

By late 1961 it was decided that the secondary schools in the project should have two agents because of the much larger geographic area to be served and three additions to the staff were made, bringing the total number of school-community agents to ten. For the next three years each agent operated as an entrepreneur, developing and expanding his role within the limitations imposed by the school to which he was posted —its administrator, teachers, school social workers, and the like—and the surrounding community.

When Ford Foundation financing terminated in 1964, the Economic Opportunity Act provided a new, broader source of support. Through Title IIA (Community Action) of the act, the Board of Education was able to get funding for an expansion of the Great Cities Project to twenty additional schools, with school-community agents as part of the educational package. A coordinator of agents was added to the project staff to provide supervision, program planning, and administrative leadership. Fifty-one more schools were introduced to the community school concept, also with OEO assistance, by being designated as extended schools. The term extended school indicated the establishment of special services in each school. These included one or more of the following after-school activities:

1. Special remedial help
2. Extended use of the school library

3. Adult education programs
4. Accelerated volunteer projects
5. Activities run by community agencies
6. Use of the school as a subcenter for the antipoverty program
7. Meetings of local organizations

The Great Cities Project had many other facets besides its community orientation. The project added a full-time specialist in remedial reading in some schools and attempted to extend school social work services. Other important programs included in-service training for teachers, special field trips, provision of additional money for supplies and equipment, and collaborative projects with a number of social agencies. Further expansion was made possible in 1966 through Title I of the Elementary and Secondary Education Act. The extended program grew by approximately one hundred schools, and six more schools were able to take on school-community agents. Thus by the spring of 1967 approximately 45 percent of Detroit's inner-city schools had been introduced to the extended and community agent approaches.[4]

The Agent's Role

Describing and defining the agent's role has been a major problem. To define it too closely is to restrict it; to leave it too loose is to provide no guidance. A "middle road" definition was needed that provided supportive structure without curtailing innovation. Currently the agent is regarded as a professional attached to a local public school and responsible administratively to the principal of that school. Each position is different because every school and community has its own character, growth patterns, and problems. The agent cannot be seen as a "captive" of the school system if he is to be effective in the community, yet in moving out into the community he must maintain his contact with the teaching and administrative staff of his school. Early in the project the agents themselves came to define their role as that of a professional trained to stimulate and guide the community development process, assist the school in fulfilling its educational goals, and help individuals and groups in the community to strengthen the attitudes, interests, and skills required for full participation in seeking

---

[4] "A Summary of the Extended Schools Program" (Detroit: Great Cities Project, 1964). (Mimeographed.)

[5] For an extended discussion of the community development process, *see* Roland L. Warren, *The Community in America* (Chicago: Rand McNally Co., 1963), pp. 303–339.

and implementing effective solutions to school-community problems.[5]

An effective community development approach in a public school setting requires the creation of a process through which a community and school can come together to meet some of the most pressing needs of the school community. This approach has included efforts that range from formation of food-buying cooperatives based in the schools, to jointly sponsored summer recreation activities, to support of community-generated housing rehabilitation programs. Projects such as these have typically been effected through cooperative (and at times vigorously debated and negotiated) planning and action between the school and community.

An Action Theory

In order to develop an action theory to guide agents, arrangements were made in 1963 for faculty members from the University of Michigan School of Social Work to meet with the agents and Great Cities administrative staff. Faculty members worked together with the agents in the schools in an effort to combine practice with social science theory. Thus the theory grew out of an examination of what the agents were actually doing.

It was found that one of the first things most agents did was to note whether the school building was accessible to the parents. This involved assessment of the extent to which the school administration recognized that many basic educational processes take place outside the school building—in the family, the peer group, community institutions, and the neighborhood. Agents also felt it was important to gauge the acceptance by teachers and administrators of the idea that sound motivation requires educational experiences related to the everyday life of the child.

In addition the agents tried to evaluate how the school was run, along such dimensions as therapeutic versus custodial styles and democratic, autocratic, or laissez-faire administrative leadership arrangements. Discussions with the consultants led to a set of guidelines for this evaluation.[6] Examining the bureaucracy in such traditional dimensions as authority structure, division of labor, interpersonal relations, performance rules and regulations, goal- and policy-setting, and the handling of personnel assignments, a general determination could be made as to

[6] *See,* for example, John Erlich, "School-Community Relations: An Action Model," Detroit Board of Education Community Agent Program, October 1970. (Mimeographed.)

whether the school tended to be rationalistic (hierarchical, specialized, impersonal), human relations oriented (collegial, generalized, personalized), or some "professional" combination of the two in which routine tasks were handled rationalistically and nonroutine ones human relations-style.[7]

Preliminary consideration was also given to the career orientations of teachers. Four broad categories were noted: "careerist"—more concerned with financial rewards than the goals of education; "old professional"—committed, but more concerned with professional standing than with students' educational needs; "new professional"—committed, deeply concerned with educational needs, and aware of new educational trends and the relevance of the local community; and finally the "missionary"—one whose major commitment is to education and who has only a secondary interest in the teaching profession.[8] Special attention had also been given to observing cliques among the teaching staff as possible sources either of support for or opposition to the initiation of change—especially in time-honored policies and tradition-bound procedures.

LINKING MECHANISMS Beyond these school-focused considerations, the most pressing problem for the agents was how to reach out into the community in the most effective and efficient ways. An examination of the agents' efforts revealed that the procedures that had been used to link school and community together could be divided into eight broad categories, often used simultaneously or sequentially. These were designated linking mechanisms.[9]

1. *Urban extension worker.* Agents went out into the community to visit families in their homes and other community gathering places. Using the warm relationships thus developed as a base, they would then attempt to involve the family in some phase of school life—after-school and evening programs, parent action groups, special events, and the like. At the same time informal efforts were made to support parental

[7] *See,* for example, Eugene Litwak, "Models of Bureaucracy which Permit Conflict," *American Journal of Sociology,* Vol. 67, No. 2 (September 1961), pp. 173–183.

[8] Eugene Litwak et al., "School-Community Manual" (Detroit: University of Michigan School of Social Work, 1966). (Mimeographed.)

[9] For an elaboration *see* Eugene Litwak and Henry J. Meyer, "The School and the Family: The Use of Theories of Linkage Between Bureaucratic Organizations and External Primary Groups," in Paul Lazarsfeld, William Sewell, and Harold Wilensky, eds., *The Uses of Sociology* (New York: Free Press, 1967).

attitudes that might promote their children's educational achievement.

2. *Opinion leader.* Using this approach the agents established communication with the neighborhood by contacting its indigenous leaders. These leaders in turn became channels for a variety of communications between the school and the community.

3. *Settlement house.* In this mechanism the agents used the physical facilities of the schools in the late afternoon and evening and provided professional staffing, thus assuring that the programs offered would be convenient to the homes of the potential participants. This sometimes also served to reduce negative associations about the school for both children and parents.

It might be noted that this procedure is closely associated with the community-school model developed in the Flint (Mich.) program sponsored by the Mott Foundation. Sometimes called the "lighted school" approach, it was used extensively early in the development of the school-community agent program. As time and experience were gained, however, the agents switched their focus away from this programmatic device and toward a broader community action orientation. Often this was necessitated by the agent's finding himself bogged down in the administrative details of running a recreation program and/or an adult night school. However, this concept continues to be the basic foundation of the community school program in Flint.

4. *Auxiliary voluntary association.* In this procedure the agents developed various kinds of voluntary groups to serve as a channel for two-way communication between the school and the community. Parent-teacher associations, homeroom mothers' clubs, police-community relations task forces, and educational advisory committees were all set up using this approach.

5. *Common messenger.* The "double agent" of the school community was, of course, the student. Children served as readily available and at times extremely effective bearers of information. As volunteers and more recently in a variety of paid positions, neighborhood mothers also held dual roles in their families and the schools.

6. *Mass media.* In an effort to broaden community awareness of school programs and events and the opportunities for parental involvement in educational (and local political) decisions, many agents made extensive use of the mass media: printed notices, mass mailings, local newspapers, and radio and television announcements.

7. *Formal authority.* At times the schools found it necessary to use a legal or strong normative basis for communication with families. As

an example, agents were occasionally asked to serve as quasi-attendance officers in order to assure continued attendance of given students.

8. *Delegated function.* Finally, it was clear that not only were there many health and welfare organizations functioning in almost every local school district, but also there were activities that the schools were just not equipped to do, such as organizing picket lines in front of the Board of Education office. Agents sought in a variety of ways to coordinate their activities with those of other local organizations, to connect residents with other organizations better equipped to deal with their problems, or to facilitate the development of new services or organizations when these seemed to be needed.

In order to make the theory operational, it remained for the agents to diagnose carefully the needs, resources, strengths, and weaknesses of the community. Without an adequate assessment of the problems to be attacked and the internal resources available to help solve them, these systematized action approaches would have been of little use.

Translating Theory into Action

The selection of a specific procedure or series of procedures is determined by linkage and a diagnostic evaluation of school and community resources and constraints. Some specific examples follow:

URBAN EXTENSION An urban extension approach was used quite effectively by one elementary school-based agent who virtually moved into the block he was attempting to link with the school. At the invitation of a block club president he began to use the home of the president as his office rather than remain in his school office, and he often had meals with the president's family. Asked for assistance by the block club, he began helping the residents to mobilize their resources to work on a problem of great urgency—installation of a traffic light at an intersection where a child had been seriously injured.

Having through the success of this endeavor come to see the potential of joint community-school efforts, the block club went on to other projects, such as a study hall for children right on the block. With the agent's help they organized a study club with mothers of the children rotating as staff. When the need for more-professional assistance arose, the school responded by sending a teacher to the block one night a week and by providing books and other essential materials. This cooperation on the part of the school has led to further joint efforts and to the inclusion of block club representatives on the school's Educational Policy Committee.

OPINION LEADER One agent found an unusual opinion leader in his community to be his most effective linkage. This person was one to whom others went when they had any kind of problem—from being terminated by the local welfare office to garbage pickups not being made. He had created his own channels of communication within city agencies; he knew how to get what "his" community needed.

It was clear to the agent that projects and programs not endorsed by this individual were unlikely to succeed. He therefore made regular visits to this leader to seek his advice and support regarding school-related issues that might be controversial, as well as community-based problems such as the establishment of relationships with the local police precinct. The opinion leader put the agent in touch with families not being reached by the school, and gradually mutual trust was established.

In turn the agent has proved his worth to this leader by gathering and organizing data for him that validated the need for a new elementary school in the area rather than the junior high school proposed by the Board of Education. The agent's technical assistance, coupled with the opinion leader's communicative powers, assured the building of a new elementary school.

SETTLEMENT HOUSE   The settlement house approach is used by many agents. As suggested earlier, this has sometimes been referred to as the lighted-school concept. Basically it means just that—the school building is used in the late afternoons and evenings by community residents.[10]   It is a procedure aimed at wide coverage in the school community because it is open to all while at the same time demanding little real commitment to follow through on the part of the participants. Many agents design programs for adults simply as a device to get people physically into the buildings; by this means they can get acquainted with community residents much more quickly than they could in a door-to-door effort and have an opportunity to determine their needs and interests. An important aspect of this mechanism is the follow-up after programs have been initiated.

In one elementary school, using a voluntary association procedure, the agent served as the catalyst. Capitalizing on a situation at a nearby high school where the quality of education was attacked by students and parents alike, the agent immediately set up a citizens' council to air concerns, not limited to but including the critical situation at the high school. As a result the school was viewed as having demonstrated a real interest in neighborhood problems. Much support was given to the citizens' group by the agent and the principal. As the group realized that many services needed by the community were not being provided, they turned to the school. Currently the school is the center of community activity, with many agencies using it as a field office for their services.

---

[10] See Henry Saltzman, "The Community School in the Urban Setting," in Passow, ed., op. cit., pp. 322–331.

USE OF PARAPROFESSIONALS   In 1965 as the school-community agents took firm hold in the major Great Cities schools, the fifty-one project schools without agents were asked to select a person indigenous to the school neighborhood who might serve as a school-community assistant for that school.   Qualifications for this job were broad, with no educational or job experience requisites.   Primarily, an opinion leader-type was being sought—a person to whom others would listen and to whom residents might go for help.

Once hired, community assistants were included in workshops that brought them together with teachers, administrators, and agents for a mutual exploration of possible roles and future training.   In 1966–67 school-community assistants were added to all Great Cities schools. By 1971–72 there were 175 agents or community assistants in 127 schools, or about 40 percent of the inner-city total.   An effort is made by agents in all schools to meet regularly with the assistants and to analyze their maximal functioning in the local situation.   Here, then, is an attempt at linkage using neighborhood people as common messengers between community and school.

The community assistants have proved able to establish contact with families not previously reached by the school, they have uncovered a multiplicity of problems not known to the school, and they have in many cases forced the school to take actions that would not otherwise have been considered.   Community assistants have achieved such changes as scheduling of parent-teacher conferences in the evening hours rather than during the day to encourage visits by working parents, arranging for parents to visit classrooms, and arranging for homework to be sent to the child's home on a regular schedule so that parents could expect homework on given subjects on certain days.   There is no doubt that the school-community assistants view themselves as outreach workers, extending the school into the community and the community into the school.

Latest Developments

Decentralization of the Detroit public schools by legislative action in 1970 (Public Act 48) called for division of the city of Detroit into eight regions, with each region having a five-member regional board elected by the registered voters; candidates are required to reside in the region from which they are elected.   The act further enlarged the Central Board by providing that the person receiving the highest number of votes in the region would be the chairman of that region and sit on the Central Board together with five members elected at large, for a total of thirteen Central Board members. Powers given to regional boards under the act include personnel selection, determination of curriculum, and budget allocation based on an allocation of funds received from the Central Board.

From the beginning school-community agents have played a vital role in holding a variety of local meetings on the form and process of decentralization and in interpreting the final legislation to concerned community groups. The regional boards have encouraged community residents to participate in regional board meetings.

In addition to the general increase in public information and public interest in education that has resulted, one region, with the help of its agents, has mandated the formation of local school-community councils to assist in the operation of local schools. Each council must have a broadly representative group that includes parents, citizens at large, agency staff members, students, and school staff members. During the 1971–72 school year the Region I school-community structure was further strengthened by the addition of region-wide committees in the areas of finance, curriculum, personnel, and school-community relations. The general objectives of these councils, as adopted by the regional board, include the following:[11]

1. Provide vehicles by which the community can engage in democratic decision-making regarding the education of children and adults.

2. Build better relationships between the school and the community.

3. Help the school to fulfill its role as a public service institution of the community.

4. Carry on a continuing evaluation of the educational process.

5. Define the educational needs of the local school community.

6. Develop concerted community action on specific school-community problems.

7. Participate in the interviewing, selection, and termination of local school personnel.

It is clear that the functions of these groups cannot negate the legal responsibilities of the regional and/or central boards as specified by state and federal law, yet the local groups have been delegated an entire

---

[11] "Objectives and Functions of Local School-Community Councils" (Detroit: Region I Ad Hoc Committee on School-Community Councils, March 8, 1971). (Mimeographed.)

range of functions that involves them directly in the life of the school.

Any community development effort must have some consistent guidance and/or technical assistance if it is to succeed. It is clear that this role of technical assistant or staff consultant cannot be played by the principal of the school. The school-community agent, trained in the community development process, is in a singular position to provide the technical assistance so necessary to both the community leaders and the school staff.

Conclusion

A new model for improving school-community relations is evolving, one that takes account of current inner-city political and social realities. It helps to make possible laying the problems of school-community relations squarely on the doorstep of the local school and its local community—not to deal with them superficially (and often politically) at some higher bureaucratic level, but indeed to involve grass-roots people in the decision-making process. If they are to survive, the public schools must be truly responsive to the people whose needs they are supposed to serve. The system of free public education has failed miserably to meet the challenge of the nation's inner cities.

Perhaps there is still a chance for the schools to serve children. As Holt points out:

> Children want, more than anything else, and even after many years of miseducation, to make sense of the world, themselves, and other human beings. Let them get at this job, with our help if they ask for it, in the way that makes most sense to them.[12]

In every urban area there can be a new opportunity for real participation of and control by community residents in the schools and through the schools. The Detroit experience suggests that it should not be missed.

---

[12] John Holt, *The Underachieving School* (New York: Pitman, 1969), p. 33.

Community Organization in School Social Work

Jeffrey Lickson

Community organization activities have become an essential part of social work in the school setting. In addition to traditional roles, the school social worker must engage in the roles of client advocate, change agent, and ombudsman or risk the growing criticisms that he is merely serving the institution or that he is failing to solve the school's social problems.

In the role of ombudsman the school social worker must be independent, committed to pursuing each problem freely with access to all pertinent data, able to represent either school or student, capable of clearly explaining his conclusions and results, and committed to pursuing whatever behavioral or policy changes he deems in the best interests of the client.[1] The client can range from the whole community or the vastly complex school system to the individual family or child. Whatever the client may be, however, the ethical responsibility of the ombudsman demands that his decisions be rooted in the intrinsic worth of the individual and in the notion of social justice and equal educational opportunity for every child.

Whenever a school social worker attempts to protect a student from the school system he takes a risk. The ombudsmanship model pre-

[1] Alfred J. Kahn, *Theory and Practice of Social Planning* (New York: Russell Sage Foundation, 1969), pp. 294–301.

sumes that the employing school system is willing to have some kind of planned change and that the school social worker is sophisticated enough to assist such change.

The schools reflect configurations of power with school board members at the top of the hierarchy and students at the bottom. How this power impinges on the individual child within the classroom has become an essential issue for school social workers.

That schools should enhance the self-image of each student while providing the best possible learning opportunities remains an essential goal of student advocacy. That schools have failed to do this is a fact. Obviously the schools must change, but the power structure that has produced the educational system persists. Therefore even when school personnel ask for assistance in planned change, the complexity of inherent issues and risks—from budget to personal attack—must be understood and dealt with delicately.

Student Field Placements

On August 3, 1970, an attempt was made to implement the objectives of the Florida State University Department of Social Work for first- and second-year graduate students in field placement in the Leon County School System, Tallahassee, Florida. These objectives include generic methods in the first year with specializations in casework, group work, and supervision for second-year students.

As the student unit began, the county school system was under federal court order to desegregate its twenty-nine schools, which had a student population of 21,000. This was accomplished in September without major incident. When the graduate students in school social work began their placements in August, an attempt was made to assess where the school system was in relation to the many economic, social, and educational problems of its children.

The initial problem was to change the image of the school social worker from truant officer and principal's helper to professional change agent. While the department coordinator and the field instructor chose schools whose administrators had expressed a desire for help, they also attempted to place the graduate students in the city's disadvantaged neighborhoods and in those schools most in need of service. After each student had been assigned, internal communication and field instruction were carried out through weekly individual conferences, weekly group meetings, field visits, participation in school and community meetings and on committees, and close liaison with the regular school social work department.

The learning process for each graduate student involved analyzing the problems in each case, setting priorities for intensive and/or brief service, and consultation with the regular school social worker and other agencies. The essential purpose was to provide direct service to individuals and groups via social casework and group work. In almost every case indirect work with teachers, principals, and other agencies was provided. Community organization was added when it seemed necessary to expand service delivery.

A vast majority of cases (172 of 260 referrals, or 70 percent) reflected home- and community-based problems. This category included referrals attributable to poor health, nonattendance, poverty, insufficient clothing, inadequate housing, poor child care, and family stress. A majority of the remaining referrals reflected behavioral problems, with manifest implications concerning the need for in-school changes.

This fact was immediately seen as significant by the graduate students, who recognized that intensive casework and group work alone could only help the child temporarily, while the real problems festered both within and outside the school. These "real" problems were poverty, unemployment, underemployment, poor health, inadequate services, lack of child care, and, most tragically, an abysmal self-image that went along with frustrated and frustrating acting-out behavior in school. As for the school system, it offered many unsuitable academic programs and appeared not fully committed to educating its disadvantaged and socially troubled students.

As part of the individual and group field instruction process, each graduate student was encouraged to analyze the child and family referred to determine what was needed to achieve legitimate service objectives. The social reality of rural and urban poverty, limited education budgets, and limited community resources did the rest of the teaching. Faced with a fraction of the frustration that teachers, disenfranchised students, and parents carry, the graduate students were encouraged in their investigative efforts to seek all existing resources for individual clients.

STUDENT PROJECTS *Stamp stores.* Responding to the need of many of the children for clothing, "Snoopy Stamp Stores" were established by some school social workers in cooperation with parents and teachers. These are student-run programs whereby children are able to earn

Snoopy Stamps from teachers as positive reinforcement for a variety of acceptable behaviors in class. They may then use these stamps to purchase clothing, books, toys, and so on, that have been contributed by local parents. The stores have been enthusiastically accepted by students, teachers, and parents. The students carry decision-making roles and demonstrate their capacity to help the school, which seems to add to a positive, student-focused atmosphere. Such in-school community organization focuses in a positive, constructive way on disadvantaged children, the public relations skills of the school social worker, and the importance of ongoing community support.

Program assessment. Another graduate student worked closely with the curriculum coordinator in an elementary school in the construction of two program assessment instruments designed to gather and compare the results of the teachers' ratings of the most pressing problems with the ratings of third-, fourth-, and fifth-grade students. The results of the survey provided two full days of in-service discussion among the teachers. One point the teachers made was their desire for more parental support. Many teachers recognized that some problems were the result of home situations and inconsistent relationships at school. The children's responses were largely positive; surprisingly, they corroborated the teachers' desire for written school-wide policies that would let them know what was expected of them. Other requests were for more books in the library and a chance to make decisions. The children's ideas proved so valuable that the principal agreed to form a student forum to review school policies and problems. Such student participation reduces the threat of administration and gives the youngsters a higher degree of self-involvement in school in a freer atmosphere.

Teachers' attitudes. A graduate student at another elementary school focused on teachers' attitudes toward poor and black students, who comprised over 50 percent of the school's population. After attempting informal discussions with teachers on poverty in the families of children referred to him, the student decided to organize an afternoon workshop to reach more teachers. The objectives of the workshop encouraged human relations sensitivity and an exchange of viewpoints, while the program itself brought together several parents, teachers, and the principal for an open discussion of poverty, self-image, and creative teaching. This activity did not permanently change the school, but it did change the image of the school social worker and stimulated the principal and teachers to ask for follow-up workshops.

Day care. In assessing the reasons for poor attendance among cases referred, it was seen that the older children in many large impoverished families were kept home from school to take turns caring for younger brothers and sisters while their parents worked. One graduate student at a school that serves a large geographic area with a population ranging from middle-class whites to low-income rural blacks plotted on a county map where the school's chronic attendance cases lived. A visit to the neighborhood and analysis of the problem prompted a project to establish a child care center in the target neighborhood. It was decided that the local community needed to be informed of what could be done, should exercise a decision-making voice in planning, and should be involved in the process. The help of the regular school social worker, who knew the community well and had excellent communications skills, was enlisted. Meetings with the local minister, visits to the neighborhood church, establishment of a parents' committee, and compilation of data led to approval of the project.

At another school where a chronic need existed for day care of pre-schoolers, the progression of a project from felt need to the opening of a new day care center took seventeen months, the persistence of four different graduate students, and sophistication in meeting each delay and setback with self-examination and necessary changes in strategy.

Consumer rights. As a result of casework with a parent, one graduate student initiated a consumer rights project. The client, who was illiterate, had signed a contract with a furniture store that charged illegal interest and violated five areas of the federal Truth in Lending Act and state consumer protection laws. The graduate student contacted the State Office of Finance and the Office of Installment Contracts and in the process located an attorney who successfully voided the illegal contract. In cooperation with a Division of Family Services caseworker, a Consumer Complaint Referral Service was organized to steer other welfare families away from companies involved in unfair trade practices.

Teen-age parents. With the help of another graduate student, the Northwest Florida Chapter of the National Association of Social Workers launched a comprehensive community organization project with a meeting focused on the "Education of Teen-age Parents," following defeat by the Leon County School Board of a proposal to change the board's restrictive policies toward married and pregnant students. After this meeting an Ad Hoc Committee for the Education of Teen-age Parents was formed. Included on this committee were agency representatives from the Division of Family Services, Health Department,

Children's Home Society, and various other local agencies and groups, as well as graduate and undergraduate social work students, teachers, parents, clergy, and high school students.

The committee was able to use a recent comprehensive study of pregnant students that had been prepared for the Florida House of Representatives Committee on Health and Rehabilitative Services. In addition research was done in two local prenatal clinics to document the number of pregnant girls in the county and the number who wanted to continue their education. One committee member was successful in finding a church willing to house a program for pregnant girls. In March 1971 the committee's three recommendations— (1) to allow married students to remain in the regular school program, (2) to permit pregnant students to attend a special comprehensive program, and (3) to allow girls to reenter their regular schools following the birth of their babies—were approved.

The school board's approval of the committee's recommendations paved the way for the establishment of a comprehensive program for teen-age parents in Leon County. A school-appointed Advisory Committee for Teen-age Parents met to propose program details and to establish a federally funded project that has been in operation since September 1971. Graduate social work students are now being assigned to work in an area that a short time ago was a major source of injustice in the school system.

Involving the Total School Community

The alarm has been sounding for the past three years for school social workers to expand traditional casework and group work roles by accepting and using differentially trained personnel and by energetically advocating that the school meet the needs of its disadvantaged children.[2] Now the school social worker, whatever his training, must be committed to restructuring the organizational hierarchy that places school board members, administrators, and teachers in vertical configurations above the student.

The transformation of the school requires a political process and a coalition between school social workers and clients in documenting

---

[2] Carl Marburger, "Measuring Social Work's Contributions Against Educational Needs," p. 8. Paper presented at the National Workshop on School Social Work, University of Pennsylvania, June 11–14, 1969.

need, strategically advocating policy change, and working together toward a healthy affective climate in the schools. No school social worker would deny the political pressures that affect public education. As Setleis says:

> The transformation of social institutions requires political processes. Unless this is understood, there can be little hope for people to find the kind of relevant responsiveness they seek from social institutions.[3]

Setleis has clearly identified social work practice as political activity, stressing the necessity for broader agency involvement with the wider community and the necessity for a horizontal organization

> . . . all on the same plane, each representing a different point on the organizational spectrum, each having direct access to each other in the vital decision-making processes.[4]

The school social worker must mediate between his clients and social institutions to enhance a mutually meaningful exchange between them. However, when a school or institution denies to an individual the power to participate directly in determining institutional outcomes as they affect his needs, the school social worker must become an ombudsman and client advocate. The client is an expert on his own situation—who knows better than the school dropout why he has left school?

> The basic reality of genuine social change rests *in the process* through which *the people affected* can bring to bear their own "human weight" upon the knowledge and expertise that informs and dictates the nature and extent of the change.[5]

If the school social worker is to be an effective advocate he must also accurately assess the power structure within the school system and formulate appropriate strategies to deal with the school.

The schools have a responsibility to educate all children, and school social work has the responsibility of providing the school system with an accurate view of its children, especially its minority group students. Because not all educators share the notion that students are capable of taking part in critical decision-making processes regarding their

---

[3] Lloyd Setleis, "Social Work Practice as Political Activity," *Journal of Social Work Process*, Vol. 17 (1969), p. 151.

[4] Ibid., p. 149.

[5] Max Silverstein, "Urban Crisis, Community Organization Practice and Mr. Pray's Questions," *Journal of Social Work Process*, Vol. 17 (1969), p. 99.

education, the school social worker must demonstrate how students, parents, and the community may join in the development of effective programs of public education. No longer can we tolerate a system that has eroded the spirit of so many misguided, disenfranchised, depersonalized children.

An essential part of the message of school social work is that each individual has the capacity for growth toward self-actualization, provided he has the proper in-school encouragement. More and more school systems are attempting to rewrite curricula and restyle their organizations to revolve around the needs of children, teachers, and parents as human beings. Everyone needs to see himself as a capable person. Public education's lingering failure is that children are still often categorized as "failures."

School social workers cannot produce a just society—or even deliver effective casework help—alone. The mandate for social workers to risk themselves on behalf of educationally and socially disadvantaged clients demands that we specify to the school system the numbers and kinds of problems that exist and explore together with students, parents, and teachers how the total community can change the school to fit the needs of its students in addition to helping children adapt to the institution. In situations outside the jurisdiction of the school, the school social worker must assume some responsibility for leading the school into a moral, ethical, and professional social reform posture vis-à-vis the community problem. School social workers and educators, as concerned citizens, have a tradition of commitment to social change. Each must recognize the contribution of the other and provide in their cooperative activities an example of mutual respect for and dedication to children.

The specific crisis that begins the internal administrative chain reaction toward referral of a child for school social work service is, of course, symptomatic of the total problem. The tragic danger social workers face today is in too rigidly specifying their competence to deliver service at the expense of pragmatic, flexible, and differential teamwork to help the child.

Most of us in public education have remained spectators in the arena of social and political change. Not wanting to be tainted by partisanship and fearful of the zealots on opposing sides of the political continuum, we have manifested a basic mistrust of ourselves, our children, and our communities. We now must become ombudsmen for the disenfranchised who feel powerless to affect the ubiquitous social institutions, because we too suffer (if less painfully) from the twin afflictions of society: dehumanization and the need to use technology to relieve man's burdens.

Summary

School social workers must learn how to engage effectively in community organization activities and add the role of change agent and ombudsman to traditional clinical functions. In the midst of rapidly changing social pressures, the school social worker is faced with the dilemma of a public demand for more and better service for less money. Larger schools and rapidly changing technology are placing children in a vulnerable position within the educational bureaucracy. Students need advocates to help them participate in decision-making so that they can take what they need from the school.

The school social worker has an opportunity to use his community organization skills to lead the school system toward greater relevance to the community and its students. A pragmatic, flexible service should also contain traditional professional services to help children. Such a program has been offered in the field placement for Florida State University Department of Social Work graduate students in the Leon County School System.

As school social workers build community responsiveness and program accountability into their service, the school and community become more fully aware of their problems, possible solutions, the manpower utilization issue, and training implications. Effective service will produce a team effort involving child, parent, school, and the total resources of the community in whatever activities are necessary to remove the obstacles in the path of the child's educational and social development.

Comprehensive Social Work in the Secondary School

Johanna M. Bielecki

A secondary school is more than a building complex where several hundred adults and several thousand adolescents gather for the purpose of education. It is a complex community larger than many cities, wherein two thousand or more individuals interact in the process of living, sometimes enhancing, sometimes retarding the process of learning, but always affecting and being affected by the larger community within which it exists. Beneath the structured façade of order runs an often unseen stream of human behavior that periodically erupts in crisis and disorder.

While the old problems of adolescence—the search for self-identity and independence, the need to act out and rebel—still exist, new problems of drug abuse, demands for rights, a relevant curriculum, and racial equality create greater challenges for the educator and the social worker. Secondary schools are increasingly becoming a mirror of the larger society, no longer able merely to educate for the future, but reflecting almost immediately the relevant issues of today.

Role of the School Social Worker

Educators are no longer able to let the form and content of education change slowly, but are forced to make adaptations virtually overnight.

While the role of the school social worker is a relatively new concept in the secondary school, school social workers must also innovate and adopt new and more flexible styles of operation or be rendered totally ineffective. The agency concept of cases referred individually to a social worker unknown to all but a select few is a tragic waste of the worker's skills.

While consultation with faculty regarding individual students, group management, or innovative classroom procedures to modify behavior or affect learning are important parts of the social worker's role, a wide range of personal contacts with the student body is also necessary if the social worker is to assess on a broader base what is really happening to all the students in a building. The total view may be seen only if the social worker listens to representative students from the total school community, not only those who are referred to him for specific problems.

Just as the sociologist assesses the feeling of a community, recommends changes, and works directly with the residents to effect change, the school social worker can play an equally vital role within the school community. Diagnosing the problems of a school is but an extension of the skills required to diagnose the problems of a family.

The high school community contains two primary groups that are the target of the social worker's service: (1) students who need individual help with personal or family problems and (2) those with basically adequate personalities whose needs are not met by the social system—that is, those for whom the curriculum is not appropriate, who must submit to dehumanizing practices, or who lack opportunities for meaningful activities. To meet the needs of both groups, the social worker must provide a comprehensive program that includes direct service to individuals in the first group and indirect service that modifies or enhances the environment for the second group.

Direct service to individuals implies service to those who are referred through any channels. Since in a large high school many students may need help but never get referred through traditional means, an opportunity should be provided for students with real but not obvious problems to refer themselves voluntarily. The unanticipated benefit of self-referral is the expansion of service to more students, since the high degree of motivation and readiness for change that typifies those who request service makes short-term counseling more effective and a more rapid turnover of cases is therefore possible.

Indirect service necessitates a comprehensive approach to the problems that affect large segments of the student population, all students in the school, or the school system as a whole. Change is most likely to be effective and valued enough to be incroporated into the system if those affected by or concerned with the problem—that is, students, community, staff, and parents—are involved in assessing the problem and planning and implementing action programs to alleviate it.

STEPS IN A PROBLEM-FOCUSED APPROACH   Both concepts are most often based on essentially the same problem-focused approach. Whether the social worker is dealing with an individual, a group, a school, or a community, the same steps are usually workable:

1. *Defining the problem.* What is the real problem? Is it situational, environmental, or societal? Does it exist because of the nature and behavior of the individual or group or because of outside forces that affect those involved?

2. *Determining the jurisdiction of the problem.* Is the problem resolvable within the limits of the school, the school system, or the community? Is it within the limits of the expanded role of the school social worker? Is the problem more appropriate for an agency, the legal or medical profession, other existing school or community resources, or committees to solve than for the social worker?

3. *Assessing who is involved in and affected by the problem.* Is the problem focused in a limited parent-child, teacher-child, or peer group setting or are larger groups of students, teachers, and administrators involved? Does the problem extend beyond the school into the school system as a whole or into the community?

4. *Planning an action program.* Who needs to be involved in planning and implementing an action program to resolve the problem? Has the plan been mutually agreed on by all concerned? Is it realistic and workable within the limits, strengths, and resources of the individuals or organizations involved?

5. *Follow-up and follow-through.* Is a casual reporting back on a one-time crisis interview all that is necessary? Does the action plan need revisions, additions, repeated follow-up by the social worker? In plans involving system change, is it the social worker who must follow through with implementation or can others do it as well? At what point may the program be turned over to others?

While the problem-focused approach may be adapted to most situations encountered by the social worker, the complex problems of a high school community cannot be programmed to fit one mode of operation. The social worker must often use an eclectic montage of many traditional social work approaches in inventive ways. The infinite variety of human problems may best be served by a variety of approaches selected to meet the needs of the individual or group. In real-life situations, confronted by the immediacy of crisis situations with individuals or in the school as a whole, the social worker often may have to rely on intuition when there is no time to develop an appropriate strategy.

OBJECTIVES The objectives of a comprehensive secondary school social work program that attempts to meet the needs of as many students as possible through direct service and system change are as follows:

1. Provide services to more students by incorporating a walk-in self-referral system into the social work program.

2. Assess the problems affecting all students on a broader base within the school and community and involve those affected in planning solutions.

3. Increase the ways social work services can be used and ensure that they will be used by presenting an image of the social worker's service that demonstrates a wide range of options.

These three objectives are interrelated and interdependent. Direct service via a walk-in operation is dependent on the accessibility of the social worker, students' knowledge of the worker's role, and an atmosphere of trust that is created through comprehensive role activities. The social worker's awareness of broad problems affecting youths emanates from his contacts with students and faculty. Time allotted to speaking in classes on problems of adolescence promulgates the role of the social worker to many, advertises the self-referral service, and also serves the needs of students with minor problems. While time devoted to system change may require periodic blocks of time during the day, temporarily limiting direct service to some individuals, students who are involved on committees with adults to plan system change are benefited by the opportunity for meaningful involvement; the resultant change itself may benefit many students.

Creating a Comprehensive Role Image

In order to work effectively in a comprehensive way, create an atmosphere that is conducive to a walk-in self-referral system, earn the confidence of staff and students in assessing problems on a broader

257

base, and be able to motivate and involve those affected by problems in planning and implementing change, the social worker must establish the image of a deliverer of multiple services and an accepted agent of change. The social worker, with his training in assessment of behavior and interpersonal relationship skills, can serve as a neutral, nonauthoritarian observer who can assess the tone and feeling of the high school community, its needs, and the possible solutions to the problem by listening to, observing, and interacting with students, faculty, and administrators. In effect this is one of the principal sources of the social worker's power—a center of information and communication.

With the skills in mediation necessary for parent-child conflicts, the social worker can become a liaison between students and faculty or administration. He must accordingly be visible and accessible not only to the faculty but to the student body as a whole, beyond the limits of the referred caseload.

In most schools the social worker is either not known or is identified as a person to whom students with problems are sent. To avoid this limited role and identification, the social worker must broaden his base of contact with students and recreate his image as a person who has a variety of services to offer to many students. The groundwork necessary to create an atmosphere of trust is time consuming, but the time is well spent. Once a tradition is established, it is nourished and promulgated from year to year by the student grapevine. The social worker's reputation, skills, confidentiality, and credibility are carried on the far-reaching, rapidly spreading branches of the grapevine within the school and out into the community. It is this same grapevine that becomes the communication link between the social worker and students and is the key source of information on the temper, tone, and tensions of the building.

There are numerous ways in which the social worker can become known to the student body. While these techniques take time away from individual casework, they enable the social worker to make an impact on hundreds of students who never have had any personal contact with the worker. They create an atmosphere in which students see mental health services as part of their daily lives rather than as something mysterious, fearful, and to be avoided at all costs. If the worker is successful, a climate is created in which a visit to the social worker is as normal as a visit to the school nurse or a guidance counselor.

Whether a student actually uses social work services during his years in school is not important. The ultimate goal is to develop an attitude that mental health services are available and desirable at whatever point in his future life they may become necessary.

The following are but a few of the techniques that may be utilized to establish and maintain an image of the social worker as a trusted person with something to offer students beyond the limits of casework:

1. Speaking to classes or student groups on whatever topics are appropriate to the mental health field, such as drug abuse, student unrest, and problems of adolescence.

2. Acting as an observer and consultant on the student council, student-faculty committees, and meetings of student activist groups, maintaining a neutral role in order to remain a more effective advocate, liaison, and adviser.

3. Becoming involved with activities or groups that encompass a broad spectrum of the student body. This may include establishing and operating a school volunteer program or helping youth groups to establish a drug hot line.

4. Enlisting the aid of journalism classes to publicize the varied school social work services offered, advertising the means by which a student can refer himself for help with any problem.

Once the social worker has become visible and acceptable as a trustworthy professional person through such practices as these, continuing the same practices will provide him with a communication link between students and faculty. The social worker then becomes a true liaison for peaceful intercommunication within the school, alert to developing tensions, aware of developing problems, and recognized as a respected change agent.

Walk-in Services

The traditional role of the school social worker is that of a caseworker or group worker accepting appropriate referrals from parents, faculty members, or agencies according to a predetermined process. Adherence to the traditional approach reduces the role of the worker to that of a microcosmic isolated unit of a mental health agency conveniently located on the school premises. The worker's impact is limited to a small percentage of the total student body, usually those whose behavior is more overt and whose symptoms are more noticeable to the staff. Since few social workers are assigned to high schools on a full-time basis, one or two days per week allotted to a school of approximately two thousand students would allow the social worker to work with only ten students, whereas two hundred might be in need of assistance.

In a large secondary school many students who need help are not noticed or reached through the normal referral systems. As professionals have continued with established systems of service and debated which profession should assume responsibility for coping with the growing drug problem, drug-abusers themselves have recognized their need for help and have created a network of self-help programs, run primarily by nonprofessionals. Hot lines, walk-in street clinics, free medical centers, and drug information centers have been established throughout the country and have drawn not only those who have drug-related problems, but a broad range of lonely, troubled, and depressed youths in the throes of a crisis or gripped with a long-range problem that may lead them to drugs. Although many of these youths are in school, they either do not know the channels through which to seek help, distrust the school as establishment oriented, or have sought help unsuccessfully.

If a professional social worker is available within a school building, students who need help should not have to rely solely on a street clinic outside the school. The school social work office should function as an initial contact for youths with crisis problems and as a cooperative resource to the local street clinic, if one exists.

The need for a walk-in service is based on the following premises:

1. Most adolescents do want to communicate with an understanding adult. When communication is inadequate or nonexistent at home, many will expend much energy seeking out and testing adults (teachers, counselors, ministers, other parents) with whom they can relate and in whom they can confide.

2. The success of hot lines, suicide prevention centers, and walk-in clinics in the community attests to this need. The increasing rates of drug abuse and of adolescent runaways are symptomatic of the unmet needs of adolescents.

STUDENT ACCEPTANCE While many adolescents tend to shy away from traditional agencies such as clinics, outpatient centers of mental health hospitals, and school-oriented psychological services, they will refer themselves in the school setting if the milieu is right. This requires a social work office in the school that is readily accessible to students without their having to obtain clearance from administrative offices, secretaries, counselors, or the like. It also requires a social worker who is known to students as an understanding adult, who will be flexible enough to tolerate the interruptions of students who drop in during noon hours and between classes and be willing to reschedule his time to accommodate crisis cases. A social worker who has spent some time in after-hours volunteer work with students is more apt to encourage self-referrals than one who views social work as a rigid, fixed-time job.

Since the greatest concentration of adolescents in the community is in the secondary school, it is logical that a walk-in service be provided on the school premises. Whether students will use and accept a walk-in facility depends on several factors:

1. The value of social work service as established by tradition and promulgated by word of mouth among students.

2. The knowledge that such a service exists as promoted through the student newspaper, orientation classes, talks by the social worker, and the student grapevine.

3. The accessibility, credibility, and confidentiality of the school social worker as assessed by the students from reports of other students who have received help, and by non-social work contacts with the social worker in clubs, classes, and school-related extracurricular activities.

4. The knowledge that they have a right to refer themselves and that this right is accepted by the administration, counselors, teachers, faculty, and parents.

5. A simple method of referral, publicized in the school newspaper —for example, dropping in at the social worker's office before school, between classes, or during the lunch hour or using an envelope posted outside the worker's office to leave a note requesting an interview.

A self-referral system can be chaotic if it is not well organized or based on adaptation to the school's function and procedures. It can be detrimental to faculty–social worker relations unless it is generally accepted.

To satisfy the demand for service and still maintain the sanity of the social worker requires skills in management, diagnosis, and amelioration; an inner sense of order; and a sense of humor. The task becomes impossible if all requests for service are routinely accepted in order. Screening of potential cases and self-referrals, adequate (and often rapid) preliminary assessment of the nature of the presenting problem, and delegation of cases to other therapeutic or supportive persons or agencies is a necessity in order to avoid entrapment in an unworkable, overburdened caseload.

INITIATING SELF-REFERRAL   If self-referral is to be initiated, the principal and assistant principal must first have a clear understanding of the comprehensive role of the social worker in the high school.   The social worker has the responsibility of clarifying the program, selling the administrators on the need for and value of social work services within the building, and proposing and delineating the expansion of service.   In addition, broad guidelines for the service are established by the local social work department and in some states by the state department of education.   The social worker is not completely autonomous in a building and the administrator has some rights in determining the most effective use of the social worker's time.   The social worker has the responsibility to negotiate the type of service to be offered, especially since a self-referral system is not as orderly a process as the usual referral system and the wholehearted approval of the administration must be obtained in order to gain faculty acceptance.

The implementation of a walk-in operation is also dependent on a flexible, understanding school administration and faculty members who have accepted the need for mental health services in the school and recognize that crisis needs of students are important enough to permit them to miss a class without undue questioning by the teacher.   Mutually agreed-on procedures must be delineated so that accountability to parents and faculty is adequate and class attendance is not disrupted.   Continuity of social work staff is a critical element of a walk-in operation, since it is based on trust and tradition, both of which are intangibles that cannot be imposed by the social worker but are earned by a lengthy process of testing over time.

Whether a student is referred through the traditional channels or refers himself, he represents a new case to be dealt with by the social worker.   Many self-referrals are temporary crisis problems—teacher-student or parent-child conflicts, peer relationship problems, or just the need to talk to a neutral adult—and the helping process may simply involve presentation of the problem, discussion of alternative behaviors or means of coping with or alleviating the problem, development of action plans, and follow-through that may require only a brief reporting back to the social worker.   Other self-referrals may involve long-range problems such as pregnancy, possible suicide, major family crises such as divorce and physical abuse, arrest, or drug abuse, and may become part of the regular caseload and treated as short-term cases until the presenting problem is resolved or action plans have been put into operation.

SCREENING Limiting a caseload to a manageable number and working with only those cases that are appropriate for a social worker can be an exceedingly difficult task in a school setting. An agency is safely removed from the battleground where life's problems are fought and can accept or reject cases or relegate them to a waiting list. The school social worker is in the open field in the midst of the action. His waiting list does not consist of featureless names but real problem-ridden people. The school social worker cannot escape the confrontations and pleas of frustrated faculty members, cannot be present at a crisis and blandly inform those involved that help will be available in two months.

The social worker must first realistically appraise his own skills, knowledge, and limitations. Second, he must direct some students to the available guidance counselors and teachers who are capable of giving therapeutic or supportive help. The training and experience of guidance counselors are variable. In any large secondary school some counselors are well equipped to handle most students' problems, especially if periodic consultative help is available from the social worker or other members of the psychological services team. Joint screening of cases by the social worker and guidance counselor or a pre-referral diagnostic interview by the social worker with the potential client can determine who can best handle a case. Many problems can be resolved or ameliorated at the screening stage by environmental manipulation, jointly planned by the social worker and counselor, but implemented and followed through by the counselor. A part-time job, meaningful voluntary or social activities, change of classes, courses, or teachers may be therapeutic enough to eliminate the need for casework.

Cases accepted by the social worker should primarily be those that require his casework skills or those needing subsequent referral for testing and evaluation or referral to clinics, other agencies, or psychiatric or medical care for which continued liaison is necessary. Some cases may need intensive short-term help from the social worker and then may be referred back to the guidance counselor for long-range follow-up with repeated consultation from the social worker.

WORKING WITH DRUG ABUSERS As the problem of drug abuse in schools has grown, surveys have attempted to determine the magnitude of the problem. A 1970 Dearborn (Mich.) Community Task Force survey of all ninth- and twelfth-graders in the school system indicated that approximately one-third were using or had used drugs for nonmedical purposes either on a one-time-only basis or repeatedly. A 1971 survey by the Lafayette Clinic of a sampling of Detroit area schools substantiated the Dearborn report. With so many students abusing drugs, the likelihood that the social worker will encounter drug abusers among the youths referred or self-referred for related problems is magnified. With the acceptance of walk-in referral services by students, the incidence of drug abusers coming to the attention of the social worker is even greater.

Casework or group work with students who use drugs is basically no different from working with students with any other problem. The normal adolescent who occasionally experiments with drugs may never need to come to the attention of the social worker. The student who uses drugs frequently with little caution or control, the drug-dependent student, or the high-risk-taker may use drugs as an escape, as a means of acting out or rebelling, as a method of self-destruction, to seek attention or status, out of an extreme need to conform to a peer group, or as a form of self-medication because he is too depressed, confused, or anxious to tolerate himself or his life situation without the aid of drugs. The self-medicating drug abuser may be the one who needs referral for psychiatric help and a supervised program of legitimate medication.

Individual students who abuse drugs are people with problems. The focus of social work is primarily to deal with the problems that are causing the individual to turn to drugs and, secondarily, to provide information on drugs and the risks involved.

Some students who abuse drugs have multiple personal problems and may need and prefer to be involved in individual casework. The high-risk-takers, self-destructive youths, and the self-medicators fall into this category. Others are best treated in a fluid group setting where peer influence can be exerted; common problems with self, school, family, and society may be aired; coping mechanisms may be shared; and alternatives to drug abuse may be explored. The social worker may need to suggest additional alternatives, direct students into meaningful activities such as volunteer work, involvement in self-help programs (walk-in centers, rap sessions, and telephone hot lines), and participation on school and community planning committees. When meaningful opportunities for responsible activities for youths do not exist, the social worker may be the one to help propose and initiate such opportunities.

Working with parents of drug abusers is the same as working with parents of any youths with problems. Once the parents' panic is dealt with, the traditional approach to family casework may be initiated, especially in cases in which the use of drugs may be directly related to or be merely one symptom of serious personal or family problems.

Since drug abuse is a problem that both reflects and creates a massive lack of understanding, alienation, and inability of adults and youths to communicate with each other, one way to work with parents of drug abusers is in group sessions involving both youths and parents. In such sessions the personal and social problems underlying the abuse of drugs by any age group may be discussed, the fact and fiction of drug information can be imparted, youth-adult confrontation and communication can be stimulated and directed by the social worker, and approaches to mutual resolution of problems may be explored.

THE FLUID GROUP   Although the traditional type of group work with a fixed, constant complement of group members may be utilized in a secondary school setting, today's youths have grown accustomed to the rap group, a more flexible group approach wherein people share ideas and experiences and probable ways of working out common problems and confront each other in an effort to communicate and to understand themselves and others. For many students a constant group is neither essential nor feasible because of scheduling problems. A fluid group that cuts across age, experience, and clique levels, includes whoever is available at a given hour, and changes members from meeting to meeting may be more comfortable and productive.

The distinguishing characteristics of a fluid group are as follows:

1. There is conscious screening by the social worker of chance encounters as well as planned groupings. When several students request service at the same time, a commonality of problems may indicate that they could be seen as a group. Some may be included, if they freely consent to meeting with the group, because the social worker knows from prior contacts that their experiences could benefit others in the group. Some may be excluded and scheduled for individual interviews because the social worker is sensitive to their need for private time, which is often communicated to him nonverbally.

2. There is consensus by the potential members of a group that they are willing to share feelings and information. The social worker asks directly whether the students know each other well enough to be honest or do not know each other at all and therefore can be honest because of their anonymity.

3. Members are briefly introduced to each other by the social worker; information about individuals known to the social worker is revealed only with the permission—often nonverbal—of the client. If some potential members are not known to the social worker, they introduce themselves and are advised that they may reserve private information and schedule an individual interview with the social worker in a more confidential setting at a later time.

4. There is rapid group induction through clarity and simplicity of group norms. Since a fluid group may meet together only once or may involve different members in subsequent sessions, group development does not proceed as in a stable group in which there is time for the establishment of roles among members and more involvement by group members in topic selection and determining the direction in which the group may proceed. In a fluid group the social worker briefly establishes the basic ground rules for group process, topic-selection (often determined by the social worker), problem-definition, goal-setting, and development of action plans. The action plans may simply be plans to try alternative behavior or to provide different ways of coping with a temporary problem.

5. There is no prior commitment by members to meet again unless a subsequent session is planned by some or all members.

6. There is a necessary limitation on the size of the group. With less structure than a stable group and more intervention and control required by the social worker, fluid groups are more manageable when limited to three to six persons.

7. There is often only limited follow-through by the social worker. Some members of the group may never need to be seen again or to report back except casually.

The fluid group concept is a natural mode of operation when walk-in social work service is available. It is not uncommon in a walk-in setting for several students with similar problems to request service on the same day. Frequently a student may ask to come for the first interview with a friend in order to relieve his initial anxiety and help him to explain the problem situation.

Prior to scheduling an interview, the social worker should inquire whether the student prefers to come in alone or whether a group meeting would be acceptable. After an initial contact at which the presenting problem of an individual is delineated, one plan of action may be to involve the student in one or more group sessions with others who are experiencing or have resolved similar problems to enable him to see his problem in a different perspective, benefit from the experiences of others, or merely to learn to relate to and interrelate with others.

Similarly, when a group has already been formed, the social worker may include in a given group session individual clients who may be of benefit to the group, at the discretion of the worker and with the consent of the group. For example, a former drug user may be invited to join a group of students who are in the beginning stages of drug experimentation, or a new user may be invited into a group of former users. A former student, a dropout, or a visiting college student may be a valuable one-time member of a group of students who want to drop out or who are discontented with school and undecided about their future.

In a fluid group session the demands on the social worker are greater, with more intervention required to keep the group on the topic being discussed, maintain a balance of roles to prevent domination by older, more experienced members, assess the needs and problems of a new member who is not known to the social worker, and constantly evaluate the tone and direction of the group's focus. Groups of drug users in particular can support and increase drug use if members use the group to eulogize their drug experiences or boast of the extent of their drug use as a source of status. Some former users are overly evangelistic and may be rejected by a group more than the most authoritarian adult.

While the fluid group is more demanding of the social worker, it can be a useful technique in a self-referral setting, since the needs of some students may be met in the fluid group alone. For others it is a good screening device for the social worker to determine which of the group members have more complex problems that may require repeated individual sessions.

THE PROBLEM-FOCUSED GROUP In a self-referral system in which students are aware of the services offered by the social worker, it is not uncommon for a group assembled by the students themselves to request consultation with the worker. These may include groups of students affected by certain disciplinary practices in the school or confrontations with a specific teacher or representatives from school clubs, organizations, or political groups who are concerned about school policies, codes of conduct, or other problems affecting many students. The sole purpose of such a group may be to consult with the social worker on appropriate means of coping with the situation or means that the students can utilize to attempt to change the situation.

In such groups the focus is not on the individual problems of the members or on behavioral change, but on the problem itself. The social worker's role is as a liaison between students and the school, representing and interpreting the system to them, and suggesting appropriate techniques to use in dealing with the system. While the group may not meet again, the social worker may be involved with more follow-through and action-planning with representative members of the group. A similar group is one in which variable groups—preselected by the students themselves or chance groups of normal adolescents who might never encounter a social worker—are allowed to sign up at an allotted time to talk over with a social worker common problems of adolescence or practices in the school of concern to them, or merely to clarify their own values and discuss ways in which they can counter peer group pressure to use drugs.

Accountability to School and Family

There are two principles of accountability that may conflict in a self-referral operation. The first is the right of a student to seek help without putting himself in jeopardy with parents or school authorities. The second is the right of parents and, to a lesser degree, school personnel to be informed about their child or student. If the presenting problem indicates the need for more than two sessions or if a threat to the health and safety of the student or others is possible or imminent, family and school involvement are necessary. When a student is seriously contemplating suicide, threatening to do bodily harm to someone, or using drugs in an extremely high-risk manner, the parents are notified immediately by the social worker, who first spends sufficient time with them to assure that their efforts will be helpful rather than punitive, in order to assuage the effect of a possible break of confidentiality with the student. The social worker is responsible for advising the guidance counselor on self-referrals necessitating more than two sessions. Minors must be advised about the range of and exceptions to confidentiality, especially when their health and safety are involved, and given the option to inform their parents themselves that they have sought social work assistance or to give the social worker permission to do so. The student may need help on the approaches to use if he elects to inform his parents himself. Two approaches that have been used effectively are these:

1. Role-playing the possible situation the student may encounter when he informs his parents.

2. Suggesting that the student notify his parents about his self-referral on the basis of problems already known to them, leaving the major issues to be dealt with by the social worker in subsequent work with the parents.

The setting for parental and faculty acceptance of self-referrals is best laid in staff and parent-teacher association meetings in which the social worker explains the system to parents and faculty and advises that there may be a time lapse of several weeks before parents of minors are notified, especially in the case of drug abusers. Most parents will accept the idea that the social worker needs to gain the trust and confidence of a student before working out ways and means of involving the parents. General acceptance by and awareness of parents of the self-referral system should be acquired via general PTA talks and other parents' group meetings before a self-referral system is initiated. With the appropriate indoctrination few parents will object to their child's voluntarily seeking help from a professional adult rather than seeking assistance from peers or less-qualified adults.

Serving Students Through System Change

The problem of drug abuse among youths and the concurrent problems of violence, strikes, and protests in the schools have forced parents, schools, communities, and professionals to take a penetrating look at the causes underlying these massive problems. Cohen, in the earlier years of the drug abuse problem, urged parents and educators not to look at drugs as the primary problem, but at what was really happening to youths in their schools and in their communities—to resolve the source of the problem, not the symptom. Dehumanizing practices, inadequate or irrelevant curricula, and the failure to teach and provide opportunities for viable alternatives to the use of drugs were cited as factors in the growth of drug abuse.[1]

The concept of a meaningful life, as adapted and implemented by Treffert, has often been advanced as a deterrent to drug abuse. This concept includes the need for youths to experience warm human rela-

[1] Allan Y. Cohen, "Inside What's Happening: Sociological, Psychological, and Spiritual Perspectives in the Contemporary Scene." Paper presented at the 42nd Annual Meeting of the American School Health Association, Detroit, Mich., November 12, 1968.

tionships, opportunities for honesty and self-expression without penalty, a sense of structure and hope for the future, a sense of belonging to something larger than oneself that is worthwhile, and a life that the individual feels he has made through his own efforts.[2]

Although critics of education have long identified other unmet needs of youths, advocating system change and the need for adults to take a closer look at what was happening to children in the school environment, change within school systems traditionally has been slow. Now the urgency of the drug problem and the threat of violence and protest in the schools have created a readiness for change.

INITIATING CHANGE Initiating system change and innovations requires first, a good working relationship among the social worker, students, faculty, administration, and community and second, the determination and energy to invest time and hard work in implementing change. A good relationship implies that the social worker is respected for the skills he has to offer but does not impose his ideas on others. Interviewing skills of listening with understanding, assessing the nature and extent of the problem, helping the client to develop insight into and understanding of his problem, and mutually arriving at a plan of action are the same skills utilized in working with larger groups to effect broad system change.

Change, whether in an individual, a small group, a school, or a community, is usually not effective unless workable action plans are developed, the persons involved are motivated to change, and change techniques are taught, demonstrated, and followed through by the one who is most concerned with the need for change. The school social worker may be not only the person who influences, persuades, and lobbies for a cause but the one who formulates plans, initiates programs, and implements them to a point at which others can take over or they are incorporated into the system.

MODELS OF CHANGE PROGRAMS The following are a few examples of social worker-initiated programs in the Dearborn (Mich.) school system that affected a broad range of students and problems.

---

[2] Dr. Darold Treffert, superintendent, Winnebago State Hospital, Winnebago, Wis., has referred to this concept in two articles: "The Mischief: Is It in Drugs or in People," *Rehabilitation Record,* Vol. 12, No. 2 (March–April 1971), pp. 5–11; and "The Mischief: Is It in Drugs or in People?" paper presented at the Western Institute on Drug Studies, Portland, Oregon, June 1972. The "meaningful life concept" was developed by a group called the Family, at Mendocino State Hospital, Mendocino, Calif.

A volunteer program. For a meaningful activity, at the request of a Future Teachers' Club in one high school the social worker initiated a small volunteer program in which twenty high school students worked as tutors with elementary school children. The following year students at a second high school asked to be involved in the program. After routine notices in the school bulletin, the social worker was deluged with a corps of seventy potential volunteers, with no workable program ready to accommodate so many. The worker obtained the approval of the administration; solicited operating funds from service clubs; developed a program involving training sessions, screening of high school students, and recruitment of children to be tutored from elementary school teachers and social workers; and recruited adult volunteers as supervisors. The social worker coordinated and supervised the overall operation on a voluntary after-school basis. As the program expanded in subsequent years to include over 150 students, the voluntary assistance of more social workers was enlisted.

A variety of proposals were developed designed to incorporate the program into the school system, including plans for credit classes with instruction, training, and supervised tutoring, various systems of coordination, and adaptations to expand the program into an overall community service program. Acceptance of the program in the schools was measured as follows:

1. The students themselves requested the program at the beginning of each year with little or no advertising. Incoming high school students, having heard of the program while in junior high school, inquired about volunteer work prior to entering high school.

2. When the social worker was involved in other business, the students themselves—prior to the social worker's involvement—advertised, recruited, posted a sign-up sheet for volunteers outside the social worker's office on which eighty students signed their names, held initial meetings, and recruited a teacher to help them.

3. Elementary school teachers and parents routinely requested volunteers.

4. PTAs and service clubs included the contribution for the volunteer program as a standing item on their budget.

When the program was too well established to be discontinued, with demonstrated value to the school and community, the Exchange Club (a community service club similar to the Rotary or Kiwanis club) offered a two-year grant to finance a pilot project to incorporate the program into the school system with possible credit offered to students,

271

expansion of community service opportunities, and a paid part-time coordinator in each of three high schools. The social workers who initiated and developed the program were to act only as consultants and referral sources, feeding into the program young children who needed the services of volunteers and high school students who needed the opportunity for meaningful activities.

School-community liaison program. Confronted with mounting problems in the schools and in the community and with poor school-police relations, the secondary school social workers promoted and effected a liaison of police, social workers, and administrators from all the secondary schools that evolved into a Youth Problems Committee—broadened to include representatives of the community and service clubs—that resulted in the formation of a police youth bureau and a variety of cooperative programs to help youths. These included talks by youth officers in elementary school classes on safety and in secondary schools on legal aspects of delinquency and drugs, and a variety of drug education programs in schools and PTAs.

A drug abuse program. Based on continuing assessment by the secondary school social workers of the increase in drug abuse owing to the greater influx of drugs into the community, the mobility of students that gave them access to drugs outside the neighborhood, and the lack of services and facilities to assist chronic or addicted drug abusers, the school administration selected one social worker to attend a concentrated drug workshop with the charge to plan an overall approach to a drug abuse program. With a preliminary proposal for a comprehensive community program prepared by the social worker, followed by talks before the PTA and service clubs to stimulate support, the school and community expanded the existing program into the extensive Dearborn Community Task Force including one hundred student, city, police, and community representatives. Among the task force's accomplishments were implementation of a walk-in counseling center and a hot line.

The youths involved in establishing the hot line requested the assistance of the two secondary school social workers to act as their liaison with the adult community, assist in training operators, set up operating procedures, and handle internal problems. The workers agreed also to act as a referral resource for difficult cases and as consultants on call when the operators felt they were not able to handle given situations.

After the first six months of the task force's operation, the school system selected a second school social worker to attend a national drug training workshop, thereby affirming their recognition of school social workers as change agents. Two social workers served concurrently as advisers to the walk-in counseling center committee to assist in planning and implementing the center. They also helped to screen applicants and select a full-time director for the center with the advice and consent of the youths from the hot line.

Both social workers, at the request of the school system administration, were selected to serve the Community Task Force in the area of professional staff development. Working through a committee composed of youths, teachers, administrators, and community representatives, the social workers led the group from its early focus on training staff members to teach drug education into a broader look at what could be done to make positive changes in the total living-learning environment. Utilizing resources from the State Department of Education, the Governor's Office on Drug Abuse, and the Wayne County Intermediate School District's Drug Abuse Reduction Through Education (DARTE) program, the committee developed workshops on communication skills and clarification of values involving an ever widening group of adults and youths. The primary objective of this mode of operation is to utilize the multiplier effect by involving a representative group of youths and adults in planning change processes, training the initial group to train secondary groups in the same process, and so on.

The objective of the social worker in any of these models is to initiate and maintain a leadership role only until other leaders are developed and the model is incorporated into the school system itself without the need for further involvement by the worker. By diminishing his leadership role in one area of system change, the social worker frees himself to approach another problem area and begin again.

Conclusion

To deviate from the traditional role, a social worker must be flexible, creative, competent in the traditional skills, and cognizant of the roles he must play and the limits of his function in the school setting. A balance must be maintained among casework, consultation on individual cases and general educational problems, and innovative involvement with a broader segment of the school and community in order to assess problems, change systems, and improve the living-learning environment.

While the school social worker is accountable to the school for handling individual students with problems, the school and community also have the right to expect that he will use his skills and knowledge in giving consultation on, planning, and innovating changes that affect a larger number of students. To avoid involvement in too many activities that might dilute the worker's effectiveness, expanded activities need to be screened and evaluated constantly to determine whether the task requires the specialized skills of the worker. If others can perform the function effectively, the task does not fall within the role of the school social worker. To provide time for expanded activities, crisis handling, and short-term drop-in self-referrals, the social worker should accept referrals for longer term casework or group work only if the resources of other members of the mental health team in the school have been exhausted and all other alternatives have been explored.

To operate an effective broad-based social work program in the secondary school, the social worker must earn the respect and trust of administration, faculty, students, and community; be willing to make a commitment of time that may involve overtime hours in crisis handling, committee work, and planning; and be able to function on a flexible schedule. The secondary school social worker is a mental health resource in the school. To work with only a few referred students is comfortable. To work with these few and also assist the school in changing the behavior and living-learning environment of many is to be accountable.

Partners in Change

Claire Gallant
Barbara Macdonald

The late 1960s produced a research study that clearly indicated the need for a new approach to school social work: expansion of the traditional one-to-one medical model to a broader base incorporating classroom meetings, consultation, and other means such as goal- and task-setting interviews and shared decision-making.[1] During that decade various articles had challenged school social work practice and many conferences had been held, but their impact was limited.[2] Clearly an intensive effort was needed to influence the majority of practitioners. Such a plan was eventually carried out in the state of Connecticut. By describing the types of workshops that were held, the development of models, and the wide range of participants, the writers intend to provide

---

[1] Lela B. Costin, *An Analysis of the Tasks in School Social Work as a Basis for Improved Use of Staff*, final report to the U.S. Department of Health, Education, and Welfare, Office of Education, Bureau of Research (Washington, D.C.: U.S. Government Printing Office, February 28, 1968).

[2] *See*, for example, Robert D. Vinter and Rosemary C. Sarri, "Malperformance in the Public School: A Group-Work Approach," *Social Work*, Vol. 10, No. 1 (January 1965), pp. 3–13; David Street, "Educators and Social Workers: Sibling Rivalry in the Inner City," *Social Service Review*, Vol. 41, No. 2 (June 1967), pp. 152–165.

an example of how change was implemented on a statewide level over a period of one year.

The problem, stated briefly, was to work out a system whereby two Connecticut Department of Education consultants (the present writers) could offer meaningful assistance to approximately seventy school systems whose social workers were requesting help or otherwise indicating some dissatisfaction. The requests for service from each community varied, but many common problems could be identified.

School social workers felt that they were not appreciated. Decisions about who would receive social work services were often made arbitrarily by the local school administration; the social workers themselves had little or no say in the matter. Much of the individual social worker's frustration could be traced to these arbitrary referrals. The worker might visit two or three elementary schools a week, receiving referrals from the principals or finding them in his mailbox. Most of the children referred represented disciplinary or learning problems, and the referrals usually requested that a home visit be made. The social worker found himself with a referral in hand but only the child available. There was no real access to the teacher or to the principal, and little access to the parents, who had already been called into the school and were not inclined to return. In the past some efforts had been made to improve this ineffective procedure—for example, requiring the teacher and the principal to be available for conferences each time a referral was accepted—but these were patchwork remedies for a service without a sound philosophical base.

Educational Workshops

In June 1970 representatives of five towns came together at the University of Connecticut School of Social Work to study the problem. Each social worker was asked to bring at least two teachers with whom he had a working relationship and the principal from each teacher's school. Pupil personnel directors were also asked to come. This one-day workshop allowed for open discussion, which emphasized class group discussions and analyzed the various techniques teachers could use to make discussions work. Some teachers had developed talk games around feelings; role-playing and the concept of contract-setting were also introduced.

A second workshop was planned to respond to social workers' expressed concern over their lack of experience in the classroom. As

276

pointed out in a recent study dealing with failures to implement change, the success of a new program depends on the training and capabilities of those involved.[3] Many of the state's school social workers had received their graduate degrees more than ten years ago and their expertise was in casework. Social systems theory, group management, contract-setting, and class meetings were new ideas to many of them.

The second workshop, held in September 1970, set about to change this. It was an action workshop—the forty participants experienced and practiced modern interviewing techniques, group management skills, and class meetings. The teacher who was present enthusiastically acknowledged the importance of a new role for school social workers after participating with the workshop leader in an actual problem-solving interview recorded on videotape. The interview demonstrated how a social worker and teacher could solve a student's problem in the classroom without a private conference between student and social worker. Perhaps most important, the focus was on the student's problem rather than on the student himself, and the issue of emotional disturbance did not enter the discussion. Papers by the workshop leader were distributed to help the participants assimilate the new concepts.[4]

Enthusiasm was generated across community lines, and the present writers were asked to speak on their findings at a variety of meetings. One of the most significant was Teachers Convention Day in late October 1970, attended by over two hundred educators. At this meeting the writers were faced with questions that established priorities for future activities.

The charge was made that class meetings could serve no function in the inner city or on the secondary level, that they were suitable only in white suburban elementary schools. There was much opposition, but it was offset by the enthusiasm and eagerness of many.

In March 1971 the University of Connecticut School of Social Work held a follow-up to the first workshop. It was decided to put on a demonstration within a school to try to help representatives of inner-city and secondary schools—and teachers and principals in general—understand the importance of the social worker's new role. A commit-

---

[3] Neal Gross, Joseph B. Giacquinta, and Marilyn Bernstein, "Failure to Implement a Major Organizational Innovation," in Matthew W. Miles and W. W. Charters, Jr., eds., *Learning in Social Settings* (Boston: Allyn & Bacon, 1970), p. 691.

[4] These consisted of three unpublished papers: Frank F. Maple and Edward J. Pawlak, "The Use of Labeling Theory in Social Work and in Educational Practice in Schools"; Maple, "Shared Decision Making: A Systematic Approach to Problem Solving"; and Maple, "A Manual for Class Meetings."

tee was formed and the result was a two-day workshop involving three hundred educators. The workshop featured live demonstrations at three schools and use of videotapes developed by participating school social workers.[5]

The writers were convinced that team involvement was essential. One of the committee members—a principal—felt that students should be included on the committee. Although this was ruled out, he kept his students totally involved on the day of the workshop, providing equipment, participating in discussions, and offering critiques. The rest of the committee realized how wise his suggestion had been— the students made a significant contribution.

A demonstration high school class meeting on the first day did not turn out well, but the poor results spurred the writers to gather more information and improve their skills with regard to the secondary level; the class meeting concept was redesigned for high school use.

On the second day an elementary school was opened to social workers and educators. In this school the children were accustomed to class discussion and had invited other adults and children to join them before; it was therefore possible to hold the workshop in the classrooms with the children sharing their ideas and experiences. At least forty principals took part in an interview training session, one of the highlights of the workshop. The innovations demonstrated by the staff at an inner-city school—in class meetings, goal-setting interviews, and on-the-spot evaluation service—more than convinced the participants about the practicality of these methods for inner-city schools. The school social workers in the three participating schools had adapted the techniques they had learned at the earlier workshop to the needs of their schools and communities, a perfect example of the value of and need for flexibility in any system.

At all the workshops the school social workers have had difficulty accepting simulation as a part of the new method. Simulations, as described by Maple, are "decision making games built to offer 'Let's Pretend' opportunities. Role playing is a well-known simulation technique." [6] The present writers concluded that this uncertainty was due to lack of understanding, and in a May 1971 workshop eight school

---

[5] The three schools were Hamden High School, Hamden; North West Elementary School, Newington; and Baldwin School, Baldwin King Project, New Haven.

[6] Frank F. Maple, "The Development of Practice Theory for School Social Workers," p. 7. Unpublished paper presented at the National Conference on Social Welfare, Chicago, June 1970.

social workers were given extra training to assist the workshop leader, who in turn simplified the model he was using. Evaluation of this workshop revealed that teachers were quite enthusiastic about the technique and anticipated using it, but social workers considered it impractical and did not expect to use it much. Some of their uneasiness was based on a feeling that the use of games was too far removed from reality.

It is significant that teachers will accept new means of reaching children more readily than social workers will. The receptiveness and enthusiasm shown by teachers should encourage school social workers to evaluate the change process with less bias.

Developing Models

The next thrust was toward the development of our own models. Three diverse communities were selected in which the school social workers had no stake in maintaining the old techniques.

Throughout the late fall and early winter of 1970–71, the authors visited these towns to observe any progress and to offer direct consultation and in-service training. But the results seemed meager in proportion to the energy and enthusiasm that had been expended; progress was spotty and inconsistent, and frequently it did not occur in the school systems where the greatest improvement had been anticipated. However, in some schools new models for school social work were developing. The following examples are illustrative:

1. Social workers were working with teachers in the classrooms and they were responding together to the needs of children, each using the different kinds of training they had received and learning from each other. Many social workers were not used to dealing with groups of children; the teachers supported their efforts to run class meetings. Many teachers, on the other hand, had avoided certain kinds of discussions in class, steering away from expressions of anger, criticism, or personal feelings because they did not know how to respond. The social worker's use of interpersonal skills in the classroom illuminated another approach to children. When a school social worker ran a class meeting or helped a teacher show children how to solve problems collectively, adults and children learned together.

2. Principals received fewer requests from teachers for individual referrals of children, since children were helped by their classmates in the open, relaxed climate of the classroom.

3. Teachers submitted requests for help in classroom management

rather than asking social workers to subdue individual children who were difficult to handle.

4. School social workers developed new referral and assessment forms in order to compare their understanding of the purpose of the service with that of the teachers.

Four towns were identified in which such models were developing. In these school systems the authors found strong principals who attracted good faculty and able social workers who were encouraged to try new methods. It was also discovered that principals and workers in neighboring schools, who were more conservative in their reactions to new methods, were willing to copy models that had been used successfully by their more adventurous colleagues. Teachers learned about classroom meetings from other teachers and asked for help in running them.

On the basis of these findings the writers worked out some ground rules for accelerating statewide change:

1. No more workshops were offered exclusively for social workers. Instead invitations went out to superintendents, principals, social workers, pupil personnel directors, and teachers.

2. Little effort was focused on school systems resistant to change. Invitations went to a number of school systems involved in new methods, including the consultants' model programs. Only a few of the more conservative towns—located near the model service—were included.

3. Concentration was on developing leadership in principals, teachers, and social workers in the model services through training them to be leaders in state workshops. More conservative educators from nearby communities were encouraged to visit the model service and watch trained leaders in action. Principals and school social workers were encouraged to include all staff members in classroom discussions and had learned to solve problems through these meetings.

Partly as a result of the writers' new way of offering consultation, school social work in Connecticut is rapidly becoming a service meaningful to administrators and classroom teachers. The partnership between educators and workers will serve to make the school community a more open society in which children and adults can learn together.

Anticipated Directions for State Consultation

The practice of limiting attendance at state workshops to those social workers who can bring the principals, teachers, and pupil personnel directors of their schools with them has been most effective. In the past the social worker has been inspired at various conferences to be an agent of change, then sent home to a group of uninspired educators who are understandably not receptive to his suggestions. When the principal, pupil personnel director, and teacher are all present at the workshop, workshop leaders feel compelled to influence them as well as the social workers, through visible demonstrations of the fresh techniques available to them. The outcome is that educators go home from a workshop committed to change, having shared the experience with their social workers. Working on problems together, even in the synthetic workshop situation, creates an atmosphere that helps the process continue. This is the key to innovation and change. The joint commitment with shared experiences elicits the energy to do the work required to keep the ideas alive.

Not enough attention has been paid to the inadequate attendance by superintendents and pupil personnel directors, and the reasons for this poor attendance have not been identified. Plans are under way to develop the participation of students and parents in workshops, thus ensuring a more intense experience than is possible with educators alone.

But why is it so difficult for some school social workers to leave the sanctuary of the one-to-one approach? In a follow-up session in the summer of 1971 with seven of the most innovative school social workers, their answer was that they had no power. But this explanation is less than satisfactory, given the authors' conclusion that workers are less responsive than teachers to suggestions for change (see Table 1). There is no simple answer to the question. Only a combination of factors—support, encouragement, recognition, and skill—will suffice to restructure an entrenched system.

It is becoming increasingly evident that the material tools of school social work services—records, manuals, referral forms, and the like—need to be upgraded to ensure the attainment of new goals. It is not possible, for example, to move from child-oriented casework service to task-oriented school community service using old referral forms that ask for a description of a single child's behavior. And, of course, it is difficult for teachers to reconcile 1940 pupil personnel manuals that offer "a mental health service for children with emotional problems" with the worker's offer to help with classroom management problems. Records are a constantly nagging issue at all levels. The writers suggest the use of class records rather than individual records, kept only until the class problem is solved.

Table 1

Average Change Scores on Questions Concerning Workshop Techniques

Techniques	Class Meeting		Teacher Interview		Game Simulation	
	Preworkshop score	Postworkshop score	Preworkshop score	Postworkshop score	Preworkshop score	Postworkshop score
Knowledge of						
School social workers	2.55	3.37	2.92	4.17	1.69	3.31
Classroom teachers	1.75	3.25	1.67	3.75	1.75	3.33
Feasible to use						
School social workers	2.95	3.51	3.42	4.08	1.97	2.74
Classroom teachers	3.00	4.27	2.70	4.20	2.60	3.80
Confidence in using						
School social workers	2.08	3.16	2.83	4.08	1.54	2.89
Classroom teachers	1.58	3.08	1.42	3.42	1.67	2.67
Commitment to use						
School social workers	3.14	3.75	3.71	4.32	2.13	3.00
Classroom teachers	2.40	3.80	2.10	3.90	2.36	3.64
Anticipate using						
School social workers	3.05	3.30	3.74	4.23	2.35	2.62
Classroom teachers	2.10	4.00	2.33	4.11	2.40	3.70
Useful to						
School social workers	3.56	4.06	3.91	4.49	2.52	3.36
Classroom teachers	2.56	4.44	2.67	4.78	2.70	4.40
Enthusiasm for						
School social workers	3.54	4.08	3.83	4.43	2.45	3.26
Classroom teachers	3.08	4.58	2.73	4.46	2.83	4.25

The rating scale used was as follows: 1, not at all; 2, not very much; 3, fairly; 4, very; 5, extremely. With the exception of social workers' anticipated use of game simulation, increases in scores between pre- and postworkshop times were significant at either the .01 or .05 level.

As state consultants the writers see their task as to impart new ideas, create new models, redefine expertise, and improve tools. Referral forms, local service manuals, job descriptions, records, and statistics all work to bind school social workers to the old procedures, and all must be revised if new procedures are to succeed.

A rough overview shows that progress has been made in changing the traditional model. Workshops have provided the primary impetus toward change; twenty-one towns had access to an area workshop.

All school social work staff in the writers' areas of the state were invited to at least one workshop during the 1970–71 school year and 66 percent of them attended at least once. Five statewide workshops were offered and two more were sponsored by the University of Connecticut School of Social Work. A film has been produced that illustrates the different models that evolved, and a monograph was prepared to accompany the film.

These new approaches—involving action-oriented workshops, the structuring of new models, and follow-up support from consultants—are unique in that they were planned and carried out on a statewide level. The sanction of the state department of education was a help; a single agency coordinating all participating towns and services provided a strong and effective framework for the program.

Further study should be undertaken on the impact the school social worker's changing role will have on the schools. Observation of the authors' model programs alone will not serve to sustain the process of change. Professional conviction must be supported by action research and evaluation.

Problem-Solving Through Shared Decision-Making

Frank F. Maple

The material in this learning package is intended to help people become effective problem-solving partners. The approach is designed for situations in which both participants in a dyadic transaction are seeking a common solution to some overall problem. When a parent-teacher interview is conducted, for example, both partners often want to change aspects of the child's behavior, whether academic or social outcomes are involved. To be effective partners, however, each participant must accept specific communication functions designed to develop a workable plan of action. One participant must present the problem as he experiences it in a given situation. The other must work to clarify the way the problem is stated, the subparts of the problem, the goal, and so forth. The process used by both partners must be systematic so that expectations for the transaction are clear to both. Shared decision-making is such a process. Thus the entire approach may be conceptualized as partners sharing responsibility for a clearly defined process to achieve a workable solution (their mutual goal).

Rationale

One of the major reasons for the failure of change efforts to work initially or to be maintained over a period of time is that the change strategy was usually conceived in an adversary transaction. That is, two or more persons sat down together to try to arrive at a solution using tried and *un*true interviewing or group decision-making procedures. By untrue it is meant that the transactions have historically proved ineffective in regard to the efficient production of workable and operable solutions between two persons who want to improve a general situation involving both parties to different degrees. Much has been written about the games people play in these transactions, but little has been done to help people learn simple, systematic procedures by which they can effectively conduct their everyday business.

The approach described in this learning package attempts to avoid two of the major limiting factors apparent in the traditional interview. The process is called shared decision-making (SDM)—a term designed to avoid the idea that seems to be present in most interviews, namely, that one person is "doing something" to the other person, so that one participant must be on the defensive. In conrast, SDM implies equal collective responsibility in arriving at a solution. This means that the step-by-step process to be followed and the basic terms of the relationship must be clearly spelled out. In the SDM process the interviewee (called the problem-poser) is provided—prior to the transaction—with a written diagram of the process, a page of clarifying comments, and a transcription of a sample interview. The process is further clarified for potential interviewees whenever possible by exposing them to a live interview. For example, an elementary school teacher might conduct an SDM transaction with a parent at a parent-teacher association meeting scheduled just prior to parent-teacher conference time.

In dyadic transactions designed to solve problems, the goal of SDM is to have the problem-poser understand as much about the problem-solving process as the helping professional does. In social work the sharing aspect is achieved through clear guidelines, a demonstrated example, and specific benefits identified for potential problem-posers. The potential problem-poser then determines whether the transaction might be useful to him.

Thus the SDM process is used with voluntary clients. The two people meeting have clear expectations of what will happen and accept different individual functions for the duration of the transaction. One partner wants a solution to a specific problem; the other partner (the process director), wants to help the problem-poser find a workable solution.

In one transaction a parent may help the teacher solve a child's problem that is focused in the classroom. In another transaction the teacher may help the parent solve a problem with the child at home. To function as an effective partnership, the parent-teacher dyad can address only one of these problems at a time. The expert on the first problem is the teacher, so the teacher is both the problem-poser and the person in charge of presenting data on the problem. When overall approaches to a solution are being considered, the parent adds relevant data about the child to help evaluate each approach under consideration, thus limiting the input and facilitating communication. Thus a premise of this approach is that communication must be limited or focused to be effective.

What Is Shared Decision-Making?

Shared decision-making is a dyadic transaction in which one person presents the content of the problem while the second person is in charge of operating the SDM process. It is a basic tool designed to provide clear expectations regarding both the power and the process of an initial problem-solving dyadic transaction.

SDM can be demonstrated to a large group of potential problem-posers in order to rehearse them for their actual transactions. It provides an opportunity for the person seeking help to see and practice the helping process he will use before he commits himself to participation.

SDM is seen as a basic minimum structure on which to build competent helping skills. It can be modified and individualized to fit varying personal styles and to fit later interviews in which progress is reported and evaluated. The SDM diagram can be made visible during interviews and charted for progress by either participant.

The basic SDM concept is that clear expectations will enhance cooperation in problem-solving transactions. The subconcepts are as follows:

1. The rights of each individual in a two-way communication must be clearly spelled out.

2. The process by which the plan of action will be developed must be clearly understood by both parties.

3. The two persons must see themselves as partners seeking a mutual goal with differential powers regarding each function in the transaction clearly prescribed.

The overall objectives of the SDM process are to (1) obtain maximum relevant information—information used in the plan of action—and avoid collecting irrelevant information, (2) maintain optimum interpersonal relations, and (3) develop an overall approach and a specific goal path designed to resolve at least one problem, difficulty, or concern presented in the transaction.

Training Program

Learning objectives of the SDM training program for the helping professional are that, given a person seeking help with one or more human performance problems stated in vague terms, the process director should be able to do the following:

1. Help the problem-poser to isolate, define, and describe one or more problem situations in his life.

2. Help select one problem for resolution at this time.

3. Help transform the problem into a goal stated in behaviorally specific terms.

4. Clearly spell out what outcome may be expected if the goal is achieved.

5. Develop and clarify two or more alternative approaches to achieving the goal.

6. Systematically select the best overall approach through listing the good and bad points of each approach.

7. Develop a feasible plan of action and obtain a commitment to implement that plan.

Learning the preceding steps will increase the process director's effectiveness in interpersonal transactions. Potential benefits to participants include an increase in knowledge and understanding of verbal communication difficulties, development of the skills necessary to demonstrate an effective SDM transaction, and development of workable solutions (plans of action) to actual problem situations.

PRETEST   *Goal:* To determine effectively the entry skills of participants regarding the basic tasks of the worker in dyadic transactions.

Means: Given one hour and a fellow student (peer, colleague), each participant will train and evaluate one learner's ability to carry out one important problem-solving task. The trainer will select the task from his past experiences, from a list of four such tasks, or through seeking information from anyone he wishes. He will then design his training and evaluative procedures and operate them during the scheduled hour.

Measurement: If the average of two observations places the learner in the top 75 percent of a scale ranging from not competent to very competent, the trainer will have successfully demonstrated that he possesses the skill to carry out the task himself.

INSTRUCTIONS TO THE TRAINER This learning package is designed to be used in conjunction with the demonstration-practice-application learning sequence. The step-by-step approach is as follows:

1. Participants read the Outline for Shared Decision-Making.
2. The trainer explains the rationale behind the process.
3. The trainer conducts a demonstration interview with a participant who presents a real problem that he is currently facing. Participants offer a critique of the interview as they observe it.
4. Observers ask questions of either the trainer or the problem-poser.
5. In Practice Session I the total group is divided into triads to practice the technique. Each triad is composed voluntarily, with the members of the triad assuming the roles of problem-poser, observer, and process director. Practice Session II immediately follows Practice Session I, with the members of each triad simply switching roles. One triad is either videotaped or audiotaped during Practice Session I and a different triad is taped during Practice Session II.

An excellent way to set up the first round is to ask the participants to think of someone they need to talk to in the coming week about a real problem. In this approach one member of each triad is asked to describe what problems he will face in that future interaction with his child, marital partner, immediate superior, teacher, colleague, or whatever. Then this participant is asked to assume the position of the person he will be confronting. The other two members of the triad become respectively the process director and observer.

After two practice sessions the participants are called back into one large group and one tape is played. A step-by-step critique of their session, with group participation, is carried out. The purpose of this exercise is to obtain clarity and consensus on the most important steps of the process.

Practice Session III involves asking the problem-poser and the process director in each triad to read aloud a transcription of the first five minutes of an actual interview between a parent and a school social worker and then to finish the transaction as they see fit. Using the SDM technique, this offers an interesting wrap-up session in which the various plans of action may be compared and a good composite plan developed.

INSTRUCTIONS TO PARTICIPANTS The SDM approach cannot be called new or totally different. However, it is up to date in the sense that it is designed to allow both participants in a dyadic transaction relatively equal knowledge about what they are doing, with power clearly delegated through explicit identification of who is in charge of each basic component of the transaction. That is, the problem-poser is the expert on the problem and on the workability of any potential solution. The process director is the expert on the process of the transaction and is in charge of operating the procedures that should lead to the development of an effective plan of action (for example, he brings the discussion back on the track, checks the clarity of the understanding, and so on).

This approach is not called interviewing, because that word implies doing something *to* someone. The emphasis of this approach is on doing something *with* someone. The dyad may be viewed as a problem-solving partnership. Communication is sideways—not up and down.

Therefore the term shared decision-making implies equal knowledge about the process to be used and about the functions each person will have in the process. Also involved is shared responsibility for the outcome, whether it is a workable plan of action or possibly a determination that the two persons are unable to develop such a plan at this time. Thus potential failure is immediately accepted as one of two possible outcomes in any SDM transaction, so that free discussion about why a plan did not develop is a normal part of the shared decision-making.

Outline for Shared Decision-Making

1. The worker utilizes the maximum level of the client's motivation to state his problem by opening with a question that elicits what the client wants to talk about in this session.

2. The worker follows up the client's opening statement with a general question designed to obtain more information about the client's initial concerns.

THE SCHOOL IN THE COMMUNITY

3. The worker prevents premature closure on the first problem or difficulty presented by asking the client to describe another area of difficulty.

4. The worker and the client collectively agree to focus on one problem by selecting from the problems presented the one that meets these two criteria:

a. It can be resolved successfully.

b. The resolution of this problem is important to the client.

5. The worker guides the first phase of the transaction so that

a. Obstacles to solutions are not discussed in this phase.

b. The time spent talking about the problem is minimized by changing the problem statement into clear specifications (behaviorally specific goals) of what has to be accomplished.

c. The worker quickly identifies two or three alternative approaches designed to achieve the objective selected. One overall approach is selected from the following criteria:

(1) It seems to be the right approach after the pros and cons of each approach have been spelled out.

(2) It has not been selected because it is the most acceptable approach (compromises are made during goal path planning, not now).

6. The worker and the client convert the decision on one overall approach into a planned goal path.

7. Finally, the goal path must include specified means for ascertaining progress and modifying the procedures accordingly.

In the following example of shared decision-making, the social worker uses all the major skills that will be learned in this training program.

Time: Early February
Place: A senior high school in an academically oriented community
Social worker: Bill Miller, a full-time social worker at this school
Teacher: Jim Shaw—biology, earth science, conservation
Situation: Jim Shaw has requested a meeting with Bill Miller because he has some questions about students in his conservation class who are doing little or no schoolwork. Jim has just arrived at Bill's office. The discussion proceeds as follows:

BILL: Come in, Jim. Pull up a chair.

JIM: Thanks, Bill. I've been troubled by a large number of kids in my conservation class who won't do any work, and I finally decided it might be helpful to talk it over with you.

290

BILL: I'd be glad to try and help. What do you think is going on in the class, Jim?

(Here the worker goes cordially but directly to the problem.)

JIM: Well, I'm not sure, Bill. I've been looking into it but I don't seem to have any answers yet. I had hoped it wouldn't last this long, but now I know it's not a temporary situation.

(This statement verifies that there is a continuing problem requiring the development of action plans.)

BILL: Can you tell me anything more about the problem?

(The worker makes sure that the teacher offers his ideas about the problem first.)

JIM: Well, they just aren't motivated to do any work. Other teachers complain about them too. You know, conservation is a dumping ground for kids the school doesn't know what else to do with. If they need a credit for graduation they stick them in with me and hope I can get them through.

BILL: Yes, I know that's one reason kids are put in your course. Can you give me an example or two of when they are acting in an unmotivated way?

(The worker seeks to clarify the problem of lack of motivation, hoping to divide it into subparts.)

JIM: Well, I can't get the kids to complete their field projects, and I can't even get them to participate in class.

BILL: Oh, in other words participating in class discussions and turning in completed field projects are what motivated pupils do?

(The worker now turns the problem behavior into clear specifications of what objectives the problem-solving discussion must accomplish.)

JIM: Yes, that's right. In this class it doesn't seem to make any difference what I do; they just sit like dead fish when I ask for questions.

BILL: What kinds of things have you tried?

(The next steps must be performed carefully, because they can downgrade the teacher's past efforts. The worker's purpose is to elicit some of the teacher's attempted solutions so that they may be modified and revised.)

JIM: Well, I have used a lot of audiovisual aids, and lately I've had slides for the first fifteen or twenty minutes of the class, hoping they would get the group going, but it hasn't worked.

BILL: Using audiovisual materials does seem like a good approach. In other words, you can't seem to get discussion started no matter how you pattern your teaching.

(The social worker first acknowledges the teacher's suggestion and provides reinforcement for it; he then summarizes what has just been said.)

JIM: Oh, some patterns have worked better than others. The slides have led four or five students to ask questions, which practically no one did before.

BILL: Did you change anything else when you got that increase in participation?

JIM: Yes, come to think of it. I started making a record of each time someone participated and I told them they could improve their grades by participating. Of course, most of these students don't care about a grade as long as they pass, so it hasn't affected them much.

BILL: I think record-keeping sounds like a good idea, but it didn't influence enough pupils. You sound like you want to solve this as soon as you can. Let's keep at it and see if we can figure this thing out, Jim. You've done a good job of bringing me up to date on the class. Let's sum up where we stand. We know that the lack of participation is a general problem for these kids and it represents a long-term situation. It doesn't appear to be related much to subject matter or teacher behavior and isn't influenced when competition for grades is stressed. Would you agree with those two statements?

JIM: Yes. In fact, that's exactly where things stand now.

BILL: OK. With that as background, what other factors—especially general factors—might affect the situation?

JIM: Well, there must be something about this school system that makes it easier to sit and do nothing than to complete work.

The kids sure don't see any connection between learning in my class and anything they want for themselves.

BILL: Good point, Jim. What might be in the system that causes boredom, or what might the system lack that would lead to pupil motivation if it existed?

JIM: Well, I can think of a few ways to turn kids off, and I guess my class and the school as a whole turn those kids off. For example, we don't offer any relevant outcomes for them in their terms for the learning behaviors we expect. I know grades don't turn these kids on, but I'm darned if I know what else I can offer them.

BILL: Could we have inadvertently led the pupils to believe we wanted them to sit quietly and not participate as they went through school? Kids often tell me how they get yelled at for talking, and in some cases I have tried to help kids learn to sit quietly in class. We've got the same coin—talking—one side is how to obtain it when it's useful to learning; the other side is how to control it when it hurts learning. Let's look at how you communicate your expectations for participation to your pupils now, Jim.

(This section was put in to demonstrate how oversummarizing and too much informational input on the part of the worker can lead the interview off the track. Note how the next paragraph could have connected to Jim's statement before the worker's summary.)

JIM: Well, when class started in January I set up a contract plan with incentives for completing projects, but I didn't connect classroom participation into it in any way. I guess I thought they would participate because of the fun of getting involved in discussing anything. After all, all teen-agers like to talk, and this gives them a chance to show that they know a little about something!

BILL: Well, your incentive plan may need simplifying or clarifying if it's not working. If the overall class is mainly concerned about getting only a passing grade, then they would——

JIM: They'd sit and do as little as possible, and they'd avoid participating because that might expose their ignorance!

293

BILL: Such a fear may be a factor. Is there anything else you can think of that might affect the situation?

JIM: Yeah, one kid told me that he and his buddies figure that's how to make the teacher feel like a failure. You know, it should be obvious that the real message they're getting from teachers is: Work for me so I'll feel successful.

BILL: That seems like an important new piece of information. Could we say, then, that the real problem is that asking pupils to put out for us is upsetting the pupils since there is no way for them to work for themselves? We need to figure some way to provide for learning opportunities that will help pupils demonstrate their own success.

JIM: I really feel sorry about this, Bill, because I can see now that much of the situation is my fault. I was so concerned about my own immediate problem of getting pupils to work that I didn't think a plan through. I didn't determine my own priorities before setting up my incentive plan, so how could my pupils know what I wanted?

BILL: Nonsense, Jim! Being a teacher means exercising judgment dozens of times a day, and you know you do a good job in most of your classes. The critical question is: Where do we go from here? To decide that we have to ask ourselves: What restrictions are there on what you can do? As I see it, you shouldn't go back on any promises to the pupils, and we can't do anything that will cost more money. Within those two restrictions, what do you think you can do about the problem?

JIM: Well, I never said what percentage of their total class grade their project would be. I could adjust the percentage so that class participation would become essential just to pass the course.

BILL: That's a possibility, but let's see if you really want to. How would it help and not help?

JIM: It would probably get participation going, but the pupils wouldn't do a good job of thinking and communicating, and it might make some of those presently participating pretty mad. No, that's no good. What I really should do is provide bonuses for evidence of good thinking as demonstrated in class participa-

294

tion. I warned the pupils that the incentive plan was an experiment and might be modified as we gained experience with it. As long as I give them notice of the change, it will be OK.

BILL: Well, let's check out your idea. How are you thinking of modifying the plan?

JIM: I don't know yet, and judging from my past experience, I'd better be darn sure I do know before I go monkeying with it! There's obviously much more to a work incentive plan than I realized. I'll want to talk with you again at some length about the implications of any revised plan.

BILL: I'll be glad to help if I can, Jim. How long do you think it will take to develop a revised plan?

JIM: About a week to ten days.

BILL: Is there anything you want to do in the meantime that will get the pupils working?

JIM: Sure there is: I think the thing to do is to lay my cards on the table with the pupils. I can explain exactly what's been happening, and why in the long run their lack of participation is harmful to them, to me, to the school. Then I can involve them in planning a revised incentive plan—heck, I should have done that in the first place—and ask for their cooperation in regard to participating in class now and in developing the plan.

BILL: Do you think that some will be angry and resent this approach?

JIM: No, I'm sure they won't as long as they understand why. You see, it should still give them the leeway they need to act in their own best interests.

BILL: Fine. Then we are saying that the best approach to solving the problem is to try to get the pupils to cooperate in increasing classroom participation and in revising the incentive plan. You can see how these two can fit together, since you can ask for group discussion as one means of revising the plan.

JIM: I sure can.

BILL: Well, let's turn these ideas into actions before we close. We each have certain things to do. I'll be available whenever you're ready to discuss a revised incentive plan. But before you draft the plan you work out with the pupils, you said you want to lay your cards on the table right away with the pupils. When can you do that?

JIM: I'll handle that in class first thing tomorrow—in fact, I'll schedule the entire period for discussion of the problem and starting to revise the incentive plan. That way I'll be ready to discuss a proposed revision of the incentive plan with you by . . . say Monday or Tuesday of next week.

BILL: Tuesday would be best for me, particularly if you can give me the draft Monday to read over before I see you.

JIM: That would be fine.

BILL: Swell, let's put it down for 2:00 during your conference period. Would you also give me a brief summary of the student response to your laying the cards on the table tomorrow?

JIM: Sure. Well, thanks a lot for your help on this, Bill. I think I know the real source of the trouble. See you on the twenty-sixth at 2:00.

BILL: You bet, Jim. I'll be looking forward to your plan—I'll bet other teachers might want to know about the outcome of your effort to increase participation. We can talk about that next time, if you want to. Thanks for coming in.

LESSON 1—WORKER-INITIATED STEPS The following steps are those initiated by the worker in shared decision-making:

1. *Defining the problem*
   a. Brief greeting.
   b. We will look at a couple of problems, then work on them one at a time.
   c. What difficulty would you like to discuss first today?
   d. Can you give me examples of when the difficulty occurs most?
   e. Who does what? . . . when? . . . where? . . . how often? . . . how much?
   f. Is there another problem you would like to cover today? (If so, repeat steps *d* and *e*.)
   g. Which problem that we both believe it is possible and important to solve should we try to work on today by developing a plan to resolve it?
   h. Summarize the problem.

2. *Specifying the goal*
   a. What behaviors would you expect to see if the problem were solved?
   b. Can we try to state two or three outcomes as behaviorally specific objectives?
   c. To clarify the goal, we will try to figure out how to achieve it.
   d. We can test whether we are specific enough by starting to talk about overall approaches we can identify that would help us move toward our goals.

3. *Developing and evaluating alternative overall approaches*
   a. Try to identify a couple of alternative approaches designed to move toward the objective. What can be done?
   b. Evaluation of the first suggestion—how it would help or not help and what new problems it might create.
   c. What else might be done?
   d. Evaluation of the second suggestion· as in *b*.
   e. Are there any other overall approaches?
   f. Summary of what the best overall approach is.

4. *Specifying the goal path*
   a. Statement of what the specific goal path is.
   b. Can this be accomplished?
   c. Restatement of the path.
   d. Closing.

5. *Process directors do the following:*
   a. Obtain maximum relevant information (and avoid collecting irrelevant information).
   b. Maintain optimum interpersonal relations.
   c. Develop an overall approach and a specific plan of action designed to resolve at least one problem, difficulty, or concern presented by the client during the interview.

LESSON 2—DEFINING THE PROBLEM   The objective of this lesson is to learn to recognize when a problem is limited and clearly defined. In learning this skill the worker should be able to recognize easily the differences among (1) broad problems clearly defined, (2) limited or focused problems clearly defined, and (3) any problem stated in general terms and/or poorly defined.

During Practice Session I each observer is asked to turn in statements from each participant about problems presented during the session. An oral reading of these statements at a collective session with group evaluation should develop group consensus regarding what is a clear and limited problem statement. Then the following examples are distributed and the correct responses discussed with the total group.

Participants are asked to indicate whether each of the following problem statements is clear, limited, not clear, or not limited (the correct answer is given in parentheses following each statement):

1. Randy seldom completes any schoolwork. (Not clear, not limited)

2. Bill is hyperactive, always busy with his hands, and disruptive in school. (Not clear, not limited)

3. Joan talks incessantly to the girls near her during desk work in mathematics. (Limited, not clear)

4. Barry has not completed one English theme this year. (Clear, limited)

5. Judy has no friends. (Not clear, not limited)

6. Helen has not been asked to participate in any activities during recess since she cried in class two weeks ago. (Clear, limited)

LESSON 3—PROBLEMS INTO GOALS The objective of this lession is, given a series of clear, limited problem statements, to transform them into feasible goal statements. A feasible goal is a goal that the problem-poser states is important and possible to achieve.

When problem statements have been generated in the group session, the group and the trainer can collectively transform the best problem statements submitted from each triad into goal statements. Then the following examples are distributed and the correct responses are discussed with the total group.

1. "Everything's wrong. Everybody is ignoring my requests for help for my son. My husband won't lift a finger. It makes me irritable, tense, and depressed." Select the appropriate goal statement:

    a. My husband should help me with my son.
    b. I want to reduce my feeling of tension.
    c. I want to be less irritable.
    d. None of the above.
(Answer a is correct.)

2. "The students in my class aren't motivated to do any work. They don't turn in their assignments and they don't participate in classroom discussions." Select the best goal statement:
    a. I want the students to increase their motivation.

298

b. I want at least a 50 percent increase in individual participation in classroom discussions following my presentations. Since only three students are now participating and I allow twenty minutes, this is a possible goal.

c. I want everyone in class to turn in at least one assignment per week.

d. None of the above.

(Either b or c is correct, since they are both measurable.)

LESSON 4—DEVELOPING OVERALL APPROACHES The objective of Lesson 4 is, given a clear, limited goal, to develop two or more overall approaches worthy of evaluation. An approach is deemed worthy if no immediate restriction is apparent to either partner.

Using two clear, limited goal statements generated from the practice sessions, the audience is asked to generate two or more overall approaches to each goal and determine which is worth spending time evaluating. Then the participants are asked to discuss briefly the approaches listed in the case examples that follow.

1. A school social worker and John, an 11-year-old boy, have been working on numerous problems for several weeks. John has run away from home several times and has been referred to the local juvenile authorities for possible residential placement. In the last transaction John asked the worker for help in dealing with the fact that his mother regularly locks him in his room when he doesn't complete his chores satisfactorily.

The worker and John are discussing possible approaches to dealing with this problem. Of course the first task is to try to transform the problem into a goal statement. One tentative attempt has been made. The goal that has been set is to increase the number of times John performs a chore satisfactorily and to decrease the number of times and the length of time he is locked in his room. This goal is clear enough to cause both the worker and John to think in terms of clarifying what a minimally acceptable performance of each chore is, developing criteria for evaluating chore performance, and linking appropriate outcomes (praise, length of punishment, and the like) to the competence of John's performance.

With these details the worker and John have to decide which approach would produce measures that the mother will actually use. This is the immediate limited goal.

Potential overall approaches are as follows:

a. John develops such measures with the worker's help.

b. John, in an SDM transaction, asks his mother to develop such measures and helps her to do it.

c. John and the worker together, in an SDM transaction, help John's mother to develop her own measures.

d. The worker sees John's mother alone and tries to develop such measures.

e. The worker teaches John's mother the SDM process and asks her to use it with John to develop such measures.

2. A 25-year-old young man reported that he weighed fifty pounds more than his doctor recommended. Select the appropriate goal statement:

a. Increase his appreciation of the dignity of food.

b. Increase the number of times he devotes himself exclusively to eating without any reinforcing consequences.

c. Give up thirty minutes of television viewing for each between-meal trip to the refrigerator.

d. None of the above.

(Answer d is correct. We do not know what the client wants, only what the doctor recommends.)

Now let us do the total job of transforming problem statements into goal statements and then developing overall approaches.

3. A 23-year-old woman complained of having no friends of her own age and of being so fearful of peer contacts that she constantly withdrew from young adults despite her intense desire to be with them. The major skill, knowledge, or attitude to be achieved in this case should be a specific statement of the goal identified by the problem-poser expressed in terms of how she would like to be able to behave in specific situations at the conclusion of treatment. This does not require the level of behavior of a highly skilled or experienced person, but the kind of performance that can reasonably be expected at the end of the treatment period.

Step I. The goals might be stated as follows:

a. The client wants to develop lasting friendships.

b. That is too broad an area to be a target. What is friendship?

Step II. Redefine the goals.

a. The client wishes to interact in social situations on a continuing basis with males and females of her own age.

b. Now friendship has been defined as involving continuing interaction among two or more people.

Step III. Try for a more specific statement. First friendship must be defined. One definition is that friendship is a series of continuing voluntary interactions among two or more people that are reinforcing to all parties. Reinforcement involves continuous requests for future interactions and the fulfillment of these requests.

Step IV. Restate the goals. The client wants to know three non-agency persons who will agree to interact with her on request and who will ask her to interact with them on a continuing and fairly equal basis.

Step V. Specification of subgoals.

a. The client can learn the skills necessary to make herself attractive to peers.

b. The client can learn skills to enable her to locate peers.

c. The client can learn approach behaviors in specific social situations.

d. The client can learn behaviors appropriate to the maintenance of new friendships.

Step VI. Selection of a single goal and statement clarification. It is necessary to check each potential goal against three elements before going further. These elements require that the following be specified:

a. The performance expected of the learner

b. The conditions under which the performance will take place

c. The proficiency level expected of the learner

The assignment to the participant is to rewrite one goal to contain these elements.

LESSON 5—EVALUATING OVERALL APPROACHES The objective of this lesson is to learn to list at least one advantage and one disadvantage of an overall approach with which two other persons will agree. Participants should divide into small groups and go through each of the goals listed in Lesson 4. Each group should agree on one advantage and disadvantage of each goal. Participants should then cite an advantage and a disadvantage for the two cases that follow. Each participant should find two other persons who will agree with one of each of the advantages and disadvantages for either case.

1. A teacher of a social problems class of thirty eleventh-graders decided to develop a series of dramatic vignettes picturing the situation at Attica State Prison before, during, and after the riot as a means of looking at injustice in prisons.

2. A third-grade teacher has been talking to the worker about the hostility between the boys and girls in her room. She has decided to set up two primitive societies in her room, one in which the women are segregated from the men and have little power, the other in which the women make most of the tribal decisions. In particular she intends to use role reversal, so that some boys will play the roles of girls and some girls will play boys' roles.

LESSON 6—DEVELOPING A GOAL PATH The objective here is to complete the total treatment approach by developing a plan of action that will be judged workable by one problem-poser. After Practice Session III each participant should read the material that follows carefully and then write out a plan to achieve the goal presented in one of the practice sessions. He should take the plan to the problem-poser and develop with him an action memo to be presented to the trainer for evaluation.

The ideal solution package requires defining not only what the problem is, but what the client wants to accomplish both in terms of the immediate transaction (the SDM process) and in relation to the total SDM transaction. The ideal single SDM transaction is a microcosm of the total transaction. The major difference involves some means of maintaining records that will provide feedback on how things are going and that will reinforce successive improvement. While going through the sample, participants are asked to try working out a strategy to solve a real treatment situation.

> Barbara is a physically small, shy eighth-grader who has trouble making friends. She will not approach other children in the lunchroom or after school. She's always alone. Other children tease her by saying, "Barbara, don't touch my desk. You'll contaminate it." Barbara has suffered this kind of rejection for over three years.

The plan developed for Barbara is as follows:

1. Define the problem. Barbara has no friends with whom to eat lunch or spend time on weekends. She is the recipient of hostile statements from peers.

2. Specify goals or behavioral changes desired.
   a. To make friends
   b. To join one extracurricular group at school
   c. To initiate invitations to peers to attend social activities
   d. To be asked by peers to attend social activities

3. Define what solution of the problem would achieve more friends for Barbara. Is this really a problem? Would attending club meet-

ings and movies with other children make school more attractive to Barbara or make her feel better?

4. Specify why these goals are not being attained.
    a. Barbara's evaluation is as follows:
        (1) No one likes her.
        (2) She is afraid of being hurt or rejected.
    b. The worker's evaluation (using client system information) is as follows:
        (1) Barbara shows a deficit of friendship-making skills.
        (2) Attention from adults and peers when Barbara is scapegoated maintains her present inappropriate behavior.

5. Specify overall approaches to achieving the objective.
    a. Conduct an SDM transaction with Barbara to determine her interests as they relate to existing extracurricular clubs.
    b. Increase Barbara's assertive behavior in social situations with her peers.
    c. Reduce the number of times Barbara complains to an adult when she is scapegoated by others from sometimes to very seldom.
    d. Increase Barbara's positive interaction with one or more selected peers.

6. List the pros and cons of each of these approaches and select one.
    a. Not complete; presents no next steps.
    b. Expects Barbara to learn skills that will be transferred.
    c. This approach may not solve the problem of Barbara's having no friends.
    d. Too narrow.

7. Develop a plan. The decision made was to combine *a, b,* and *d* into one plan of action. First, what was needed was specified:
    a. Sharing of Barbara's goals with selected members of existing peer groups
    b. Entry skills for specific social situations
    c. Maintenance skills to increase enjoyment when participating
    d. Identification of benefits to Barbara from initiating and maintaining social situations
    e. Feedback on how Barbara was doing

8. Apply the procedure. On Monday Barbara was to watch a recess activity that she selected; on Tuesday she was to join the group and stay for two minutes. On Wednesday and Thursday she was to eat lunch with her peers. On Friday she was to join the recess group and stay for twenty minutes and to complete a self-management planning sheet.

9. Make progress charts.

10. Review the results.

   a. Did I reach my goal?

     (1) If yes, maintain behavior, make a new graph.

     (2) If no, reanalyze, modify strategy, and apply an improvement procedure.

   b. Am I moving in the right direction?

     (1) If yes, maintain behavior and continue graphing.

     (2) If yes, but too slowly, modify and graph.

     (3) If no, analyze, then develop another plan, apply the new technique for a set time period, graph progress, and evaluate as before.

Summary and Post-test

The major purposes of shared decision-making are as follows:

1. To increase the client's commitment to an interventive strategy designed in a dyadic transaction by increasing his involvement in planning the goal and strategy for achieving the goal.

2. To enhance efficient perception of the problem, the solution, and the process utilized to move from where the client is to where he wants to be.

3. To create useful means for determining when the goal has been achieved.

4. To develop a written action memo describing explicitly the first steps each partner will take to implement the action plan.

The following questions are an effort to discover if the participant has learned the basic information and concepts in this learning package. If there is any problem in answering a question, perhaps another reading of the package or of supplementary material will clarify the issue. The student should write out the answers to this post-test and then take it to the instructor, who will discuss and explain the answers to the questions.

1. What are three ways in which SDM differs from most types of interviewing?

2. Select one type of interview (be specific) and show three specific means by which the interviewer exercises control over the interviewee.

3. From your practice interviews, cite one example of the process director's leading of the problem-poser.

4. List three specific ways in which the efficiency of the problem-poser's perception of the major facets of the interview may be measured.

5. Name three basic prerequisites for conducting an SDM interview.

6. Explain two reasons for utilizing SDM.

3M 11/72–2/74—P.D.
6/76—1M